SYMBOLIC CRUSADE

UNIVERSITY OF ILLINOIS PRESS, URBANA, CHICAGO, AND LONDON

SYMBOLIC CRUSADE

Status Politics and the American Temperance Movement

JOSEPH R. GUSFIELD

Third printing of the paperback edition, 1972
Originally published in a clothbound edition, 1963.

© 1963 by the Board of Trustees of the University
of Illinois. Manufactured in the United States of America.
Library of Congress Catalog Card No. 63-10314.

ISBN 0-252-74518-3

TO IRMA

Acknowledgments

My interest in the political significance of the American Temperance movement was first awakened in the course of an earlier study concerned with organizational and doctrinal changes in the Woman's Christian Temperance Union. The present book is an effort to answer theoretical questions about moral reform movements to which the earlier study had led me. Thus it was necessary to consider the entire scope of Temperance in American politics and history.

I have drawn on my earlier work (Ph.D. dissertation, University of Chicago, 1954) in certain sections of this book. Some aspects of that work discussed here were reported in my "Social Structure and Moral Reform: A Study of the Woman's Christian Temperance Union," *American Journal of Sociology*, 61 (November, 1955), 221-232.

In the course of my studies of Temperance I have benefited from the use of the Frances Willard Library at the National Woman's Christian Temperance Union in Evanston, Illinois. The cooperation of former presidents of the organization, Mrs. D. L. Colvin and Mrs. Glenn Hays, in initial parts of this study was both gracious and indispensable. I am thankful to them and to the officers of WCTU units who helped me to understand their views. Grants from the University of Illinois Graduate Research Board provided a Summer Faculty Fellowship, during which the initial draft of this book was written, and the costs of typing the various versions of manuscript. I am grateful to the National Council for the Prevention of Alcoholism and the U.S. Department of Health, Education and Welfare for sponsoring my attendance at special meetings of the Committee on Alcoholism of the Society for the Study of Social Problems, in 1960 and 1961. Both meetings added significantly to my knowledge of current research on drinking behavior. The Distilled Spirits Institute kindly made available to me their *Annual Reports*. Some aspects of the present study were discussed by me in "Status Conflicts and the Changing Ideologies of the American Temperance Movement," in David Pittman and Charles Snyder (eds.), *Society, Culture, and Drinking Patterns* (New York: John Wiley and Sons, 1962), pp. 101-120.

No author can recall everyone from whom he has borrowed unfootnoted thoughts. We can only mention those whose criticisms and suggestions have been especially noteworthy. Herbert Blumer and Everett Hughes were responsible for stimulating and guiding my early interest in this area of study. The following have been helpful in suggesting ideas and avenues of exploration: Bernard Farber, Erving Goffman, Norman Graebner, Robert Habenstein, Donald Horton, Edward Hulett, Jr., Bernard Karsh, David Pittman, David Riesman, Charles Snyder, and W. Lloyd Warner. The following, in addition, gave the last full measure of collegial devotion and read all or part of early or final drafts of the manuscript: Bennett Berger, John Clark, Barbara Dennis, Murray Edelman, Alvin Gouldner, Mark Keller, Louis Schneider, and R. Richard Wohl. Louise Bindman helped in the preparation of footnotes.

I owe a special debt to R. Richard Wohl that, unfortunately, can never be repaid. More than anyone, he encouraged me to continue my earlier interest in Temperance. His death at the early age of 36 was a loss to American scholarship and a personal blow. His many friends will always remember his erudition, wit, and lively enthusiasm for the play of the intellect.

Two very recent and significant monographs appeared after this manuscript had gone to press. We were thus unable to utilize these works by Andrew Sinclair *(Prohibition)* and James Timberlake *(Prohibition and the Progressive Movement)* in the body of the text.

Contents

Introduction

For many observers of American life the Temperance movement is evidence for an excessive moral perfectionism and an overly legalistic bent to American culture. It seems the action of devoted sectarians who are unable to compromise with human impulse. The legal measures taken to enforce abstinence display the reputed American faith in the power of Law to correct all evils. This moralism and utopianism bring smiles to the cynical and fear to the sinners. Such a movement seems at once naive, intolerant, saintly, and silly.

Although controversies of morality, religion, and culture have been recognized as endemic elements of American politics, they have generally been viewed as minor themes in the interplay of economic and class conflicts. Only in recent years have American historians and social scientists de-emphasized economic issues as the major points of dissension in American society.[1] We share this newer point of view, especially in its insistence on the significant role of cultural conflicts in American politics. Our social system has not experienced the sharp class organization and class conflict which have been so salient in European history. Under continuous conditions of relative affluence and without a feudal resistance to nineteenth-century commercialism and industry, Amer-

[1] For manifestations of this viewpoint in American history see Lee Benson, *The Concept of Jacksonian Democracy* (Princeton, N.J.: Princeton University Press, 1961), and Louis Hartz, *The Liberal Tradition in America* (New York: Harcourt, Brace and Co., 1955). These trends in historiography are discussed in John Higham (ed.), *The Reconstruction of American History* (New York: Harper Torch Books, 1962).

ican society has possessed a comparatively high degree of consensus on economic matters. In its bland attitude toward class
issues, political controversy in the United States has given only a
limited role to strong economic antagonisms. Controversies of personality, cultural difference, and the nuances of style and morality
have occupied part of the political stage. Consensus about fundamentals of governmental form, free enterprise economy, and
church power has left a political vacuum which moral issues have
partially filled. Differences between ethnic groups, cultures, and
religious organizations have been able to assume a greater importance than has been true of societies marked by deeper economic divisions. ". . . agreement on fundamentals will permit almost
every kind of social conflict, tension and difference to find political
expression." [2]

It is within an analytical context of concern with noneconomic
issues that we have studied the Temperance movement. This is
a study of moral reform as a political and social issue. We have
chosen the Temperance movement because of its persistence and
power in the history of the United States. Typical of moral reform
efforts, Temperance has usually been the attempt of the moral
people, in this case the abstainers, to correct the behavior of the
immoral people, in this case the drinkers. The issue has appeared
as a moral one, divorced from any direct economic interests in
abstinence or indulgence. This quality of "disinterested reform"
is the analytical focus of our study.

This book is an interpretation rather than a history because our
interest is largely with the analysis of what is already known of
the movement rather than with the presentation of new data.
Some new field data will be presented and some new primary
historical material has been gathered. A large number of already
published materials has been utilized. Our interest is not in a
definitive history of the movement. We have written within the
methodological perspective of the sociologist interested in the
general process of moral reform. Our concern is with the structural
and cultural roots of the movement and with the consequences of
Temperance activities and goals for its adherents, its "victims,"
and the relations between these two.

The sociologist picks up where the historian closes. Put in

[2] Benson, *op. cit.*, p. 275.

another way, he delves into the assumptions with which the historian begins (see Chapter 2, pp. 57-60, "A Note on Religious Motives and Sociological Reductionism"). The amount written about Temperance is monumentally staggering to someone who tries to read it all. Claims, counterclaims, factual histories, and proceedings of organizations overwhelm us in their immensity. Despite this plethora of documents and analyses, we are left with either partisan writings, histories which preach, or analyses which fail to go beyond general remarks about moral perfectionism, rural-urban conflict, or the Protestant envy of the sinner.[3] It is here, in the analysis of the process, that the sociologist focuses his interest. He studies just that which is so often *ad hoc* to the interpretation of the historian.

In this book we will describe the relation between Temperance attitudes, the organized Temperance movement, and the conflicts between divergent subcultures in American society. Issues of moral reform are analyzed as one way through which a cultural group acts to preserve, defend, or enhance the dominance and prestige of its own style of living within the total society. In the set of religious, ethnic, and cultural communities that have made up American society, drinking (and abstinence) has been one of the significant consumption habits distinguishing one subculture from another. It has been one of the major characteristics through which Americans have defined their own cultural commitments. The "drunken bum," "the sophisticated gourmet," or the "blue-nosed teetotaler" are all terms by which we express our approval or disapproval of cultures by reference to the moral position they accord drinking. Horace Greeley recognized this cultural base to political loyalties and animosities in the 1844 elections in New York state: "Upon those Working Men who stick to their business, hope to improve their circumstances by honest industry and *go on Sundays to church rather than to the grog-shop* [italics added] the appeals of Loco-Focoism fell comparatively harmless; while the opposite class were rallied with unprecedented unanimity against us."[4]

---

[3] A major exception to this is John A. Krout, *The Origins of Prohibition* (New York: A. A. Knopf, 1925). Even Peter Odegard's otherwise excellent work on *Pressure Politics* (New York: Columbia University Press, 1928) is marred by his utter lack of sympathy with Temperance goals. The same moralistic condemnation of moralism limits the utility of the very recent work of Andrew Sinclair, *Prohibition* (Boston: Little, Brown and Co., 1962).

[4] Quoted in Benson, *op. cit.*, p. 199.

Precisely because drinking and nondrinking have been ways to identify the members of a subculture, drinking and abstinence became symbols of social status, identifying social levels of the society whose styles of life separated them culturally. They indicated to what culture the actor was committed and hence what social groups he took as his models of imitation and avoidance and his points of positive and negative reference for judging his behavior. The rural, native American Protestant of the nineteenth century respected Temperance ideals. He adhered to a culture in which self-control, industriousness, and impulse renunciation were both praised and made necessary. Any lapse was a serious threat to his system of respect. Sobriety was virtuous and, in a community dominated by middle-class Protestants, necessary to social acceptance and to self-esteem. In the twentieth century this is less often true. As Americans are less work-minded, more urban, and less theological, the same behavior which once brought rewards and self-assurance to the abstainer today more often brings contempt and rejection. The demands for self-control and individual industry count for less in an atmosphere of teamwork where tolerance, good interpersonal relations, and the ability to relax oneself and others are greatly prized. Abstinence has lost much of its utility to confer prestige and esteem.

Our attention to the significance of drink and abstinence as symbols of membership in status groups does not imply that religious and moral beliefs have not been important in the Temperance movement. We are not reducing moral reform to something else. Instead, we are adding something. Religious motives and moral fervor do not happen *in vacuo*, apart from a specific setting. We have examined the social conditions which made the facts of other people's drinking especially galling to the abstainer and the need for reformist action acutely pressing to him. These conditions are found in the development of threats to the socially dominant position of the Temperance adherent by those whose style of life differs from his. As his own claim to social respect and honor are diminished, the sober, abstaining citizen seeks for public acts through which he may reaffirm the dominance and prestige of his style of life. Converting the sinner to virtue is one way; law is another. Even if the law is not enforced or enforceable, the symbolic import of its passage is important to the reformer. It settles the controversies between those who represent clashing cultures.

The public support of one conception of morality at the expense of another enhances the prestige and self-esteem of the victors and degrades the culture of the losers.

In its earliest development, Temperance [5] was one way in which a declining social elite tried to retain some of its social power and leadership. The New England Federalist "aristocracy" was alarmed by the political defeats of the early nineteenth century and by the decreased deference shown their clergy. The rural farmer, the evangelical Protestant, and the uneducated middle class appeared as a rising social group who rejected the social status, as well as political power, of the Federalist leadership. In the first quarter of the nineteenth century, the moral supremacy of the educated was under attack by the frontiersman, the artisan, and the independent farmer. The Federalist saw his own declining status in the increased power of the drinker, the ignorant, the secularist, and the religious revivalist. During the 1820's, the men who founded the Temperance movement sought to make Americans into a clean, sober, godly, and decorous people whose aspirations and style of living would reflect the moral leadership of New England Federalism. If they could not control the politics of the country, they reasoned that they might at least control its morals.

Spurred by religious revivalism, Temperance became more ultraist than its founders had intended. The settling of frontiers and the influx of non-Protestant cultures increased the symbolic importance of morality and religious behavior in distinguishing between the reputable and the disreputable. During the 1830's and 1840's, it became a large and influential movement, composed of several major organizations. Religious dedication and a sober life were becoming touchstones of middle-class respectability. Large numbers of men were attracted to Temperance organizations as a means of self-help. In the interests of social and economic mobility, they sought to preserve their abstinence or reform their own drinking habits. Abstinence was becoming a symbol of middle-class membership and a necessity for ambitious and aspiring young men. It was one of the ways society could distinguish the industrious from the ne'er-do-well; the steady worker from the unreliable

[5] The term "Temperance" is an inadequate name for a movement which preaches total abstinence rather than "temperate" use of alcohol. The word was affixed to the movement in its early years (1820's) when its doctrine was not yet as extreme as it later came to be.

drifter; the good credit risk from the bad gamble; the native American from the immigrant. In this process the movement lost its association with New England upper classes and became democratized.

The political role of Temperance emerged in the 1840's in its use as a symbol of native and immigrant, Protestant and Catholic tensions. The "disinterested reformer" of the 1840's was likely to see the curtailment of alcohol sales as a way of solving the problems presented by an immigrant, urban poor whose culture clashed with American Protestantism. He sensed the rising power of these strange, alien peoples and used Temperance legislation as one means of impressing upon the immigrant the central power and dominance of native American Protestant morality. Along with Abolition and Nativism, Temperance formed one of a trio of major movements during the 1840's and 1850's.

Throughout its history, Temperance has revealed two diverse types of disinterested reform. By the last quarter of the nineteenth century, these had become clear and somewhat distinct elements within the movement. One was an *assimilative reform*. Here the reformer was sympathetic to the plight of the urban poor and critical of the conditions produced by industry and the factory system. This urban, progressivist impulse in Temperance reflected the fears of an older, established social group at the sight of rising industrialism. While commercial and professional men saw America changing from a country of small towns to one of cities, they were still socially dominant. The norm of abstinence had become the public morality after the Civil War. In the doctrines of abstinence they could still offer the poor and the immigrants a way of living which had the sanction of respect and success attached to it. Through reform of the drinker, the middle-class professional and businessman coped with urban problems in a way which affirmed his sense of cultural dominance. He could feel his own social position affirmed by a Temperance argument that invited the drinker (whom he largely identified with the poor, the alien, and the downtrodden) to follow the reformer's habits and lift himself to middle-class respect and income. He was even able to denounce the rich for their sumptuary sophistication. He could do this because he felt secure that abstinence was still the public morality. It was not yet somebody else's America.

A more hostile attitude to reform is found when the object of the reformer's efforts is no longer someone he can pity or help.

Coercive reform emerges when the object of reform is seen as an intractable defender of another culture, someone who rejects the reformer's values and really doesn't want to change. The champion of assimilative reform viewed the drinker as part of a social system in which the reformer's culture was dominant. On this assumption, his invitation to the drinker to reform made sense. The champion of coercive reform cannot make this assumption. He sees the object of reform as someone who rejects the social dominance of the reformer and denies the legitimacy of his life style. Since the dominance of his culture and the social status of his group are denied, the coercive reformer turns to law and force as ways to affirm it.

In the last quarter of the nineteenth century, coercive reform was most evident in the Populist wing of the Temperance movement. As a phase of the rural distrust of the city, it was allied to an agrarian radicalism which fought the power of industrial and urban political and economic forces. Already convinced that the old, rural middle class was losing out in the sweep of history, the Populist as Temperance adherent could not assume that his way of life was still dominant in America. He had to fight it out by political action which would coerce the public definition of what is moral and respectable. He had to shore up his waning self-esteem by inflicting his morality on everybody.

As America became more urban, more secular, and more Catholic, the sense of declining status intensified the coercive, Populist elements in the Temperance movement. The political defeat of Populism in both North and South heightened the decline, so evident in the drama of William Jennings Bryan. With the development of the Anti-Saloon League in 1896, the Temperance movement began to separate itself from a complex of economic and social reforms and concentrate on the cultural struggle of the traditional rural Protestant society against the developing urban and industrial social system. Coercive reform became the dominating theme of Temperance. It culminated in the drive for national Prohibition. The Eighteenth Amendment was the high point of the struggle to assert the public dominance of old middle-class values. It established the victory of Protestant over Catholic, rural over urban, tradition over modernity, the middle class over both the lower and the upper strata.

The significance of Prohibition is in the fact that it happened. The establishment of Prohibition laws was a battle in the struggle for status between two divergent styles of life. It marked the public affirmation of the abstemious, ascetic qualities of American Protestantism. In this sense, it was an act of ceremonial deference toward old middle-class culture. If the law was often disobeyed and not enforced, the respectability of its adherents was honored in the breach. After all, it was *their* law that drinkers had to avoid.

If Prohibition was the high point of old middle-class defense, Repeal was the nadir. As the Prohibition period lengthened and resistance solidified, Temperance forces grew more hostile, coercive, and nativist. The more assimilative, progressivist adherents were alienated from a movement of such soured Populism. In 1928, anti-Catholic and anti-urban forces led the movement with a "knockout punch" thrown at Al Smith in an open ring. By 1933, they had lost their power and their fight. In the Great Depression both the old order of nineteenth-century economics and the culture of the Temperance ethic were cruelly discredited.

The repeal of the Eighteenth Amendment gave the final push to the decline of old middle-class values in American culture. Since 1933, the Temperance movement has seen itself fighting a losing battle against old enemies and new ones. In contemporary American society, even in his own local communities, it is the total abstainer who is the despised nonconformist. The Protestant churches and the public schools are no longer his allies. The respectable, upper middle-class citizen can no longer be safely counted upon to support abstinence.

What underlies the tragic dilemmas of the Temperance movement are basic changes in the American social system and culture during the past half-century. As we have changed from a commercial society to an industrial one, we have developed a new set of values in which self-control, impulse renunciation, discipline, and sobriety are no longer such hallowed virtues. Thorstein Veblen, himself the epitome of the rural, middle-class Protestant, saw the new society of consumers coming into being. In his satirical fashion, he depicted a society in which leisure and consumption fixed men's status and took precedence over the work-mindedness and efficiency concerns of his own Swedish-American farm communities. More recently, David Riesman has brilliantly depicted the major outlines of this society by pointing to the intensity with which modern Americans are replacing an interest in work and morality with an interest in interpersonal relations and styles of consuming leisure.

For the "other-directed" man neither the intolerance nor the seriousness of the abstainer is acceptable. Nor is the intense rebelliousness and social isolation of the hard drinker acceptable. Analysis of American alcohol consumption is consistent with this. The contemporary American is less likely than his nineteenth-century ancestor to be either a total abstainer or a hard drinker. Moderation is his drinking watchword. One must get along with others and liquor has proven to be a necessary and effective facilitator to sociability. It relaxes reserve and permits fellowship at the same time that it displays the drinker's tolerance for some moral lapse in himself and others.

For those who have grown up to believe in the validity of the Temperance ethic, American culture today seems a strange system in which Truth is condemned as Falsehood and Vice as Virtue. The total abstainer finds himself the exponent of a point of view which is rejected in the centers of urban and national society and among their followers at all levels of American communities. Self-control and foresight made sense in a scarcity, production-minded economy. In an easygoing, affluent society, the credit mechanism has made the Ant a fool and the Grasshopper a hero of the counter-cyclical maintenance of consumer demand. In a consumption-centered society, people must learn to have fun and be good mixers if they are to achieve respect. Not Horatio Alger but *Playboy* magazine is the instructor of the college boy who wants to learn the skills of social ascent. Though they have their noses to the grindstone, their feet must tap to the sound of the dance.

It is at this point that the study of Temperance assumes significance for a general understanding of contemporary American politics and social tensions. Social systems and cultures die slowly, leaving their rear guards behind to fight delaying action. Even after they have ceased to be relevant economic groups, the old middle classes of America are still searching for some way to restore a sense of lost respect. The dishonoring of their values is a part of the process of cultural and social change. A heightened stress on the importance of tradition is a major response of such "doomed classes."

This fundamentalist defense is a primary motif in the current phase of Temperance. To different degrees and within different areas, the contemporary Temperance adherent is part of the rear guard with which small-town America and commercial capitalism fight their losing battle against a nationalized culture and an industrial economy of mass organizations. Increasingly, he fights alone. Churches, schools, and public officials are disdainful of "rigid" attitudes and doctrines. Within the American middle class, in almost all communities, there is a sharp split between two stylistic components. In one the abstainer can feel at home. Here the local community of neighbors and townsmen is the point of reference for behavior. In the other, the more cosmopolitan centers of urban institutions are mediated to the town through national institutions, communications media, and the two-way geographical mobility which brings in newcomers and sends out college students for training elsewhere. The clash between the drinker and the abstainer reflects these diverse references. The localistic culture clings to the traditional while the easier, relaxed, modern ways are the province of the national culture. It is this national culture which becomes the more prestigeful and powerful as America becomes more homogeneous.

The anger and bitterness of the "doomed class" is by no means an "irrational" reaction. There *has* been a decline in the social status of the old middle class and in the dominance of his values. This sense of anger at the loss of status and bitterness about lowered self-esteem pervades the entire Temperance movement today. It takes a number of forms. At one extreme and within certain Temperance elements, it is expressed as a general, diffuse criticism of modern political and social doctrines and a defense of tradition in almost all areas of American life. At the other extreme, within other parts of the Temperance movement, it is part of the intense nationalism, economic conservatism, and social stagnation of the radical right. (This latter is especially true of the Prohibition Party.)

The study of the American Temperance movement is a phase of the process by which, as Richard Hofstadter expressed it, "a large part of the Populist-Progressive tradition has turned sour, become ill-liberal and ill-tempered." [6] The values and the economic position of the native American Protestant, old middle class of individual enterprisers have been losing out in the shuffle of time and social change. The efforts of the old middle class and of those who have built their self-conceptions on their values to defend

[6] Richard Hofstadter, *The Age of Reform* (New York: A. A. Knopf, 1955), pp. 19-20.

and restore their lost prestige have taken a number of forms. In fluoridation, domestic Communism, school curricula, and the United Nations, they have found issues which range tradition against modernity. Temperance has been one of the classic issues on which divergent cultures have faced each other in America. Such issues of style have been significant because they have been ways through which groups have tried to handle the problems which have been important to them.

It is this conception of political acts as symbolic acts that is, for us, the most valuable part of this book and the most significant fruit of studying Temperance. We consider Temperance as one form which the politics of status goals has taken in the United States. Far from being a pointless interruption of the American political system, it has exemplified one of its characteristic processes. Since governmental actions symbolize the position of groups in the status structure, seemingly ceremonial or ritual acts of government are often of great importance to many social groups. Issues which seem foolish or impractical items are often important for what they symbolize about the style or culture which is being recognized or derogated. Being acts of deference or degradation, the individual finds in governmental action that his own perceptions of his status in the society are confirmed or rejected.

These considerations take us a long way toward understanding why and how social status has been a provocative and frequent source of political tensions in the United States. Issues like fluoridation or domestic Communism or Temperance may seem to generate "irrational" emotions and excessive zeal if we fail to recognize them as symbolic rather than instrumental, pragmatic issues. If we conceive of status as somehow an unfit issue for political controversy, we are simply ignoring a clash of interests which generate a high order of emotion and political action in the United States. When a society experiences profound changes, the fortunes and the respect of people undergo loss or gain. We have always understood the desire to defend fortune. We should also understand the desire to defend respect. It is less clear because it is symbolic in nature but it is not less significant.

In the pages ahead we have subjected the Temperance movement to an analysis as a movement of social status. We see it as a reflection of clashes and conflicts between rival social systems, cultures, and status groups. Sometimes the abstainer was winning.

Sometimes, as in the present generation, he lost. The issues may seem slight to those for whom self-esteem has no relation to social esteem or to those for whom ritual, ceremony, and symbol are meaningless actions. For us, however, the study of Temperance has illuminated much that is often both problematic and unique in American life.

The point of view taken in this study reflects the interest of sociologists in the implications of the status structure for political processes. Temperance has been both a protest against a changing status system and a mechanism for influencing the distribution of prestige. This study is consequently a contribution to the theory of status conflict and its relation to political and social movements.

1

Social Status
and the
Temperance Ethic

Our aim in this work is to understand how one issue of moral reform, that of alcohol consumption, has operated in the context of American political and social conflict. Some of the deepest struggles in American politics have emerged over issues which are not directly related to economic divisions in the society. Questions of civil liberties and civil rights have moved men and changed political institutions in the past.

These movements are not easily understood by sociological models of economic class conflict. The division of the political spectrum into an economic right and left, middle class and working class, conservative and liberal has little relevance for issues of race relations, civil liberties, or moral standards. While studies of voting behavior show a high correlation between economic position and opinion toward economic issues, the same categories of class are not correlated with attitudes or votes on noneconomic questions.[1] Differences between rich and poor are clearly drawn when problems of the distribution of income are posed. On other issues the distinctions are less clear.

CLASS AND STATUS

The concept of "class" has generally been used among sociologists to refer to the control and allocation of goods and services. Classes

[1] Bernard Berelson, Paul Lazarsfeld, and William McPhee, *Voting* (Chicago: University of Chicago Press, 1959), Ch. 9; Samuel Stouffer, *Communism, Conformity and Civil Liberties* (New York: Doubleday and Co., Inc., 1955); Seymour Lipset, *Political Man* (New York: Doubleday and Co., Inc., 1960), pp. 97-130, 298-301.

are distinguished by different degrees of control over products. Categories of bourgeoisie and proletariat, middle and working class, labor and management, farmer and banker are relevant to the analysis of the division of labor and its relation to the division of economic power. A class is a sociological group in the sense that its members, by virtue of their common placement in the economic structure, share common interests. They are subject to a similar fate on the market. When people in similar economic positions organize around common symbols and through associations they assume a degree of unity and organization.² A class structure is the system of relationships between the different classes in a society, including their differential power and the extent of organization into politically relevant associations.

Social status refers to the distribution of prestige, sometimes also called social honor. By "prestige" we mean "the approval, respect, admiration, or deference a person or group is able to command by virtue of his or its imputed qualities or performances." ³ A status hierarchy tends to develop among groups which differ in characteristic ways of life. It is the essence of a status hierarchy that within it, some groups can successfully claim greater prestige than others. Insofar as such groups are identifiable and owe their unity to other than class elements it is analytically useful to call them "status groups." In American society we are used to designating groups such as Protestants, Catholics, and Jews, native and immigrant, Negro and white as status groups. We are also familiar with less explicit groupings such as "the old aristocracy," "the nouveau riche," or "the lumpenproletariat," designations by which we refer to the subtle interrelation between dimensions of status and dimensions of class.

It is by no means the case that classes and status groups are equivalent. One is not always the reflection of the other. The lack of fit, and even conflict, between principles of class designation and those of status designation is the source of Max Weber's multidimensional approach to social stratification, which is followed in this study. For Weber, although social status might be closely re-

² This meaning of "class" is in keeping with both traditional sociological and Marxist literature, as in Max Weber, *Theory of Social and Economic Organization*, tr. A. M. Henderson and Talcott Parsons (New York: Oxford University Press, 1947), and Nikolai Bukharin, *Historical Materialism* (New York: International Publishers, 1925), Ch. 8.

³ Harry M. Johnson, *Sociology: A Systematic Introduction* (New York: Harcourt, Brace and Co., 1960), p. 469.

lated to economic bases, it was not determined by this exclusively or primarily. Hereditary charisma, political authority, and, above all, distinctive styles of life gave rise to status-bearing groups which claimed and were given a specific place in the distribution of prestige. "The class status of an officer, a civil servant, and a student as determined by their income may be widely different while their social status remains the same, because they adhere to the same mode of life in all relevant respects as a result of their common education." [4]

The two dimensions of class and status make up two analytically separate orders of social structure. In the class order economic power and products are distributed. Men have their positions on the basis of functions in the division of labor. Prestige, however, is distributed within the status order on the basis of group qualities. In the long run, it may be true that class shapes and limits the existence of status. In the short run the crystallization of class into status is hardly precise. The wealthy lawyer possesses more prestige than the wealthy gangster; the third-generation rich more than the first-generation very rich; the college graduate more than the high school dropout. The classic accounts of the *nouveau riche* in the novels of Stendhal or of C. P. Snow attest to the lag between changing economic power and changing forms of respect and admiration. Only cardplayers and economists are forced to concentrate on the long run.

Symbols of Status

Since the social status of a group consists in the evaluation and respect which it receives from others, the status structure is necessarily "subjective." Approval, respect, and admiration are attitudes rather than actions. They are conveyed through acts, including language, which express prestige by symbolizing an attitudinal state of respect. Sociologists label such prestige-laden acts as instances of deference or, in negative terms, instances of degradation. The employee who holds the door open for the employer is performing an act of deference. He expresses the subordinate nature of his position by acting out the prestige of the employer. The function of the act is only incidentally economic. The saving in energy for the employer is trivial. The entire act is ceremonial, marking the imputed prestige of the employer vis-à-vis his employee. Many acts of deference and degradation, of course, become institutionalized,

[4] Weber, *op. cit.*, p. 428.

serving as signs of status without necessarily connoting the attitudinal respect.

A status system involves at least two persons, one who confers prestige and one who receives it. Insofar as the system is composed of groups rather than persons, the prestige-receiver must be "placed" as a member of the prestigeful group by those who confer prestige. "A sign of position can be a status symbol only if it is used with some regularity as a means of 'placing' socially the person who makes it." [5]

Status groups are communal. They share a common culture in the form of standards of behavior, including patterns of consumption and work orientations. This culture, or style of life, is normative for members of the group. It constitutes the "canons of decency" by which group members live. For those outside of the group, who are potential prestige-givers, these items of behavior become symbols of the status of members, who are potential prestige-receivers. The styles of home furnishings, for example, in upper middle-class homes are matters of proper taste which appear appealing to those who share this culture. To "outsiders" they are signs of the group membership of the user.

Two forms of symbolic action are thus involved in our analysis of the relation between groups at different prestige levels. One is the system of values, customs, and habits distinctive to a status group, which we shall call its "style of life." Such behavior serves as a symbol of membership in the group. Veblen's accounts of conspicuous consumption are illustrative of this symbolism. The other form of symbolic action is that involved in ceremonies of deference when one group interacts with another above or below it in rank. In the United States, a myriad of racial customs serve to dramatize the lower status of the Negro. The use of the back door when entering a white man's home in the South is just one such instance.[6]

CLASS AND STATUS POLITICS

So far we have used the terms "class" and "status" in a static fashion, as if the degrees of income, power, and prestige were distributed in accordance with the shared expectations and values of rich and

[5] Erving Goffman, "Symbols of Class Status," *British Journal of Sociology*, 2 (December, 1951), 294-304, at 295.

[6] Negro-white interaction as symbolic of status difference is analyzed in Bertram Doyle, *The Etiquette of Race Relations in the South* (Chicago: University of Chicago Press, 1937), *passim*, and Gunnar Myrdal, *An American Dilemma* (New York: Harper and Bros., 1944), Chs. 28-30.

poor, controllers and controlled, prestige-givers and prestige-receivers. We can imagine a society in which there is such consensus, where classes and status groups are content with a system. Often this is not the case in complex, industrial societies or in societies undergoing intensive changes. The idea of class conflict and class struggle is well established in the analytical apparatus of political science, history, and sociology. The idea of status struggle is somewhat newer and is implicit in the distinction between class politics and status politics.

This distinction between politics of class and of status has been developed by both Richard Hofstadter and Seymour Lipset in an effort to analyze the various movements associated with Senator McCarthy and extreme right-wing political organizations in the 1950's.[7] They have both argued that there are two different, though interrelated, processes at work in American politics. In class politics (Hofstadter uses the term "interest politics") we have the conflict between the material goals and aspirations of different social groups such as is found in the traditional right and left. In status politics the conflict arises from status aspirations and discontents. "Status politics refers to political movements whose appeal is to the not uncommon resentments of individuals or groups who desire to maintain or improve their social status."[8] Both Lipset and Hofstadter believed that periods of economic recession accentuated conflicts of class politics while periods of relative prosperity brought issues of status discontent to the forefront of political struggle. Both maintained that status politics was characterized by hostility to outgroups, ultradogmatism, and extremist attacks on democratic procedure. ". . . the political movements which have successfully appealed to status resentments have been irrational in character and have sought scapegoats which conveniently serve to symbolize the status threat."[9]

Status discontents are likely to appear when the prestige accorded to persons and groups by prestige-givers is perceived as less than that which the person or group expects. The self-esteem of the group member is belied by the failure of others to grant him the respect, approval, admiration, and deference he feels that he justly

---

[7] Richard Hofstadter, "The Pseudo-Conservative Revolt," in Daniel Bell (ed.), *The New American Right* (New York: Criterion Books, 1955), pp. 33-55; Seymour Lipset, "The Sources of the Radical Right," in *ibid.*, pp. 166-234.

[8] *Ibid.*, p. 168.

[9] *Ibid.*

deserves. This may occur when a segment of the society is losing status and finds that prestige-givers withhold expected deference. It may occur when a group is making claims to greater prestige than it has made in the past and finds that prestige-givers do not comply with the new claims. The effort of ethnic groups to raise status through political recognition of candidates, of occupational groups to raise their status through changes of names (as "janitor" to "custodian"), or of the nobility to prevent the purchase of titles and use of luxury goods by a rising middle class are all instances of attempts to enhance or defend a level of prestige under conflict.

If status systems depend on the acts of prestige-givers in relation to prestige-receivers, then efforts to redistribute prestige depend upon the ability to control the giving of prestige against the reluctance of the prestige-givers to grant it. Only in this sense can social status be a subject of political conflict. In our usage class politics is political conflict over the allocation of material resources. Status politics is political conflict over the allocation of prestige. In specific cases the two processes overlap and effect each other. Resources bring prestige and prestige often leads to material advantages.

The importance of the distinction has more than analytical value, however. Classes and status groups are different collections of people, different ways to slice the cake of societies. Just how we perceive political struggles, as matters of class or of status, has a great bearing on the groups we perceive as parties to a political conflict. The thrust of status politics lies precisely in identifying noneconomic segments as crucial in certain social and political conflicts.

When divergent styles of life claim equal or superior prestige, the bearers of these styles are involved in a clash to establish prestige dominance and subordination. Status concepts lead us to focus upon just such elements of values, beliefs, consumption habits, and the cultural items differentiating nonclass groups from each other. Thus David Riesman has described many of the social and political struggles in contemporary America not as conflicts between groups defined in economic terms but as a "characterological struggle" between people who are both nominal members of the middle class but whose cultural and characterological commitments are sharply dissimilar.[10]

There is another form of politics which has been confusingly

[10] David Riesman, *The Lonely Crowd* (New Haven, Conn: Yale University Press, 1950), pp. 31-36.

represented in the discussion of status resentments. This is the expressive element in political action. Hofstadter's usage of status politics illustrates the confusion between status and expressive elements: "Political life is not simply an arena in which the conflicting interests of various social groups in concrete material gains are fought out; it is also an arena into which status aspirations and frustrations are, as the psychologist would say, projected . . . status politics [is] the clash of various projective rationalizations arising from status aspirations and other personal motives." [11] In this characterization, class politics is an effort to influence material gain, to rectify discontents by directly affecting the distribution of wealth. Status discontents, however, are seen as sources of affect or emotion, generating action which, in the use of the psychological concepts of "projection" and "rationalization," need not affect the distribution of prestige. In our usage, this latter sense of politics as an arena in which feelings, emotions, and affect are displaced and expressed is what we mean by "expressive politics"—political action for the sake of expression rather than for the sake of influencing or controlling the distribution of valued objects. The goal of the action, the object of hostility or love, is not a "solution" to the problems which have generated the action. Politics, in this usage, is a means to express how the actors feel about their situation. Studies which have attempted to "explain" lynchings of Negroes by whites in America as consequences of the low price of cotton are the classic example. The frustrations of economic setback give rise to aggressive feelings which are then displaced against targets with little power to resist.[12]

Expressive elements may, of course, often be found in conjunction with elements of class or status even when expression is not the primary characteristic of the action. This study emphasizes the analytical distinctiveness of status as a concept in political analysis. The crucial idea is that political action can, and often has, influenced the distribution of prestige. Status politics is an effort to control the status of a group by acts which function to raise, lower, or maintain the social status of the acting group vis-à-vis others in the society. Conflicts of status in society are fought out in public arenas as are conflicts of class.

[11] Hofstadter, *op. cit.,* p. 43.
[12] Neal Miller, John Dollard, *et al., Frustration and Aggression* (New Haven, Conn.: Yale University Press, 1939), Chs. 2-3, esp. pp. 30-31.

STATUS MOVEMENTS

Status movements are collective actions which attempt to raise or maintain the prestige of a group. They can be distinguished from class movements and expressive movements by the nature of their goals and by the character of the groups to whose values and welfare the movement is oriented.[13]

Class movements are oriented toward the "interests" of particular groups in the economic system of production and distribution. The Townsend movement sought to enhance the economic security of the aged; the Labor movement aims at increasing the well-being of the employee in his relations to the employer; the Saskatchewan C.C.F. is representative of the aims of independent wheat farmers. The membership of a class movement may be wide, as in the case of the Labor movement, or relatively narrowed, as in the case of the C.C.F. In all cases, however, class movements encompass aims in the name of groups located in the economic structure.

Class movements are instrumental in their goals. Their goals are statable as alterations in the system of behavior characterizing the society. The Populists pressed the aims of farmers in demanding greater regulation of banks and railroads. The Labor movement favored the minimum wage act. The Townsendites were after pensions. The movement is presented as a solution to the discontents from which it arose. Achievement of objectives will change the situation in ways which remove the sources of frustration, resentment, or anger. Even a religious movement can be interpreted as instrumental, as a means to a tangible, material end, as in H. Richard Niebuhr's description of Christian sects in the nineteenth century: "Ethically, as well as psychologically, such religion bears a distinct character. The salvation which it seeks and sets forth is the salvation of the socially disinherited. Intellectual naïveté and practical need combine to create a marked propensity toward millenarianism, with its promise of tangible goods and of the reversal of all present systems of social rank." [14]

Status movements are oriented toward the enhancement of the

[13] The adherents of a movement need not be a constituency which directly gains rewards from achievement of the goals of the movement. The movement to outlaw child labor is neither led by nor composed of children nor is the humane society the work of animals.

[14] H. Richard Niebuhr, *The Social Sources of Denominationalism* (New York: Meridian Books, 1937; orig. pub., 1929), pp. 30-31.

prestige of groups. The carriers of the status movement may be *status communities*—status groups such as Protestants, Catholics, and Jews, or Negroes and whites. Status communities are sharply delineated segments of the status system, with associations, institutions, and a group life akin to a subcommunity within the society. The conflicts between religious and ethnic groups in American politics are good examples of conflicts about relative prestige between status communities. Groups may be less explicit than these. They may consist of *status collectivities*—status groups which, like status communities, share a common style of life, but lack the explicit definition and the associational unity of status communities.[15] Unlike groups such as religious and ethnic communities they have no church, no political unit, and no associational units which explicitly defend their interests. They possess subcultures without being subcommunities. Examples of these are cultural generations, such as the traditional and the modern; characterological types, such as "inner-directed and other-directed"; and reference orientations, such as "cosmopolitans and locals."[16] The examples used above are also cases of conflicts between paired opposites. Each subculture in the pair is the contradiction of the other, its carriers denying the claims of the other to prestige.

As status groups vie with each other to change or defend their prestige allocation, they do so through symbolic rather than instrumental goals. The significant meanings are not given in the intrinsic properties of the action but in what it has come to signify for the participants. It is symbolic behavior in the sense that we speak of the cross as the symbol of Christianity, of pens as phallic symbols, and of clothing styles as symbols of social status. In symbolic behavior the action is ritualistic and ceremonial in that the goal is reached in the behavior itself rather than in any state which it brings about.

[15] In this distinction I am helped by the work of Gregory Stone and William Form. Their report of a study of status levels in an American community has been influential throughout this section as well as elsewhere in this book. See their "Instabilities in Status," *American Sociological Review,* 18 (April, 1953), 149-162.

[16] For analyses utilizing these distinctions see David Riesman, *op. cit.*; Karl Mannheim, "The Problem of Generations," in his *Essays on the Sociology of Knowledge* (London: Oxford University Press, 1952), pp. 276-320; C. Wright Mills, *The Power Elite* (New York: Oxford University Press, 1961), Ch. 2.

Two illustrations from recent politics will illustrate symbolic goals in status conflicts. In the election of 1960 Protestant-Catholic conflict was a major source of candidate loyalties.[17] Were Protestants protecting the White House from papal domination? Were Catholics trying to enhance Catholic doctrines by a Catholic president? Only the naive and the stupid will accept either of these suggestions. At stake, however, was the relative prestige of being Protestant in American life. The ability of a Catholic to break the traditional restriction in American politics does mean that prestige accruing from being Protestant has diminished; the prestige of being Catholic is enhanced. This meaning attaches no matter what President Kennedy might do in his official acts. It is a symbolic meaning given to the election of 1960. In a similar fashion the current school desegregation struggle is symbolic rather than instrumental. Whether or not most Negroes will actually be attending integrated schools in the near future is not the issue. Northern cities have developed little more than token integration. Public acceptance of the principle of integration, expressed in token integration, is an act of deference which raises the prestige of the Negro. Whether better educational conditions for Negroes will result is not the significant issue. It is that of equal rights. It is pointless to criticize token integration in instrumental terms, as not worth the intensive struggle to obtain it. To miss the symbolic goal of the token is to miss the crucial quality of it.

In both of the illustrations we have used status communities—Catholics and Negroes. When we analyze the less explicitly formed status collectivities, we also recognize the existence of symbolic goals of the same order. In his study of reform movements, Richard Hofstadter provides us with an excellent example. Men of the Mugwump type—old family, college-educated, well-off people—found their status in American society slipping while those whose moralities they detested were ascending. ". . . they [the Mugwumps] tended to have positions in which the initiative was not their own, or in which they could not feel themselves acting in harmony with their highest ideals. They no longer called the tune, no longer commanded their old deference. They were expropriated, not so much economically as morally."[18] In our interpretation, the acts of this

[17] Philip E. Converse, "The Currents of Religion in the 1961 Presidential Election," *Institute for Social Research Newsletter* (June, 1961), pp. 1-2.

[18] Richard Hofstadter, *The Age of Reform* (New York: A. A. Knopf, 1925), p. 140.

group, which Hofstadter sees as the basis of the Progressive movement, were attempts to restore that deference by actions symbolizing the lowered prestige of the corporate businessman, the machine politician, and the newly rich. They attempted, in acts such as the merit system, antitrust legislation, and enforcement of municipal anticorruption laws, to "cut down to size" the newly ascending status elements. The fact of political victory against the "enemy" shows where social and political dominance lie. The legislative victory, whatever its factual consequences, confers respect and approval on its supporters. It is at once an act of deference to the victors and of degradation to the losers. It is a symbolic rather than an instrumental act.

Expressive movements are marked by goalless behavior or by pursuit of goals which are unrelated to the discontents from which the movement had its source. The dancing mania of the Middle Ages, one result of the Black Death, is a classic instance of an expressive movement without any defined goal beyond release of tension, anxiety, and unrest. Men and women danced in the streets until they dropped. Expressive movements in their "pure" form are divorced from any goal in terms of changes demanded in the social system. Interpretations of movements as expressive are likely to utilize psychological mechanisms of displacement, projection, or rationalization to explain the actions in which they are interested. Thus Mannheim explains the rise of German Fascism as the eruption of irrationalities which had not been integrated into the social structure and which were now forcing their way into political life. When original instrumental expectations fail, a movement often succeeds in developing symbols which are substitute goals for the "real" aims. "In the first stage men flee to symbols and cling to them mainly because they want to avoid that anxiety which, according to Freud, overwhelms us whenever the libidinous energy remains for long without an object." [19]

These distinctions between types of movements should not hide the interconnections between types which empirical reality gives us. The Temperance movement has contained class elements and expressive elements which have been significant in its history. Nevertheless the dominant motif has been that of status enhance-

[19] Karl Mannheim, *Man and Society in an Age of Reconstruction* (London: Routledge and Kegan Paul, Ltd., 1940), p. 133.

ment or defense. Because abstinence has been symbolic of a style of life, conflicts about drinking and nondrinking have assumed symbolic properties and hence affected the distribution of prestige in American society. Our analysis of the Temperance movement must accordingly begin with a discussion of the significance of drinking and nondrinking in the conferral of respect, approval, admiration, and deference.

THE STATUS SIGNIFICANCE OF ALCOHOL AND ABSTINENCE

Any item of consumption can assume properties as an indication of the social position of its consumers.[20] Veblen's analysis of "conspicuous consumption" is a classic description of the functions of such commodities as furniture, dress, house type, and food as symbols of status. The consumption or nonconsumption of alcoholic beverages have often delineated group affiliation and status identity in American society. We cannot understand the history of the Temperance movement without placing liquor, beer, and wine in the context of social classes, ethnic cultures, and differential styles of life.

Consumption of intoxicating beverages is a cultural variable as are other items such as food, clothing, and shelter. There is no universal pattern of alcohol use. In some primitive tribes, such as the Zuni and the Hopi, drinking is tabooed. In many other tribes it is an integral part of religious and social ceremony, sometimes accompanied by intensive drinking bouts. There are great differences in the drinking behavior of various cultures. Studies of modern cultures and subcultures in the United States and elsewhere have found considerable difference among ethnic groups in the frequency and function of drinking.[21] The Mormons in the United States have

[20] For descriptions by various authors of drinking practices in ancient, modern, and primitive societies see Raymond McCarthy (ed.), *Drinking and Intoxication* (Glencoe, Ill.: The Free Press, and New Haven, Conn.: Yale Center of Alcohol Studies, 1959).

[21] Studies of class, religion, sex, and ethnicity as significant variables in American drinking behavior are reported in John W. Riley, Jr., and Charles F. Marden, "The Social Pattern of Alcoholic Drinking," *Quarterly Journal of Studies on Alcohol*, 8 (September, 1947), 265-273; John Dollard, "Drinking Mores of Social Classes," in Yale Center of Alcohol Studies, *Alcohol, Science and Society* (New Haven, Conn.: Quarterly Journal of Studies on Alcohol, 1945), pp. 95-104; Robert Straus and Selden Bacon, *Drinking in College* (New Haven, Conn.: Yale University Press, 1953); Charles Snyder, *Alcohol and the Jews* (Glencoe, Ill.: The Free Press, and New Haven, Conn.: Yale Center of Alcohol Studies, 1958).

a much higher rate of abstinence than have the Italian-Americans or the American Jews, although rates of chronic alcoholism are not any higher.

The evidence of cross-cultural and subcultural studies clearly indicates that the act of drinking is socially controlled for most people in most societies. A proper and improper use of alcohol is socially defined and transmitted in almost every society. The concern of social scientists with drinking has largely been with what, in American society, is defined as improper and deviant behavior. Our analysis of alcohol use is not concerned with deviant behavior but with customary usage—usage that is sanctioned, accepted, and expected in cultures and social groups.

While we recognize that drinking (or nondrinking) is socially organized behavior, we cannot ignore the physiological attributes of alcohol, although their consequences, appearance, and degree of effect may be influenced by cultural and social prescriptions. The depressant effects of alcohol on the human nervous system are universal properties of alcohol consumption. These anti-inhibiting properties set the stage within which the meaning and symbolism of drinking occur. We must, however, separate the physiological effects of alcohol from the meaning and significance attached to those effects.

Personal Functions of Alcohol Use

Functional interpretations of alcohol use have often maintained that drinking is a means to reduce personal tensions. The depressant effects, it is argued, permit relaxation of internalized social controls and, as a consequence, reduce the anxiety of internal control and permit the satisfaction of frustrated impulses. In his cross-cultural study of primitive societies, Donald Horton found that the customary degree and frequency of drunkenness varied directly with the anxiety level of the society. He concluded that "the primary function of alcoholic beverages in all societies is the reduction of anxiety." [22]

Even in Horton's study drinking is not a direct result of anxiety. Where the anxiety level of the culture was high but drinking was prohibited, it did not occur. Drinking was, in most cultures, per-

---

[22] Donald Horton, "The Functions of Alcohol in Primitive Societies: A Cross Cultural Study," *Quarterly Journal of Studies on Alcohol,* 4 (September, 1943), 199-320, at 223.

formed in a group setting and controlled by the social norms of the society. Our analysis suggests a series of social functions which Horton did not investigate. Whatever may be the *primary* functions of alcohol use, we are oriented to the functions which it serves as a differentiator of social and cultural groups, over and above its possible function in the dynamics of personailty.

Group Solidarity Functions of Alcohol

A Sliammon Indian drinking song illustrates the use of drink in establishing a sense of equality and solidarity in the group:

> Come closer to me, come closer to me, my slave.
> We are drinking now, we feel pretty good.
> Now you feel just like me.[23]

Precisely because alcohol may produce physiological and neurological effects which diminish inhibitions of ego and superego, it may serve to reduce the reserve and distance with which conventional social norms and personal structure often prevent a sense of group affiliation and a mood of intimacy. American hosts and hostesses often speak of liquor as a social "icebreaker." It provides the social director with the means to manipulate a mood of relaxation in which personal reserve and shyness are reduced among guests or committee members. The resultant convivality promotes what Edwin Lemert has termed the process of "intimitization"—the appearance of close and friendly relations among participants in a social situation.[24] Social statuses and roles, being prescriptive rules, prevent the intense cohesion and sociability which intimacy produces.

While physiological elements are important in the development, group solidarity is often promoted by the symbolic attributes of alcohol. According to Lemert, among the Northwest Coast Indians the drinking party was a symbol of political rebellion and cultural loyalty among the Indians. Since white authorities had banned the use and sale of liquor or beer to Indians, those who sought to preserve independence and a native culture demonstrated their loyalties through drinking. In the United States this significance has often been found in the differentiation of groups who demonstrate their attachment to traditional or modern norms by nondrinking or

[23] Edwin Lemert, *Alcohol and the Northwest Coast Indians,* University of California Publications in Culture and Society, 2, No. 6 (1954), 303-406, at 330.
[24] *Ibid.,* p. 332.

drinking. The act of drinking serves to bind the group together by being a sign of membership.

Two other aspects of alcohol as a symbol of solidarity are especially significant in American society. As a reflection of Temperance doctrine, in some segments of the society, drinking and drunkenness carry a connotation of tabooed action. Participation in a common "crime" promotes the solidarity of the "criminals." Failure to join a drinking group is often a more reprehensible "snub" than other acts of social deviance. Guests who refuse alcohol often "explain away" their refusal by some statements which remove the onus of possible "moral superiority." Failure to "join the crowd" in drinking is too fraught with possible overtones of moral rejection to be forgiven easily.

The Status Functions of Alcohol Use

Any element of behavior is capable of symbolizing the social status and group identity of the actor. What is essential is that it actually does differentiate between social levels and that it is so perceived. While people may, and often do, use types of alcoholic beverages and amount as ways of displaying income and training in consumership, the most significant distinction has been between drinking and abstinence and between moderate drinking and the acceptance of occasional drunkenness.

The idea of a *contrast conception* is useful in understanding the role of alcohol as a symbol of social status. The term is taken from usage in racial and cultural relations. It describes the ways in which groups impute significance to differences between their behavior and that of other social groups: "Wherever the groups and classes are set in sharp juxtaposition, the values and mores of each are juxtaposed. Out of group opposition there arises an intense opposition of values, which comes to be projected through the social order and serves to solidify social stratification." [25]

Each status group operates with an image of correct behavior which it prizes and with a contrast conception in the behavior of despised groups whose status is beneath theirs. Studies of consumption habits have given much attention to the pacesetters who occupy positions of high status and honor and who are emulated by those below them in the social structure. It is often overlooked that persons and groups of low social status are also sources of behavior

[25] Lewis Copeland, "The Negro as a Contrast Conception," in Edgar Thompson (ed.), *Race Relations and the Race Problem* (Durham, N.C.: Duke University Press, 1939), pp. 152-179, at 161.

for those above them, although in negative terms. They are negative reference groups, models of what *not* to do.[26] We look in two directions in gaining cues to status-producing behavior. We look upward or across at those above or on a par with us and downward at those whose social levels are lower. We emulate but we also avoid. Although much consumer behavior may be "keeping up with the Joneses," much is also "getting away from the Smiths."

Both age and sex have been utilized as sources of differentiation in drinking. By law and by informal norms, the use of alcohol is reserved for persons of maturity. This is often one element in the explanation of juvenile drinking. It is an attempt to signify adulthood. Sexual distinctions are found in many societies. Veblen pointed out that the taboo against female drinking was one way in which American men symbolized their higher status.[27] (It is a sore point in the Temperance movement that the Feminist movement, which was so closely allied to Temperance, has led to an increase in feminine drinking rather than a decrease among men.)

Drinking, and nondrinking, appear as crucial signs of the contrasts and similarities with which the differentiations of group membership are made into the substance of a social class system. In their break with established churches, new sects often react against the customs and morals of their opposition, as well as against their theology. The Lollardists of sixteenth-century England prohibited drinking, gambling, and sports—the prized leisure-time pursuits of the upper-class Catholics against whom they rebelled.[28] The Pentecostalists of Gastonia, North Carolina, expressed their revolt against the organized churches of the 1920's by a stringent set of restrictions on dancing, drinking, and movies.[29] Gregory Stone and William

[26] The concept of negative reference is discussed in Robert K. Merton, *Social Theory and Social Structure,* rev. ed. (Glencoe, Ill.: The Free Press, 1957), pp. 300-302. ". . . the negative type involves motivated rejection, i.e., not merely non-acceptance of norms but the formation of counter-norms" (p. 300).

[27] Veblen felt that the norm against female drinking was likely to be most intense wherever the patriarchal tradition persisted in which women were one form of chattel. Since drink was costly, its use was honorific and those of lowly status could not presume to use it. *Theory of the Leisure Class* (New York: Modern Library, 1934), pp. 70-72.

[28] Thomas Hall, *The Religious Background of American Culture* (Boston: Little, Brown and Co., 1940), pp. 27-39.

[29] Liston Pope, *Millhands and Preachers* (New Haven, Conn.: Yale University Press, 1943), pp. 84-91; Walter Goldschmidt, "Class Denominationalism in Rural California Churches," *American Journal of Sociology,* 9 (January, 1944), 348-355.

Form have shown that drinking and nondrinking have become salient demarcators of the leisure-time styles of "old" and "new" middle classes in one American city. The "drinking crowd" and the "temperance people" were clear and significant criteria for differentiating social groups in Vansburg.[30]

The place of alcohol consumption as an indicator of social status and group identity is borne out by a series of surveys of national and state populations and by several studies of specific American populations.[31] The highest frequency of abstainers is found among the Protestant lower middle classes. Here both sentiment and behavior are most favorable to abstention from alcohol. While the status levels associated with alcohol use have changed during the past 100 years, the use of alcohol as a means of identifying social class membership has been persistent, as we will show in later chapters. The relations between cultural membership and drinking are still existent. The rural and small-town Protestant is more likely to follow the prescriptions of abstinence than is the urban Catholic or Jew.

Drinking, however, is more than a convenient sign of group custom. It has a moral connotation associated with a style of life— a patterned system of behavior regulating a wide range of actions and distinguishing one group from another. Alcohol, we are arguing, has had a special function as a symbol of a general style of life associated with levels of social status. It has been a symbol of group membership because it has communicated to observers the set of commitments of the drinker or abstainer to ways of moral conduct in realms of work, play, and familial association. It is in this relationship that Temperance has drawn on a deep source of affect in its doctrine and activities.

The relation between drinking and types of life styles in America is best portrayed through a discussion of the moral basis of abstinence doctrine and the ethical basis of Temperance.

LIFE STYLES AND THE ETHIC OF TEMPERANCE

Life styles function in two ways to support a given system of social status. On one level they are signs to others that the actor does indeed occupy the social position attributed to him. In fashions, for example, the décolletage of the upper-class lady would be "out of

[30] Stone and Form, op. cit., p. 155.
[31] See footnote 21.

place" among a group of lower middle-class housewives. The lower middle-class pattern of activities and roles is built around the tasks and expectations of family roles in housekeeping and motherhood rather than the romantic and sexual roles of female glamour.[32] Indeed, signs of status membership are most stable and communicative when they indicate the moral commitments of persons. It is precisely in this fashion that drinking and abstinence have been able to function as marks of participation or rejection. Temperance has been an ethical position and, consequently, a sign of life style commitment and status group membership.

The Cult of Character

The recent attitude of psychologists, social workers, and medical authorities is that chronic alcoholism is a disease rather than a moral failing. This is a radical change from the attitude of the nineteenth century toward drinking and alcoholism. From the ethical precepts of Temperance adherents the use of alcohol in all forms and in all degrees was a moral problem. The drinker or the drunkard was neither sick nor foolish. He was sinful. An anonymous Temperance pamphlet of the early 1830's expresses the wickedness of the drinker: "The Holy Spirit will not visit, much less will He dwell with him who is under the polluting, debasing, effects of intoxicating drink. The state of heart and mind which this occasions is to Him loathsome and an utter abomination." [33]

The moral intensity of Temperance belief has reflected the premium placed on ascetic character and the condemnation of the pursuit of pleasure. The title of a sermon by a popular mid-nineteenth-century minister states the dualism of the elect and the damned in typical fashion: "Christian Recreation and Unchristian Amusements." In the sermon, Rev. Theodore Cuyler attacks a number of "sinful enjoyments," with special reference to the theater. He argues that there is a difference between *recreation*, which is purposeful and utilitarian, and *amusement*, which is pleasure for its own sake. Recreation strengthens us for the work of the world. The pleasure-loving "want stimulant and excitement" rather than

[32] Bernard Barber and Lyle Lobel have made this point in their study of fashions, " 'Fashion' in Women's Clothes and the American Social System," in Seymour Lipset and Reinhard Bendix (eds.), *Class, Status and Power* (Glencoe, Ill.: The Free Press, 1953), pp. 323-332.

[33] *Temperance Manual* (no publisher listed, 1836), p. 46.

refreshment.[34] Amusement, implies Cuyler, has no relationship to man's function as a member of society or as a spiritual being; it does not improve him in his capacities or responsibilities.

The concept of Temperance has rested on similar approaches to a specific vision of man's character in which self-mastery, industry, and moral consistency are prized virtues. Impulsive action is at the opposite pole from virtue. The good man is able, through his character, to win the victory of Will over Impulse. Ralph Barton Perry has coined an apt description for this ascetic quality. He calls it "moral athleticism." [35] Through acts of denial, restriction, and self-control the moral athlete both trains himself and displays to others that he possesses the stern virtues of character which enable him to conquer his impulsive demands. The decline in inhibition and reserve and the relaxation of moral censoriousness through artificial, uncontrolled means is thus anathema to a viewpoint in which man must prove himself through his own efforts. Not the effacement of self, but the continuous and systematic triumph of Reason over Desire is the desideratum of character. In the dictum of Sigmund Freud, whose own steadfast devotion to work might well have qualified him for honors on this score, "Where Id is, there shall Ego be."

The argument of the moderate drinker or the occasional drunkard is often that men need some release from their inhibitions. Such viewpoints are foreign to the ethic of Temperance. If the control of desire and spontaneity is the key to moral conduct, then drinking is a profound threat because it may engulf the drinker in demands which he cannot control. Anything less than perfect regulation of behavior, anything less than command is a concession to Nature and a sin of great magnitude. "Everything that rests my body or mind; improves my health and elevates my soul is commendable. Everything that stimulates the nervous system until I become a walking maniac; everything that debauches my body, weakens my conscience, excites impure thoughts, and makes my soul a terrible house of imagery; and everything that makes me

[34] A sermon preached at Cooper Institute, New York, on October 24, 1858. Reprint contained in the Fahnstock Collection of pre–Civil War pamphlets, Vol. 6, University of Illinois Library, Urbana.

[35] Ralph Barton Perry, *Puritanism and Democracy* (New York: Vanguard Press, 1944), p. 245.

forget God and eternity is dangerous and in the last damnable." [36] Whatever is unrelated or antagonistic to the development or functioning of the moral character is wasteful and immoral. Play, leisure, fun, and gaiety are, in themselves, without utility and hence to be avoided. They are acceptable only as adjuncts needed for better work. Sobriety is a cornerstone of this ethic because it insures the cardinal quality of self-command.

Temperance fiction of the nineteenth century supported this ethic in its depiction of the drinker as a man of weak character. The fact that a man drank was a sign of moral defect even before he suffered the always excruciating ravages of chronic drunkenness. Such a figure of weakness is Joe Morgan in the most famous of Temperance novels, *Ten Nights in a Barroom.*[37] We see him at the opening of the novel described as a friendly, easygoing person, inclined toward a certain irresponsibility in his work and not as successful in business as he might be. Morgan is an easy prey to alcohol addiction as a solution to his problems. The author of this classic implies that although Joe Morgan's self-indulgence led him to lose ownership of his mill, he wasn't much of a businessman anyway. His character was already spotted and drinking was as much a sign of this as a contributor to further decline.

In the ethical system of Temperance, drink is sinful. Its appearance is a sign of defective character. The ascetic qualities of nineteenth-century American ideals had no room for behavior which failed to improve and perfect man's ability to improve and perfect himself as a producer of goods and a performer of roles.

Institutional Constraints

Any style of life may be supported or rejected by the institutions of the society as well as by the status groups which adhere to the style. The style of life which Temperance values have manifested has been supported, in the past, by the constraints of institutional regulation, especially in economic and religious areas of society.

---

[36] Cuyler, *op. cit.*, pp. 12-13. This ascetic strain in Protestantism has, of course, received a classic statement in Max Weber, *The Protestant Ethic and the Spirit of Capitalism*, tr. Talcott Parsons (New York: Charles Scribner's Sons, 1956). For a specific study of the relation of ascetic Protestantism to amusements and consumption see Isidor Thorner, "Christian Science and Ascetic Protestantism" (unpublished Ph.D. dissertation, Harvard University, 1950).

[37] Timothy Shay Arthur, *Ten Nights in a Barroom* (Chicago: Union School Furnishing Co., 1854).

Such constraints, as we shall see, have diminished in scope and intensity during the past 25 years.

The value system of Temperance has been linked to institutional constraints through the cult of character and its empirical consequences for behavior. Beginning with Max Weber, a large body of writings has made clear the affinity between economic individualism and the Protestant doctrines of the virtue of ascetic qualities of industry, thrift, discipline, punctuality, and *sobriety*. While Temperance, as a movement, appears much later than Puritanism or the other ascetic sects, its ethical foundations are deep in this stream of Protestant thought and its resonance in the economic institutions of nineteenth-century America is profound.

There are two types of relationship between institutions and values which are exemplified in the Temperance cult of character. In one type the institution is a manifestation and developer of the form of character prized in Temperance doctrine. In the other, the institution provides sanctions which enforce the behavior enunciated in the value system.

The first relationship is discoverable in the assertions that Temperance aided economic success because the economic institutions were tests of moral character. The logic of this argument is found in an early form in the classic statement of economic individualism—Thomas Malthus' *Essay on Population*.[38] Malthus argued that population imbalance was an inevitable result of defeat in the struggle between Will and Desire. The sexual impulse was responsible for the fact that population outran the capacity of the economy to sustain the reproduced population. Malthus was a minister and he sought to reconcile his gloomy prediction with the image of a good and charitable Deity. His solution was one of moral character: if men would master their sexual appetites, marry late, and live in accordance with economic logic, then population would exist in balance with economic capacities. In other words, economic distress is a result of moral defect. Abstinence is the clue to economic welfare and indulgence the clue to depressions.

As the character traits of the Temperance ethic were useful to economic success, the values of character were also values in the economy. Institutions were but the proving grounds within which persons revealed character traits that brought about success or

[38] Thomas Malthus, *Essay on Population* (New York: E. P. Dutton, 1914).

failure.[39] Abstinence from intoxicating beverages was a sign that the person possessed the requisite character. They were positive aids to economic triumph, because the economy demanded the character which prized sobriety.

The economic and social ruin of the drunkard is a ubiquitous story, repeated over and over in the pages of Temperance fiction. The drunkard yields to impulse, loses his savings, his job, or his credit. He squanders his salary and loses the love of wife and child. Drink causes him to be late to work, to disobey orders, to endanger his health, and to miss business opportunities. Economic and social failure are inevitable results of intemperance from Lucius Sargent's *Temperance Tales* (1830's) to Upton Sinclair's *Cup of Fury* (1956). Sobriety is valuable, both as a moral virtue and as a necessary adjunct to economic capability.

The second form of relationship between institution and value system was manifest when sobriety was demanded as a trait of the would-be successful man. It was a necessary form of role behavior. To the employer, the sober worker was a promise of industry and reliability. Abstinence was a sign of economic worth. To the employee, a hint of insobriety might spell ruin to the prospects of a bright career. For the creditor abstinence was a sign that the debtor merited trust.

In this manner institutional constraints bolstered the moral training of church, school, and family. Pulpit, press, and business saw eye to eye. Theodore Cuyler was most explicit about the way in which the moral code was supported by economic rewards: "Would a sensible merchant take a young man into his counting house, make him his bookkeeper, confidant or cashier on the strength of his knowledge that that young man regularly attended the theatre?" [40]

In the period of the last half of the nineteenth century the Temperance ethic was in the heyday of its institutional resonance. The abstinence doctrine of the Temperance advocate was embedded in a style of life in which ascetic character was prized both institutionally and culturally. As we shall see, this style of life represented a contrast to the life style of groups below him in honor and pres-

---

[39] Irvin Wyllie has shown that this view of institutions was implicit in much of the self-help literature of the nineteenth century. See his *The Self-Made Man in America* (New Brunswick, N.J.: Rutgers University Press, 1954), Ch. 3.

[40] Cuyler, *op. cit.*, p. 15.

tige. Threats to the cultural and institutional dominance of the ethic of Temperance emerged in the twentieth century. As they did so, the status commanded by the life style of the Protestant middle classes, the primary carriers of the Temperance movement, possessed less and less resonance in American society.

The position of a style of life in the status structure is an important clue to the significance of attempts to persuade, influence, or force others to emulate it. In understanding the American Temperance movement in the different periods of its history, we shall observe how it has functioned to preserve, maintain, or defend the social status of its adherents.

2

Social Control
and Mobility,
1826-60

In descriptions of American Temperance, abstinence is often attributed to the effects of Puritan doctrine.[1] This view is contradicted by the facts of history. Puritan and other colonial leaders did not advocate total abstinence. They stood for the moderate and regulated use of alcohol, not its eradication. The development of Temperance doctrine and organization is best understood in the context of the social and cultural changes of the pre–Civil War period. It was especially influenced by the decline of Federalist aristocracy and the rise to social and political importance of the "common man" in the United States.

TEMPERANCE AS SOCIAL CONTROL

There are two phases to the development of the American Temperance movement in the period 1826-60. Although these phases overlap, each is connected with the status aspirations of a different social class. In the first phase, described in this section, Temperance represents the reaction of the old Federalist aristocracy to loss of political, social, and religious dominance in American society. It is an effort to re-establish control over the increasingly powerful middle classes making up the American "common man." In the second phase Temperance represents the efforts of urban, native Americans to consolidate their middle-class respectability through a sharpened distinction between the native, middle-class

[1] An example of this is found in Andre Seigfried, *America Comes of Age*, tr. H. H. and Doris Hemming (New York: Harcourt, Brace and Co., 1927).

life styles and those of the immigrant and the marginal laborer or farmer.

The Breakdown of the Colonial Social Order

The use of alcohol in colonial America was governed by legal and moral sanctions which maintained a norm of moderate drinking. Taverns were licensed, not to deter their use but to regulate inns for the benefit of the traveler. Moderate use of alcohol was approved. Taverns were social centers and innkeepers respected members of the community. Although drunkenness occurred and was punished, it was seldom frequent.[2] The controlled drinking of the American colonies was largely a result of a social order in which an elite of religious, economic, and political leadership was able to develop codes of conduct which were influential at most levels of the society. The American colonial society was rigidly divided into discrete classes and status levels. ". . . democracy was new; men were still described as gentlemen and simplemen . . . disparities of rank were still sustained by those of property."[3] Political and social power were in the hands of an aristocracy of wealth, based on the commercial capitalism of the East and the plantation ownership of the South.

The power of the colonial aristocracy cut across the institutions of the society. The same families and social groups were represented in the holders of leadership in the courts, in the governments, and in the churches. The power of the clergy as arbiters of morality was enhanced by the direct relationship between Federalist aristocracy and church leadership. The clergy, like the judiciary, were stabilizing influences in the social order. The codes of moderated drinking which were enunciated by them were reasonably well followed. Even after the development of towns and port cities, drinking in America, before the Revolution, was not a problem to which great attention was paid. Compared to the

[2] John A. Krout, *The Origins of Prohibition* (New York: A. A. Knopf, 1925), pp. 1-25; Alice Earle, *Home Life in Colonial Days* (New York: Macmillan, 1937), pp. 148-149, 156-165; Alice Earle, *Customs and Fashions in Old New England* (New York: Charles Scribner's Sons, 1893), pp. 163-213.

[3] Dixon Ryan Fox, *Decline of Aristocracy in the Politics of New York* (New York: Columbia University Press, 1919), p. v. Accounts of this social structure can also be found in Charles and Mary Beard, *Rise of American Civilization* (New York: Macmillan, 1937), pp. 125-138; John A. Krout, *The Completion of Independence* (New York: Macmillan, 1944); Clinton Rossiter, *The First American Revolution* (Harcourt, Brace and Co., 1956), pp. 138-187.

drunkenness of British cities at the same time and to the post-Revolutionary period, it was a remarkably sober era. ". . . against the dark background of conditions in England . . . town life in America stands out as a model of orderliness and sobriety." [4]

The breakdown of the old order of town life was manifested in the decline of Calvinist church leadership and aristocratic political power after the Revolution and in the first two decades of the nineteenth century. The American Revolution was a great solvent working to dissolve the rigid class and status structure of colonial society.[5] The period of post-Revolutionary ferment was also one of religious dissent, decline, and irreverence. In the process of change the established institutions of church power lost a great deal of their dominance in matters of moral behavior:

The trying years of the Revolution were critical for New England orthodoxy. It was an unsettled period filled with demoralizing tendencies. The use of intoxicants was well-nigh universal. Sabbath violations were winked at by the authorities; swearing, profanity and night-walking passed all but unnoticed. Depreciated money encouraged speculation and avarice. . . . Men were becoming materialistic. The minister was fast losing his autocratic sway in the parish. Congregationalism was seriously weakened. The Church of England was all but destroyed. . . . Hence one is not surprised at the inroads "nothingarianism" made into the established order.[6]

Perhaps nothing illustrates the tolerance of excessive drinking in the late eighteenth century as much as the heavy use of whiskey at ministerial ordinations, where considerable drinking and frequent drunkenness became customary. This was so much a feature of ministerial conduct that those who tried to apply the earlier norms of moderation were liable to criticism by superiors. Rev. John Marsh, Secretary of the American Temperance Society in the 1840's, recalled the fate of a minister who had scolded his colleagues for their intemperance. His superiors in the church called him a "pest" and a "blackguard" for his excessive moralism.[7]

By the end of the eighteenth and the early nineteenth century a

[4] Carl Bridenbaugh, *Cities in the Wilderness* (New York: Ronald Press, 1938), p. 30, also pp. 55-93, 249-302; Krout, *Origins of Prohibition*, p. 30.

[5] J. Franklin Jameson, *The American Revolution Considered as a Social Movement* (Princeton, N.J.: Princeton University Press, 1926), esp. Ch. 1.

[6] Richard Purcell, *Connecticut in Transition, 1775-1818* (Washington, D.C.: American Historical Association, 1918), p. 8.

[7] John Marsh, *Temperance Recollections* (New York: Charles Scribner and Co., 1867), p. 15.

"drinking problem" had developed in many American states. The old norms of moderation were less effective as the Calvinist clergy lost its political and social position as an elite. The increase in transient populations, especially in the seaport cities, added to the familiar complex of urban crime, poverty, and drinking. Alcoholic beverages were more potent than they had been before the Revolution. The separation from England deprived the Americans of access to good maltsters and high-quality beer, leading drinkers to use the distilled spirits, especially rum. Whiskey became an important part of the economy. Distilling spirits from grain and then shipping the distilled product was a convenient and profitable way to market the crop. Its use as a medium of exchange made liquor an important adjunct to the slave trade. All these factors, plus the impact of war on traditional moralities, help explain the decline of controlled drinking and the increased frequency of drinking and drunkenness in the post-Revolutionary period. Excessive drinking had become the custom at weddings, funerals, and christenings. A great many people considered drinking essential to health. No doctrine of abstinence or even temperance had yet emerged.

Temperance and the Federalist Response

The period in which Temperance doctrine and organization emerged was also the period of Jeffersonian and Jacksonian victories in politics. The Revolution and the developing frontier life spelled eventual defeat for the aristocrat at the hands of egalitarian forces. In politics, as well as religion, the dominance of the rich, the well-educated, and the wellborn of the Eastern seaboard was coming to an end. An uncultured and uneducated mass of farmers and mechanics was grasping the reins of supremacy and throwing off the controls of Federalist power. To the old aristocracy these developments were understandably frightening. If the Whiskey Rebellion and the acts of state legislatures had thrown them into panic, the election of Jefferson was a deathblow and the threatened presidency of Andy Jackson the nail in the coffin.

Increased drinking was symbolic of decline in the power and prestige of the old aristocracy in the new social order. Both in the settled areas and on the frontier, the independent farmer and the artisan no longer looked to the Federalist clergy for guides to their conduct, as they no longer followed the doctrines of Federalist politics. If their role as dominant economic class was at an end, the Federalists could attempt to hold on to the prestige of the old order by a bid for their disappearing moral leadership. The manners and morals of the "common man" now had consequences for their political actions. Accordingly it was necessary to reform the citizen so that he might follow the moral convictions set by the old aristocracy. The seeming capriciousness and indecorousness of popular government was symbolized in the figure of the drunken voter. To make him respond to the moral ideals of the old order was both a way of maintaining the prestige of the old aristocracy and an attempt to control the character of the political electorate. It is in this sense that we can speak of the early stages of Temperance as a means by which a declining status group attempted to maintain social control. "If the rule of the country by the rich, the well-born and the able was ended, at least the United States might have the government of the moral, the virtuous and the sanctified." [8]

We are aware that the political contest between the Federalists and the Jeffersonians-Jacksonians was far from a simple one between democratic virtue and aristocratic vice or a struggle between the "common man" and the forces of anti-egalitarianism. Recent historical research has shown much similarity in the economic and political views of both sides. This makes simple dichotomies unacceptable.[9] Nevertheless, it was true that the Federalists still formed a cohesive and distinctive social stratum. As such, they did see their social and political domination waning in American society.

In his study of the Abolitionist movement, David Donald has given a very similar picture of Federalist response to declining social status. Examining biographical data on Abolitionist leaders, Donald found that almost all of them were born between 1790 and 1810, were New Englanders, and were children of steadfast Federalists.[10] Through Abolitionism and other reforms they tried to

[8] Clifford S. Griffin, "Religious Benevolence as Social Control, 1815-1860," *Mississippi Valley Historical Review*, 44 (December, 1957), 423-444, at 432.

[9] This research is summarized by John William Ward in "The Age of the Common Man," in John Higham (ed.), *The Reconstruction of American History* (New York: Harper Torch Books, 1962), pp. 82-97. For partial criticism of the "new approach" see Marcus Cunliffe's discussion in his *The Nation Takes Shape: 1789-1837* (Chicago: University of Chicago Press, 1959), pp. 150-180.

[10] David Donald, "Towards a Reconsideration of Abolitionists," in his *Lincoln Reconsidered* (New York: Vintage Books, 1961), pp. 19-36.

regain their lost positions of leadership. They were men who felt the demise of the traditional values of their social class and, in trying to restore those values, attempted to recoup their dwindled status. They were out of place in a society beginning to be led by a commercial middle class. "Too distinguished a family, too gentle an education, too nice a morality were handicaps in a bustling world of business. Expecting to lead, these young people found no followers. They were an elite without function, a displaced class in American society." [11]

The dominance of the old elite of Federalists-Calvinists in the early Temperance movement is evident in the leadership of Temperance organizations and other groups devoted to moral improvement. As was true of other movements of religious benevolence in the early nineteenth century, the major efforts to reform American drinking habits were first led by the Calvinist ministry of New England. These were not spontaneous uprisings of self-reform among the poor, the sinful, or the drunkards. The Connecticut Society for the Reformation of Morals and the Massachusetts Society for the Suppression of Intemperance (both founded in 1813) were formed and led by clergymen and laymen of wealth, prominence, and Federalist politics. The first national Temperance association, the American Temperance Society (founded in 1826), was led by Congregationalist and nonevangelical Presbyterian ministers of Federalist commitment, such as Jedidiah Morse.[12] They turned to the Whigs for legislative support. Despite commitment to Temperance as a doctrine, the Methodists of western Massachusetts, who were staunch Jacksonians, advised their adherents against contributing to the society.[13]

[11] *Ibid.*, p. 33.

[12] The leaders of the organizations included such prominent Calvinists and Federalists as Jedidiah Morse, Jeremiah Evarts, and Eliphalet Porter. The lists of officers of these organizations included few who are not identified with this complex political and religious outlook. See the lists of officers in George Clark, *History of the Temperance Reform in Massachusetts, 1813-1883* (Boston: Clarke and Carruth, 1888), Ch. 1, and Krout, *Origins of Prohibition*, pp. 88-92. This is discussed in John R. Bodo, *The Protestant Clergy and Public Issues* (Princeton, N.J.: Princeton University Press, 1954), pp. 183-187. The same social base of the Temperance organization in Brooklyn in 1815 is noted in Ralph Weld, *Brooklyn Village* (New York: Columbia University Press, 1938), p. 94.

[13] Henry Wheeler, *Methodism and the Temperance Reformation* (Cincinnati, Ohio: Walden and Stowe, 1882), p. 73; George C. Baker, Jr., *An Introduction to the History of New England Methodism* (Durham, N.C.: Duke University Press, 1941), pp. 61-66.

The aims and doctrine of the early movement reveal its function as an attempt to control the newly powerful electorate, both in the cities and on the frontier.[14] In aiming to reform the "common man," the movement attempted to re-establish prestige by "lifting" the rude mass to styles of life enunciated by an aristocratic moral authority. The movement was not viewed primarily as self-reform but as the reform of others below the status and economic level of the organizational adherents. Temperance supporters were men of religious conviction and moral righteousness whose own codes of moderate drinking were made models for the lives of the poor souls who had not yet achieved perfection.

This relationship between the early Temperance movement and status discontents is apparent in the writings of its leading spokesman Lyman Beecher, the New England minister. Beecher was the inheritor of Calvinist and Federalist church leadership and the leading opponent of revivalist methods. By 1810 he had become a leading critic of contemporary drinking habits and a supporter of abstinence from whiskey, beer, and other spirits. Under his leadership the Connecticut Society for the Reformation of Morals was established. Most moral reform movements of the 1810's and 1820's included him among their prominent officials. For Beecher, reform was clearly part of the defense of the old order against republican political sentiment and religious infidelity. In 1812 he voiced his fear at the growing power of the masses and his dismay at the decline of ecclesiastical control:

Our institutions, civil and religious, have outlived that domestic discipline and official vigilance in magistrates which rendered obedience easy and habitual. The laws are now beginning to operate extensively upon necks unaccustomed to their yoke, and when they shall become irksome to the majority, their execution will become impracticable. . . . To this situation we are already reduced in some districts of the land. Drunkards reel through the streets day after day . . . with entire impunity. Profane swearing is heard.[15]

For Beecher the Temperance movement was an effort to reform the masses. He saw drinking in its political consequences. Reiterating the Federalist image of an ordered society in which the church was a powerful arbiter of morals, Beecher viewed intem-

---

[14] Clifford S. Griffin, *His Brother's Keeper* (New Brunswick, N.J.: Rutgers University Press, 1960).

[15] *Autobiography of Lyman Beecher*, 1 (New York: Harper and Bros., 1864), 255-256.

perance as politically dangerous. In *Six Sermons on Intemperance* (1826), the leading statement of Temperance doctrine in the period, he wrote that intemperance fostered irreligion and, by undermining the church, endangered the political health of the nation. His writings displayed the classic fear the creditor has of the debtor, the propertied of the propertyless, and the dominant of the subordinate—the fear of disobedience, renunciation, and rebellion:

When the laboring classes are contaminated, the right of suffrage becomes the engine of destruction. . . . Such is the influence of interest and ambition, fear and indolence that one violent partisan, with a handful of disciplined troops, may overrule the influence of five hundred temperate men who are without concert. Already is the disposition to temporize, to tolerate, and even to court the intemperate too apparent on account of the apprehended retribution of their perverted suffrage. . . . As intemperance increases, the power of taxation will come more and more into the hands of men of intemperate habits and desperate fortunes; of course the laws will gradually become subservient to the debtor and less efficacious in protecting the rights of property.[16]

Temperance doctrine also made an appeal as a means for controlling subordinates. Even in the colonial social order, there were two qualifications to the permissive attitude toward alcohol use. The American Indian was "out of bounds" to liquor sales, both on grounds of moral welfare and because the colonists feared rebellion as a result of intoxication.[17] The American Negro was similarly restricted, as were apprentices and servants in many states, "lest the time of the master be spent in dissolute idleness."[18] In some states there were legal limits to the amount of credit obtainable at liquor stores. In this fashion the poor, having less cash, were less able than the rich to purchase large quantities of alcohol. In the two earliest

[16] Lyman Beecher, *Six Sermons on Intemperance* (New York: American Tract Society, 1843), pp. 57-58.

[17] The Indian's use of alcohol went well beyond the limits of restraint inculcated in the colonists. Those concerned for the moral welfare of the Indians were consequently involved in Temperance activities. The first Temperance publication in American history, *The Mighty Destroyer Displayed*, stemmed from such considerations. Its author, Anthony Benezet, was a Philadelphia Quaker much concerned with charities. He had been active in the education of free Negroes. From this he moved into work to aid the living conditions of American Negroes. As an accompaniment to this welfare interest, Benezet became involved in the welfare of the American Indian. It was this concern which first prompted his interest in the alcohol problem. See Krout, *Origins of Prohibition*, pp. 64-65.

[18] *Ibid.*, p. 17.

known local Temperance societies, improvement of employee efficiency was a major argument for Temperance reform. Both groups made pleas to employers for the discontinuance of the custom by which employers provided alcoholic refreshment as part of wages or as an accompaniment to farm labor.[19]

In the 1820's, when the Temperance movement began its organization and initiated its doctrine, the drive toward abstinence from distilled spirits (beer, wine, and cider were still permitted) functioned as a means to restore a superior position to the declining Federalist elite. As decline in moral behavior symbolized the sad facts of a waning social power, the old aristocracy sought to retain their prestige and power by upholding the standards by which the nation might then live. It was not an effort to reform the habits and behavior of those who made up its membership. The lowly, the small farmer, the wage earner, the craftsman—these were the objects of reform. This is not to maintain that there was no conviction of sin among the responsible citizens who made up the Temperance associations. What it implies is that such associations sought to disseminate and strengthen the norms of life which were part of the style of the old elite.

TEMPERANCE AS SOCIAL MOBILITY

The Temperance movement became a major social and political force in American life only as it was freed of the symbols of aristocratic dominance and converted into a popular movement to achieve self-perfection among the middle and lower classes of the nation. In the second phase of the movement Temperance became a sign of middle-class respectability and a symbol of egalitarianism.

Revivalism and "Bourgeoisification"

The great waves of religious revivalism occurring during the first third of the nineteenth century destroyed whatever leadership the old aristocracy had over American religion. Paradoxically, they made possible the moral reforms which that aristocracy had tried to bring about. As the revivalist waves of Methodism, Baptism, and the "new Presbyterianism" rolled up adherents and dried the pools of religious indifference, America underwent an intense change in

[19] *Ibid.*, pp. 79-80; Daniel Dorchester, *The Liquor Problem in All Ages* (New York: Phillips and Hunt, 1887), pp. 181-186; Charles A. Ingraham, "The Birth at Moreau of the Temperance Reformation," *New York State Historical Association, Proceedings*, 6 (1906), 115-133.

moral climate. The dissolute and secular nature of the post-Revolutionary period was replaced by the condemnation of moral infidelity. Abstinence became a part of necessary moral action rather than a matter of personal choice. Intemperance became sinful and the sober, nondrinking man a model of community respectability.

The relation between Temperance and the status system was influenced by revivalist activities. Embracing religion meant that the "convert" was now subject to the strict moral codes of evangelical Protestantism. Indulgence and idleness were among the major vices which the religious man swore to avoid. Chief among these was the vice of insobriety.

Religion and individual perfectionism went hand in hand. To be saved was evidenced through a change in habits. The man of spiritual conviction could be known by his style of living. If frontier life emphasized the roughness, liberty, and dissoluteness of a society without settled institutions, then there was all the more reason to stress the need for moral rigidity and an enthusiastic response to perfectionist standards. The organizers and directors of the major benevolent societies of the frontiers believed that moral and religious reform would make the convert a less radical voter and a more trustworthy credit risk.[20]

The assumption was quite clear. Sanctified men make better borrowers, better workers, better citizens. The corollary of this was not a glorification of the humble poor, obediently carrying out the dictates of the lordly. Rather, the corollary was the doctrine of self-improvement through the Lord. In the thick of Methodist development, John Wesley had been concerned with this consequence of the religious movement. As men became more industrious, sober, thrifty, methodical, and responsible they also improved their income through work. Pure religion might decay, "for the Methodists in every place grow diligent and frugal; consequently they increase in goods."[21]

It is in this sense that the revivalist movements of the 1820's and 1830's contributed to Temperance and to the function of abstinence as a mark of the man bent on improving his conditions of income and his status in the community. As an aspect of religious revivalism, Temperance was enjoined as a moral virtue. As a matter of self-improvement it designated the man of middle-class habits and

---

[20] Griffin, *His Brother's Keeper*, pp. 55-60.
[21] Quoted in Weber, *The Protestant Ethic and the Spirit of Capitalism*, p. 175.

aspirations. In this sense revivalism was part of the process of "bourgeoisification," a process in which the worker or the farmer takes on a middle-class (bourgeois) mode of life.

Temperance and Self-Improvement

That Temperance was one part of improving status was evident in several changes in the movement during the 1830's and 1840's. In this period it changed from one in which the rich aimed at reforming the poor into one in which members aimed at their own reformation.

During the 1830's, and especially in the 1840's, Temperance organizations and doctrine began to appear more often among groups not previously touched by the movement. Organized Temperance units emerged without the auspices of churches or ministers. A popular literature developed which used an emotional and dramatic quality of music, drama, and fiction. Even the form of the Temperance meeting was borrowed from revivalist experiences—hymn singing, vernacular speech, open-air meetings, and personal confession, all characteristics of the American revival, were put to use in eradicating Demon Rum.

The self-improvement motif is clearly observable in the Washingtonian movement and in its subsequent results. The Washingtonians began in Washington, D.C., in 1840, with a small group of reformed drunkards. Like the current Alcoholics Anonymous, the movement was addressed to people who were, or were close to becoming, alcoholics. In their pledge the Washingtonians displayed the growing importance of Temperance as a sign of middle-class status: "We, whose names are annexed, desirous of forming a society for our mutual benefit, and to safeguard against a pernicious practice injurious to our health, *standing* [italics added] and families, do pledge ourselves as gentlemen, that we will not drink any spirituous or malt liquors, wine or cider." [22]

The success of the Washingtonians in establishing a large number of units and followers among reformed drinkers and drunkards was an important element in the development of that most typical American self-improvement institution—the fraternal lodge. Even with the demise of the Washingtonians after the spread of internal conflict in the major Temperance societies, Temperance found an important source in the development of such organizations as the

[22] Krout, *Origins of Prohibition*, p. 183.

Good Templars, the Rechabites, and, most prominently, the Sons of Temperance. Like the Washingtonians, these groups were efforts to effect temperate habits among those who joined. In seeking to reform their own members these organizations differ sharply in attitude from the earlier Temperance societies of the 1820's. An excerpt from the 1842 report of the New York division of the Sons of Temperance is illustrative of the self-oriented tone of these societies:

The Order of the Sons of Temperance has three distinct objects. . . . To shield us from the evils of intemperance, to afford mutual assistance in cases of sickness and to elevate our characters as men.

We find the necessity of closer union . . . to be cemented by the ties of closer alliance and mutual benefit; to keep up and fully maintain an unrelaxed spirit of perseverance. . . .

The Order of the Sons of Temperance is merely intended as another link in the chain . . . to bind those who may have been so unfortunate as to acquire the insatiable thirst for alcoholic drinks more securely to the paths of rectitude and honor.[23]

Membership was both a sign of commitment to middle-class values and a step in the process of changing a life style. Like the Washingtonians these groups often consisted of many former drinkers and drunkards and were led by laymen rather than ministers. Like the fraternal lodges of today, of which they were forerunners, the Temperance brotherhoods were also mutual societies which conferred insurance and other economic benefits on members. They became so popular that the leading organization, the Sons of Temperance, had grown in six years from a single unit to one of 6,000 units and 200,000 paying members all pledged to total abstinence.[24]

The Decline of Aristocratic Dominance

Evangelical Protestantism recruited large numbers of soldiers for the Temperance army. Converted to a more sober behavior, they pushed aside the traditional leadership of orthodox ministers in the Temperance organizations and replaced them with a lay leadership drawn from far lower social ranks than the earlier organizations had encompassed. Revivalism had flourished among the churches of the common people where emotional expression was customary. When Temperance began to reflect the methods of the revivalist

[23] "Proceedings of the New York Division, Sons of Temperance, 1842," in Sons of Temperance, *Journal of the Proceedings of the National Division,* 1 (1844-49), 10-11.
[24] *Ibid.,* p. 211.

it acquired an appeal that had been lacking in the colder attempts of an Eastern, upper-class clergy to convert the poor to the life of righteousness. The original movement had developed in the East and its leadership remained Eastern until the late 1830's. By 1831 the American Temperance Society had 2,200 local societies with a reported membership of 170,000. Although one-sixth of the population lived in the six states northeast of the Hudson River, the area contained one-third of the Temperance organizations and one-third of the national membership. The center of Temperance was in the East, with all that this symbolized socially and politically to a nation whose political axis had begun to move westward.[25]

As the small property holder and the propertyless were drawn to the movement, they brought to it a higher level of self-demand than had been true of the earlier movement. Concerned with self-improvement, they could not compromise with evil as those more righteously trained could have done. The entry of the West into Temperance organizations was followed by ultraist doctrines. The new Temperance adherents were not content with moral suasion alone. In its beginnings, the American Temperance Society had declared for total abstinence from all spirits, but it drew the line at beer, wines, and cider. "This," said one member, "was impolitic and carrying the thing too far." [26] The Western units pushed for a wider conception of total abstinence, in the tradition since known as "teetotaling." In at least one Eastern state, New York, demand for total abstinence resulted in the loss of wealthy supporters.[27] By the late 1830's, however, internal conflicts were resolved in favor of the ultraists. Total abstinence from all alcoholic beverages was the primary doctrine of Temperance organizations everywhere in the United States. There would be no compromise with Evil in any of its forms.

Another result of the decline in aristocratic leadership and the conversion of the movement into one of "common man" identification was the rise of lay leadership. The Washingtonian movement was disapproved by the good people who had formed the Temper-

[25] Krout, *Origins of Prohibition*, pp. 128-131. D. L. Colvin, *The Prohibition Party in the United States* (New York: George H. Doran Co., 1926), Ch. 1, gives slightly different figures for the same year. These figures must be qualified by the fact that the Southern units did not keep accurate records.

[26] Dorchester, *op. cit.*, pp. 235-236.

[27] Whitney Cross, *The Burned-Over District* (Ithaca, N.Y.: Cornell University Press, 1950), pp. 211-216.

ance organizations of the 1820's and early 1830's. "Many of the leaders were uneducated and their addresses were not always of an elevating character." [28] There was much criticism of the informal character of meetings, in which people arose from the audience to narrate their experiences with King Alcohol. Men who emerged as leaders of this movement often gained great fame as orators. These men, such as John Gough and John H. W. Hawkins, had little background in public speaking and little education. They had no connection with organized religion and they based their appeal for sobriety and temperance on grounds of personal welfare rather than religion alone. In their evangelical techniques, indifference to theology, and vulgar identification with the manners and language of the masses, they were anathema to the more conservative and sedate leaders of the earlier movement.[29]

The Washingtonians, and the newer Temperance associations of the 1840's, brought a common touch to the movement. After that Temperance activities were couched in a more popular vein. An emotional and dramatic quality appeared in Temperance ceremony, music, drama, and fiction. Parades became a standard form of persuasion, and banners, flags, and outdoor meetings were typical parts of the program. Temperance songs were written and children enlisted in the cause. Perhaps the most vivid instance of this appeal to the emotional sensitivities of mass response is seen in the development of a children's group, the Cold Water Army. With songs, parades, and demonstrations by children the virtues of water and the iniquities of drink were dramatized to the public.[30]

Abstinence as Status Symbol

The quest for self-improvement implies a gap between those who

[28] Clark, op. cit., p. 53.

[29] Rev. John Marsh complained of the demand from audiences for recounting of experiences. It led to the exclusion of clergymen and other early Temperance speakers from the platforms of Temperance meetings. Marsh, op. cit., p. 297. This autobiography is an interesting statement of the coolness with which the organized Temperance movement greeted the Washingtonians. Marsh criticized the indecorous character of their meetings, the tobacco smoking of leaders, and the failure of the Washingtonians to open meetings with prayer. Ibid., pp. 94-99, 130, 230-232. The anticlerical nature of the Washingtonians is also evident in the account of one of its leading orators. See John Gough, Autobiography (London: W. Tweedle & Co., 1875).

[30] See the description of Temperance activities in Chicago during the 1840's in Bessie Louise Pierce, A History of Chicago, 1 (New York: A. A. Knopf, 1937), 258-263.

remain dissolute and those who have achieved respectability. By the 1850's, sobriety and abstinence were no longer rare examples of unique fidelity to saintly virtues. Drinking was at best tolerated and sobriety had become a necessary aspect of respectable, middle-class status. If not universally good, Americans were becoming, in this respect at least, somewhat better. Abstinence and sobriety had become public virtues. For reputation, if for nothing else, it was not expedient to be thought to be anything more than a moderate drinker. Abstinence had become part of the national religious faith. "Sunday morning all the land is still. Broadway is a quiet stream, looking sober, even dull." [31]

Temperance fiction was probably the most effective media of mass persuasion in the Temperance cause. It often played on the theme of drinking as an indication of outcast or low social position and abstinence as a symbol of middle-class life. In Temperance tales the drinker is not only an immoral and sinful man in his alcoholic vice. He is also about to be ruined. With drink comes economic deprivation. The drinker loses his industrious devotion to work. He loses his reputation for reliability. Finally he is without any employment at all. Retribution is possible. Reform, sobriety, and the pledge to abstain are rewarded by the return of economic virtues and the reappearance of economic reward.

Along with the vision of the drinker as the ruined man went the belief that the solution to poverty lay along the road to Temperance. The benefits of reformation and improvement were not pictured in terms of what they could do for the employer but for the employee. In one of his most famous stories, "Wild Dick and Good Little Robin," L. M. Sargent described the basic contrast of character between drinkers and abstainers. Dick, having reformed his drinking ways, "continued to grow in favor with God and man. He gave farmer Little complete satisfaction, by his obedience, industry and sobriety. He was permitted to cultivate a small patch of ground, on his own account." [32]

The significance of abstinence as a symbol of respectability was enhanced when large numbers of Irish and German immigrants

[31] From a review of Henry Ward Beecher's *Sermons* published in *The Atlantic Monthly* in 1858, quoted in Timothy L. Smith, *Revivalism and Social Reform* (New York: Abingdon Press, 1957), p. 37.

[32] Lucius Manius Sargent, "Wild Dick and Good Little Robin," in his *Temperance Tales* (Boston: Whipple and Damrell, 1836), p. 33.

entered the United States and made up the unskilled labor forces of the growing urban centers during the 1840's and 1850's. In the culture of the Irish and the Germans, use of whiskey or beer was customary and often a staple part of the diet. Both groups were at the bottom of the class and status structure in American society. In the evolution of status symbols, the groups at the lowest rungs of the ladder affect the behavior of those above by a process of depletion in which those traits originally shared by both groups become progressively deprized among the more prestigeful. The incoming group thus widens the status gap between it and the natives. If the lowly Irish and Germans were the drinkers and the drunkards of the community, it was more necessary than ever that the aspirant to middle-class membership not risk the possibility that he might be classed with the immigrants. He must hew more closely to the norms which provided cultural distinctiveness. As the narrator of *Ten Nights in a Barroom* phrased it, "Between quiet, thrifty, substantial farmers and drinking bar-room loungers there are many degrees of comparison." [33]

TEMPERANCE AS A POLITICAL SYMBOL

The Temperance movement began as one solely of moral suasion. By the 1840's it had become a significant part of American politics, capable of affecting local and state elections. As Temperance doctrine reached larger segments of the population, demands arose to limit the sale and use of intoxicants by legislation. Both the enforcement of existing laws and the passage of new, restrictive measures became important issues in many states. The drive to restrict liquor and beer consumption reached its heights in the state prohibition drive of the 1850's. By 1856, eight states had passed some form of Prohibition legislation.

As the sale and use of alcoholic beverages became a political issue, consumption and abstinence took on even greater meaning as symbols of group loyalty and differentiation. Political opposition reinforced the already evident contrasts of culture in which the daily fare of one group was the dangerous poison of the other. The supporter of anti-alcohol legislation was not simply someone who issued a moral condemnation of drinking. He was trying to make it more difficult for the drinker to follow his customary habits.

[33] Timothy Shay Arthur, *Ten Nights in a Barroom* (Chicago: Union School Furnishing Co., 1854), p. 85.

There was another way in which the emergence of Temperance
in politics deepened group conflicts. It linked Temperance and anti-
Temperance adherence to other class, cultural, and sectional conflicts on which it was superimposed. The supporter of legislation
encouraging Temperance was also likely to be a supporter of religious benevolence movements, of Abolition, and of nativist measures. His opponents were likely to oppose these measures as well.

Federalist Conservatism and Early Temperance

The heavily Eastern and upper-class support of the American Temperance Society was one aspect of the identification of the early
movement with anti-Jacksonianism. In Beecher and in the officials
of the leading Temperance associations, the commitment to the
struggle against Jackson was evident. Although the Temperance
movement did not seek legislative results until the 1840's, earlier
it had a political tone which made it suspect by the Jacksonian, who
was also likely to be a Westerner and religiously evangelical. In
Congress, for example, Senator Theodore Frelinghuysen was the
outstanding exponent of Temperance and the other goals of benevolent societies. He was one of Jackson's major opponents. Like
Beecher, he was explicit in viewing moral benevolence and religion
as a way of controlling the sources of Jacksonian support in the
West.[34]

In terms of practical party politics this meant that Temperance
supporters tended to find allies among the Whigs during the 1820's
and 1830's. This relation between political conservatism and Temperance appears in the career of one of the leading Temperance
agitators of the pre–Civil War period, Neal Dow.[35] Dow was sympathetic to the Federalists. In 1824 he voted for John Quincy
Adams, whose protectionist policy he favored. He was always an
intense foe of Jackson. In 1832 he found political refuge within
the anti-Masonic movement. He supported Harrison in 1840 though
he bitterly disliked the "log cabin" appeal to the average man.

Until 1838 the American Temperance movement did not attempt
direct political action. In that year the Massachusetts legislature
passed the first major Temperance bill, the Fifteen-Gallon law,
which prohibited purchase of liquor in quantities of less than 15

---

[34] Griffin, *His Brother's Keeper*, p. 58.
[35] Neal Dow, *Reminiscences* (Portland, Me.: Express Publishing Co., 1898),
pp. 120-141.

gallons. Since cash was scarest among the poorer sections of the state, the law restricted drinking among the poor more than among the rich.[36] It was repealed two years later but the precedent of seeking Temperance through law was established. It was the first wave in a campaign to outlaw taverns and to limit the sale of alcoholic beverages.

As the movement gained adherents in the West, Temperance organizations increasingly saw legislation as a mechanism through which reform could be accomplished. During this period (1840's) neither the Whigs nor the Democrats were clearly pro- or anti-Temperance, although it was still among the Whigs that most support might be found. The remnant of Jacksonian issues was still strong enough so that Horace Greeley characterized the Whigs as pro-Temperance and the Loco-Focos as anti-Temperance in the New York No-License campaign of 1845.[37]

The Reformist Movement and Temperance

Party splits were overshadowed by the growing relationship between Temperance and other political issues of the late 1840's and the 1850's. The activities of church groups had made Temperance one aspect of movements to improve the country's religious adherence. Sabbatarianism, the home missionary movements, Bible tract societies, and the move to abolish drink, as we have seen, had affinities for those who feared the common man as the new source of power. The issues of the pre–Civil War era, however, involved conflicts of economic interest and cultural differences to a vaster extent than the narrower moral problems of the churches.

The period from 1830 to 1860 has been referred to by some historians as "the era of reform" because there were so many organizations and movements devoted to improving mankind, changing social conditions, and reforming the character of human beings. These movements were seldom separate affairs. Indeed, the same people were often involved in a great many of the movements.[38] People like Geritt Smith, Theodore Weld, and Arthur Tappan were

---

[36]Krout, *Origins of Prohibition*, pp. 268-269.

[37] *Ibid.*, p. 283.

[38] The general quality of the reform movement is discussed in Arthur Bestor, Jr., "The Ferment of Reform," in Richard Leopold and Arthur Link (eds.), *Problems in American History* (New York: Prentice-Hall, 1952), Ch. 8, and Carl Fish, *The Rise of the Common Man, 1830-1850* (New York: Macmillan, 1937), p. 256.

found in the moral benevolence societies, the Abolitionists, and the Temperance societies, as well as less flamboyant movements such as peace and the abolition of Sunday mail. Among these, only the antislavery movement surpassed Temperance in the intensity of its support and the influence of its political power.

As American politics underwent a reformulation on the eve of the Civil War, Temperance and Abolitionism went hand in hand. Neal Dow is again an illustration of the process. Although a Whig during most of his life, Dow became a Free Soiler in 1848 and a Republican in 1856. His antislavery feeling was deep and had existed since his youth, when his home was a stop on the Underground Railroad. He had an immense admiration for Lincoln and an intense hatred of the South.[39] In Dow's successful Temperance campaigns for statewide Prohibition in Maine, the Liberty Party and the Free Soilers were his strongest supporters. "The one group in the state on which the Prohibitionists could count was the antislavery element." [40] Temperance and antislavery were united in the Massachusetts victory of the Know-Nothings as they were in similar victories in the United States.[41]

Temperance emerged in the 1850's in political association with forces which were breaking away from the old parties. Perhaps there were ideological similarities between Abolition and Temperance. They were both highly moralistic and perfectionist. Perhaps it was the occurrence of both in the same parts of the society—the native American independent farmer of the Midwest and East. The identification with antislavery was strong enough to stifle completely the organization of the Temperance movement in the South. Although Temperance agitation had developed in Southern states during the 1820's, by the late 1830's Temperance was unable to gain any strength in the South. Temperance was emerging as a point of union between segments of politics splitting off from the major parties. "While Whigs and Democrats split over anti-slaveryism and other matters, former partisans of both groups became Know-Nothings. These politicians also became Prohibitionists, and out of such ingredients came the potpourri of Republicanism." [42]

[39] Dow, *op. cit.*, pp. 20-21.
[40] *Ibid.*, p. 289.
[41] Oscar Handlin, *Boston's Immigrants* (Cambridge, Mass: Harvard University Press, 1941), pp. 201-209; Ray Billington, *The Protestant Crusade, 1800-1860* (New York: Macmillan, 1938).
[42] Griffin, *His Brother's Keeper*, p. 218.

Temperance and Nativism

The association of the Irish and Germans with opposition to Temperance programs added a significant meaning to Temperance in the political arena. It widened the cultural gap between native and immigrant by placing each as opponent to the other's way of life. The American Protestant and immigrant Catholic were not simply two people of somewhat different cultures. When Temperance sought legislative ends, each group became the impediment to the other's victories. The alliance between Temperance and the anti-alien movement of the Know-Nothings completed a polarization process in which political defeat was tantamount to a loss of status and power for the cultural group that bore the loss.

The relation between the native American and the immigrant populations of the cities added a third orientation—a welfare orientation—to the two already described as major sources of Temperance doctrine and sentiment. The upper-class, displaced power-elite of the Eastern seaboard attempted to shore up a fading control through the moral regeneration of the new electorate. The "common man" sought his own self-improvement through the Temperance societies. Both sought to assimilate the immigrant to American society and to solve the problems of urban poverty through Temperance. They viewed the immigrant as an object of benevolence; someone they would help to achieve the morally sanctified habits of the native American, of which abstinence had become so cardinal a virtue. Here, as in the antislavery movement, Temperance was again an effort of those who practiced virtue to make their style of life a universal one.[43]

That the immigrant was an object for the commiseration and concern of native Protestants was logical enough if one examined his standards of welfare, as well as morality. During the 1840's and 1850's the American labor force began to develop significant industrial characteristics as the American economy became larger, more urbanized, and more composed of unskilled labor. The Irish and German immigrants were the backbone of that industrial expansion. Wherever cities developed, so did the complex of criminality, intemperance, poverty, and ill-health. It was more typical of the Irish than of the Germans but it was an apparent problem in Ger-

[43] Gilbert Hobbs Barnes, *The Anti-Slavery Impulse* (New York: Appleton-Century-Crofts, 1933), p. 25.

man Ohio as well as Irish Massachusetts.[44] During the 1840's the cost of intemperance to the society was one important theme in Temperance literature. One of the leading tracts of the late 1840's was Samuel Chipman's "Temperance Lecturer: being facts gathered from a personal examination of all the jails and poor-houses in the State of New York, showing the effects of intoxicating drinks in producing Taxes, Pauperism, and Crime." The subtitle of this work was typical of this genre in its stress on Temperance as a solution to a perplexing public problem of both moral and financial dimensions. In Boston and other parts of Massachusetts, rural areas resented the large state tax bill, resulting in part from the high rates of pauperism among the Irish immigrants.[45]

Benevolence and hostility, as we point out throughout this book, are dual ways of responding to the existence of a different culture in our midst. We can feel sorry for the poor, ignorant heathen who know no better, and try to lift them to our standards. We also can see them as immoral creatures who threaten our safety and institutions and who must be stopped and restrained. In the 1840's and 1850's the Temperance movement engaged in both moral benevolence and nativistic hostility. The hostility was evidenced in the political affinities between Prohibition and anti-alienism, as well as antislavery.

The Know-Nothings and the Free Soilers made considerable headway through the combination of Abolitionism, Temperance, and an appeal to nativism. The Know-Nothings, and the other new parties of the 1850's, can justly be called "a collection of men looking for new political homes." [46] There was a pronounced affinity between the three elements of opposition to immigration, drink, and slavery. The same people were not always found in each other's company but the tendency was considerable.

The political confrontation between native and immigrant was a real one, based on real cultural differences. Temperance, to the Irish Catholic and the German Lutheran, was a tyranny over their ways of life and not a move to uplift the society. The "grogshop"

[44] This portrait of the Irish in Massachusetts in based on Handlin, *op. cit.*, and on Vera Shlakman, *Economic History of a Factory Town*, Smith College Studies in History (October, 1934), Ch. 4. The situation of the German immigrants was different. Although they displayed no affinity for temperance, their skills, industrial habits, and cultural norms were closer to those of the native American.

[45] Handlin, *op. cit.*, pp. 191-192.

[46] Billington, *op. cit.*, Ch. 15.

and beer stein were accepted parts of Irish and German group life. There was no experience with revivalism nor any tradition of moderate drinking to be revived. When the Temperance reform swept the Americans, heavy drinking was a falling off from a once-accepted moral standard. This was not the case among the immigrants, where drinking patterns were not viewed as a severe problem.

Politically, the immigrant populations were the most powerful opponents of the Temperance forces. The fear of losing immigrant support was a major source of political compromise on Prohibition issues in the 1850's, as it was to be in the twentieth century. In 1854 the Republicans had been outspokenly for Prohibition. As they became a national party, this was a liability which they dropped when immigrant opposition proved strong enough to cost state elections.

Out of the political conflicts of the 1840's and 1850's nondrinking had become more and more a symbol of middle-class, native American respectability. The urban, immigrant, lower class had emerged as both the counterimage to the Temperance hero and a political opponent of significant concern.

A NOTE ON RELIGIOUS MOTIVES
AND SOCIOLOGICAL REDUCTIONISM

Historians are likely to register an objection to our mode of analysis. They are apt to accuse us of the sociological error of reductionism. The argument might be advanced that in emphasizing the functions of Temperance for the status structure, we have distorted the importance of religious and moral motives in a movement that aimed to bring men to a higher level of moral perfection. Granted that one aspect of Temperance activities was actuated by needs for economic and status rewards, much of the attempt to produce an abstinent society was based on a desire to enhance the moral character of self and others. Religious compulsion drove men to build a more perfect world because it was right, not because it was instrumental. Duty, not utility, played a major hand in the reformist upsurge. When the sociologist finds economic or social considerations at work, he is often accused of having "reduced" religious motives to self-interested status needs. Temperance is, as we have admitted, the offspring of religious revivalism. The process of "reduction" hides and belittles that fact, or so the argument would run.

Two aspects of our method must be understood if we are to avoid the possible errors upon which such criticism focuses our attention. First, this book is not a history of the Temperance movement. Its aims are not those of the historian. Second, sociological method need not "reduce" one analytical concept to another. There are different orientations to subject matter which need not be contradictory.

This is not a history of the Temperance movement. While we have used primary materials in many parts of the study, there is much use of published materials which are part of historical and sociological literature. Our aim is interpretative. We are interested in the relations between social structure and the moral reform movements. We are not trying to develop a balanced account of the many facets of the movement in this case study. To do so in a work covering 150 years would be a most gigantic task. If we were interested in Temperance as a vehicle of religious conversion we would assay that area with greater depth. This is, however, an interpretative work and, as such, the interest is in the general knowledge to which study of this movement can contribute.

This point needs expansion. One useful way of distinguishing sociological from historical method is to say that sociology is a generalizing study while history is not. (We are, of course, referring to methods, not to individual scholars who are identified as sociologists or historians.) The historian who studies the Industrial Revolution in England attempts to discover how it came to be and what it contributed to the later events in that society. His emphasis is upon that slice of time as a unique set of events, not reproducible. The sociologist interested in the same slice of time is stimulated by a concern with the process of industrialization. He wants to know what he can discover from the British experience that will illuminate industrial change in general. This is not an "either-or" difference. Every set of events has its unique properties and its general properties. Which properties you emphasize depends upon your aims and, to some extent, upon the utility of your method for the kinds of aims you possess. A methodology is chosen for a task. If the tasks are different, the methodologies need not be the same.

The generalizing aims of the sociologist make comparative methods essential. He has to look at several societies or at several periods of history in order to observe what happens under different conditions to a common class of objects. The historian who tried to develop a scholarly account of the Temperance movement from

1826 to 1960 would be involved in a massive work. It is necessary to his aim of developing the total set of events which have brought about the present movement or of transmitting the appreciation of the past. This is not our aim. We are forced into study of the movement at different points in time precisely because we need comparison and contrast if the work is to have a sociological significance. We are not interested in Temperance per se but in status reform and political action under varying conditions.

Second, the sociologist is not "reducing" religious or reformist motivations to status or class interests. The charge of reductionism implies that the reducer finds the claims of his subjects to disinterested benevolence to be false ones. It suggests that we see religion as a "front" behind which men stalked after power, status, and income. This fails to appreciate the sociologist's concern for functional rather than descriptive questions.

We are not asserting that Temperance adherents during the 1840's were not deeply moved by the emotional appeals of religious revivals, that they did not "feel" benevolent toward those who were not abstinent, that they were not motivated by ideas and ideals. When we maintain that drinking had become a status symbol, we do not imply that religious reasons were merely cloaks for status interests. We mean that as a consequence of revivals, parts of the population that had been drinkers now were abstinent; that where drinking had been legitimate for middle-class people, now it was disapproved and sanctions placed against it. A function of Temperance activities was to enhance the symbolic properties of liquor and abstinence as marks of status. This is not an assertion that this was its only function nor is it an assertion about motives. It is merely pointing out that as a consequence of such activities, abstinence became symbolic of a status level.

A similar logic underlies our analysis of Temperance as a system of social control in the 1820's. When we assert that the Federalist elite sought to control the newly powerful democratic electorate through Temperance we are not "debunking" the movement nor reducing it to political motives. We are maintaining that the lost position of power and prestige which the old elite had suffered made them sensitive to the moral failings of the formerly subservient classes. It represented a problem which had not existed in the past. Their conviction of the righteousness of their way of life rested on religious ideas, but to "feel" the need to help those not sharing it meant that the victims of intemperance were being "bettered" by the moral values of the old elite, which implies that those values were becoming dominant.

Such functions of actions are generally latent rather than manifest. At times, as in Beecher's statements, they become explicit.[47] Such times often help the sociologist to see the significance for the structure of the actions performed.

Let us bring this section to a close with an illustration taken from a historian's analysis of the Social Gospel:

> The discovery that the doctrine of sanctification and the methods of mass evangelism played an increasingly important role in the program of the churches after 1842 compels a revaluation of their impact on every facet of the contemporary religious scene . . . whatever may have been the role of other factors, the quest for perfection joined with compassion for poor and needy sinners and a rebirth of millennial expectation to make popular Protestantism a mighty social force. . . .[48]

The sociologist is not denying the existence of a quest for perfection or compassion for the poor as factors in a social situation. He wants to know the groups within the social structure in which they arise and why they arose in that part. He wants to know how and why the vision of perfection of one group is the standard upheld for others to follow. Such questions are not reductions of one set of factors to another set. They are bridges through which the sociologist attempts to develop general schemes of analysis of structure by looking for the functions which a given set of ideas performs and the conditions within which they arise. The ideas have an independent existence but not an existence *in vacuo*. Weber wrote that although religious forces were an essential element in the development of modern capitalism, one could not deduce the economic institution from the Reformation.[49] No more are we attempting to deduce Temperance from status structure or reduce one to the other.

---

[47] See the discussion of Beecher above, pp. 42-43.
[48] Smith, *op. cit.*, p. 149.
[49] Weber, *The Protestant Ethic and the Spirit of Capitalism*, pp. 90-91.

3
Assimilative Reform
and
Social Dominance

The period roughly between 1830 and 1850 is the only phase of Temperance reform during which large numbers of adherents were attempting to curb their own drinking propensities and become self-abstinent. During the past century Temperance has been a movement by abstainers to reform drinkers. Temperance supporters have come from families, communities, and cultures in which drinking was a condemned custom and drunkenness rare among friends or relatives. Temperance people are not a segment of the society likely to have suffered directly from their own or another's drinking behavior. Eradication of intoxicating beverages is not likely to change the behavior of the abstainer. He is already abstaining. Neither is it likely to change his personal welfare, economic well-being, or emotional security in any direct fashion. The Temperance movement has sought to make others conform to the norms of the Temperance follower. As was true of the Abolitionist, "their greatest execution was among earnest young people predisposed to morality and reform." [1]

It is in this sense of action which has little direct effect upon the reformers that we speak of a "disinterested" reform. "They have little or nothing to lose by the deviant's departure from norms . . . their personal situation is not appreciably damaged by his misbehavior." [2]

[1] Gilbert Hobbs Barnes, *The Anti-Slavery Impulse* (New York: Appleton-Century-Crofts, 1933), p. 25.

[2] Robert K. Merton, "Social Problems and Sociological Theory," in R. Merton and R. Nisbet (eds.), *Contemporary Social Problems* (New York: Harcourt, Brace and Co., 1961), pp. 697-738, at 724.

Within the Temperance movement reactions to the drinker as the object of reform have depended upon the relation between the violation of the norm of abstinence and the status of that norm within the society. Where violation did not threaten the legitimacy and dominance of the Temperance standards it had different connotations than when it represented an attack upon the validity of the abstainer's criteria of moral behavior. In order to make this central point clear we must examine some characteristics of norms and norms-violation as attributes of social status. This is a necessary prelude to the analysis of the major types of Temperance reform, to be presented in the remainder of this and the next chapters.

DISINTERESTED REFORM AND TYPES OF NONCONFORMITY

The criteria of proper behavior in any subgroup or subculture may be rejected or accepted by most people in the total society. The norms of the segment may be viewed as legitimate modes of behavior by others or they may be labeled deviant, aberrant, and criminal. Some aspects of "youth culture," for example its dating and athletic concerns, are viewed by adults as legitimate ways for the young to behave. Other aspects of the same culture are seen by adults as "problems," as violations of normative standards, even though shared by many young people.[3]

The fact that the approved modes of behavior in one group may be disapproved by another in the same society is the root of the difficulty in defining the rules-breaker or the criminal. Two problems connected with this are pertinent to our concerns: (1) Whose norms shall be used to define behavior as nonconforming? (2) At what level shall we define the appropriate norms—at the level of behavioral regularities, what most people do—or at the level of moral standards—what most people think they should do?

Research in criminology has led to the conclusion that delinquent and criminal action often conforms to norms of gang, community, or neighborhood although delinquent behavior is nonconformist

---

[3] The concept of "youth" as a subculture, contrasting with adult values, is discussed in Talcott Parsons, "Age and Sex in the Social Structure of the United States," *American Sociological Review*, 7 (October, 1942), 604-616; J. Milton Yinger, "Culture, Subculture, and Contraculture," *ibid.*, 25 (October, 1960), 625-635, esp. 630-631; Bennett Berger, "On the Youthfulness of Youth Cultures" (unpublished manuscript, University of Illinois, 1961).

from the standpoint of legal norms.[4] The delinquent or criminal may deviate from the standards of other social classes but he is often true to his own. "Every delinquent subculture . . . is based upon a set of dominant roles which involve the performance of delinquent acts."[5]

When different groups in the same society adhere to opposing and contradictory norms is there any rationale or utility in referring to legitimate and illegitimate acts? The existence of normative differences might lead us to speak only of conflict with no designation of one set of rules as in any sense superior to another. Yet we recognize that in many societies the relations between contradictory sets of norms is not only conflict. One set may take precedence over the other; one group's standards have greater weight than another's, for both groups. If the delinquent persists in perceiving his behavior as sanctioned and nondelinquent behavior as a violation of norms he will find less social support for his views and actions than will those who condemn his delinquencies. Some standards are more "legitimate" than others within the total society.

Clarity can be increased if we distinguish between legitimacy as a subjective and as an objective term. As a subjective term it refers to the approval or disapproval which the actor bestows on the norm. It is a question of consensus about the moral obligation to perform an act. Max Weber's classic discussion of legitimacy contains both a subjective and an objective connotation. ". . . an order will only be called 'valid' if the orientation to such maxims includes, no matter to what extent, the recognition that they are binding on the actor *or* [italics added] the corresponding action constitutes a desirable model for him to imitate."[6] As Weber indicates, the binding nature of norms-obedience depends on accept-

[4] This is now a persistent theme in American criminology beginning with the work of Edwin Sutherland. A summation of this view and recent reformulations can be found in Donald R. Cressey, "Crime," in Merton and Nisbet (eds.), *op. cit.*, pp. 21-76, at 52-66. Other recent theories of crime and delinquency using some form of reference group theory are Albert Cohen, *Delinquent Boys* (Chicago: The Free Press, 1955); Daniel Glaser, "Criminality Theories and Behavioral Images," *American Journal of Sociology,* 61 (March, 1956), 433-445; Richard Cloward and Lloyd Ohlin, *Delinquency and Opportunity* (Glencoe, Ill.: The Free Press, 1960), Chs. 1, 3.

[5] Cloward and Ohlin, *op. cit.*, pp. 13-14.

[6] Max Weber, *Theory of Social and Economic Organization,* tr. A. M. Henderson and Talcott Parsons (New York: Oxford University Press, 1947), p. 124.

ance of the authority of the norm-giver. It is not solely dependent on the moral approval which the conformer grants to the norm itself. Weber gives as an example of this the person who fights a duel. He orients his behavior to the codes of dueling honor, but he also takes into account the police and the criminal law which he is violating, whatever may be his moral agreement with the antidueling law. "The fact that the order is recognized as valid in his society is made evident by the fact that he cannot violate it openly without punishment."[7] In this latter case, where the actor accepts the norm even though he disapproves it, legitimacy is objective. In order to distinguish these two situations we will use the term "legitimacy" to mean the moral approval of the norm by the actor. We will use the term "domination" to refer to the situation in which the actor obeys norms of which he does not approve.[8]

Norms become legitimate when the actors view them as right, proper, and appropriate. Temperance norms are legitimate to the members of the Temperance movement. To many nonabstainers they may be illegitimate. Domination rests on the power, prestige, authority of one person, group, or official over another. The content of the norm may be disapproved but, as in the case of the duelers, the nonbeliever recognizes its force. The individual may accept a given authority as legitimate even though a specific norm enunciated by that authority represents domination, that is, is not morally approved of by the subordinate. An institution may be dominated by norms which some group or person does not share. For example, the norms of patriotic commitment are dominant in the school system. Patriotic rites are performed and patriotism is taught as a revered and appropriate set of attitudes. Patriotism is dominant in American schools. The nonpatriot may disapprove of this; he

[7] *Ibid.*, p. 125.

[8] This distinction between order based on domination and order based on legitimacy in Weber is discussed in Reinhard Bendix, *Max Weber* (New York: Doubleday and Co., Inc., 1960), pp. 294-300. Our usage is slightly different. Weber viewed subjective acceptance of authority as a general condition of domination. We are placing our emphasis on the norm, rather than the norm-giver, and analyze just that case in which subjective acceptance is absent. This case, as in the clash of cultures, is by no means exceptional in modern societies. Our distinction between obedience based on moral consensus (legitimacy) and obedience based on the power or prestige of the norm-giver (domination) is essential. Without it we impute much more "subjective acceptance" to institutional behavior than is the case. Cloward and Ohlin recognize this problem and try to solve it by a distinction between moral validity and legitimacy, but this only leads them back into the difficulty since they define legitimacy in terms of acceptance of authority. Cloward and Ohlin, *op. cit.*, pp. 16-20.

may organize to influence changes; he may even withdraw his child from the school. One thing he cannot sanely do. He cannot act as if *his* norms were binding in the schools. A system of domination may rest upon legitimacy in some areas of the society but not in others. What is essential to the fact of orderly and recurrent behavior is the recognition in all areas that *one* set of norms and not its alternative is likely to prevail. It is not a question of whose ox is gored but of who holds the plow.

Levels of Normative Order

The second problem of norms-violation is that of the level at which a rule is broken. We recognize that few, if any, norms are obeyed at all times by all persons. We also recognize an important ambiguity in the concept of norm. Sometimes the term refers to a model of behavior, a standard toward which behavior should be directed. In this sense it is a moral judgment. Sometimes the term refers to the average, median, or typical pattern of behavior, as in the term "normal."[9] Norms are both ideal statements of behavior *and* regularities of action.

These two levels often diverge. Both individuals and groups support standards which are more honored in their breach than in their performance. Sexual morals are a glaring example of such discrepancies. The standards of sexual morality which law, church, school, and communications media constantly support as right and proper are disobeyed by large segments of the American population.[10]

The fact that a norm is frequently violated by no means necessarily diminishes its position as an ideal. Religious standards of charity, mercy, and justice may be daily dishonored yet remain important statements of what people of the United States perceive as the most acceptable and approved behavior. "Don't do as I do; do as I say" is a perfectly understandable maxim with which one generation frequently instructs another.

[9] Webster's dictionary shares this ambiguity, defining "norm" as "1. A rule or authoritative standard. . . . 2. *Educ.* A set standard of development or achievement, usually the average or median achievement of a large group." *Webster's Collegiate Dictionary*, 5th ed., p. 677. The concept of a standard is here, as in sociological usage, often used both as "ideal" and as "typical." See Philip Selznick, "Sociological Theory and Natural Law," *Natural Law Forum*, 6 (1961), 84-108.

[10] Alfred Kinsey *et al.*, *The Sexual Behavior of the Human Male* (Philadelphia: Saunders, 1948).

The idealized normative standards are those most likely to be acceptable in public statements and actions. In customary behavior, where there is a degree of consensus about expectations, informal understandings enable people to develop norms which violate the ideals with impunity. Where the action or statement involves the total society, the ideals are likely to be the most common denominator, the safest ways to act because they are the ways least likely to be punishable. We are less apt to go wrong in public by being saintly than by being ourselves.

The public acceptance of a set of ideal norms confers prestige and respect on them. It stamps them as those which are set forth as most worthy of obedience in the society. Correspondingly, acceptance of such ideal norms confers respect and prestige on those groups whose behavior is closest to them. It stamps such groups as those most worthy of emulation.

Types of Norms-Violators

From this standpoint, what is crucial to our analysis of disinterested reform is the impact of the violation on the acceptance of the norms as legitimate or as dominant and the implications of violation for the norms as ideal standards. We can best explain this by analyzing several different kinds of violators.

1. *The repentent deviant.* Here the violator admits that his act is morally reprehensible, to himself as well as to those who dominate institutions. The murderer admits that murder is immoral, the speeding motorist admits the legitimacy of the traffic laws he has broken, and the chronic alcoholic admits that it would be much finer to be sober. This kind of deviant may persist in his action without threatening the legitimacy or domination of the norms he violates. The homosexual who seeks a psychiatrist to rid himself of his habits has defined his action in ways that imply consensus between himself and those who condemn him.

2. *The dominated deviant.* This is the case already analyzed in our discussion of Weber's concept of legitimacy. Here the norms-violator does not attack the dominant position of the norms-upholder as more prestigeful and powerful. The criminal takes account of the law; he does not quarrel with it. The drug addict does not boast in public that he is a drug addict, although the addict who has cured himself may do so. Juvenile delinquents, as Sykes

and Matza have shown,[11] are adept in using neutralizing techniques to influence legal officials. They excuse their behavior in such ways that it is not repudiation of the law as a legitimate ideal. Even the rebel grants the domination of those he rebels against. Marx recognized this in his contempt for Bohemianism, which he saw as inverted convention "emphasizing and paying homage to the very same false values by exaggerated protest against them." [12]

We consider these two kinds of rules-violation as deviant behavior because they recognize the legitimacy or domination of the norms they have violated. They "pay homage" to them as occupying a dominant position at either an ideal or a behavioral level. Deviant behavior is not, in fact, a matter of public controversy. Nobody can publicly, institutionally, side with the deviant. The delinquent, the homosexual, the radical, the drug addict—all these cease to be deviants the moment their behavior can be problematically legitimate; the moment their behavior is held out as publicly emulative. Perhaps this is best illustrated by a current comic strip in which an elementary classroom is informed that next week there will be a panel of speakers discussing juvenile delinquency. "Oh, goody," says one of the girls. "Are they for it or against it?"

3. *Enemies.* In a society that had perfect consensus, everybody would be agreed on the moral value of any possible norm. The only kind of norms-violators would be repentent deviants. Such consensus is seldom obtained, least of all in rapidly changing or in complex societies. When one group acts in a manner contradicting the other's beliefs in the legitimacy and domination of its own norms, the situation becomes that of a conflict between enemies. One side of this conflict anticipates that its norms will be dominant in the major institutions of the society; that its norms will have public validity; that the other side will respect these norms as the "official" prescriptions of the society. The "rightness" of the norms is not accepted by the norms-violator either as legitimate or as an institutional fact, as dominant. From the perspective of the norms-violator, the norms-proscribers (those who have expected dominance) are deviant, illegitimate, and themselves norms-violators.

[11] Gresham Sykes and David Matza, "Techniques of Neutralization," *American Sociological Review,* 22 (December, 1957), 664-670.

[12] Isaiah Berlin, *Karl Marx,* quoted by Merton, *Contemporary Social Problems,* p. 728.

Each contradicts the cultural and institutional expectations of the other. Neither "pays homage" to the other, by attitude or action. Each is a repudiation of the power and prestige of the other.

An example of this form of social conflict is given in many educational issues. Issues of educational content often range groups against each other as enemies, each denying the legitimacy and dominance of the other's values and beliefs. Those who want school curricula to reflect controversy and those who want a greater degree of censorship are drawn from diverging cultures and social strata.[13] When the school system is organized along the principles of either side, the other sees the situation as morally wrong and as "shocking" to their expectations of how the schools are operated. The domination of the other side is not accepted or taken as given. The situation is in conflict.

Norms-Violation and the Reform Reaction

When the object of moral reform, the person who has violated the norm of the reformers, can be perceived as a deviant rather than an enemy, the social status of the reformer is supported and enhanced. His norms are the ideal and the dominant operative standards for his society. When the norms-violator is seen as an enemy the social status of the reformer is threatened. The dominant position of his culture is under attack. It is possible that his sources of respect and deference may be degraded. Groups obtain prestige and self-respect, in part, from the resonance between their norms and those which achieve dominance in the society.

This relation between norms-violation and response means that as objects of reform deviants and enemies are regarded differently. A social group that perceives its culture as defining the ideal and publicly valid norms of the society will approach the deviant as someone to be helped in attaining the habits which can assure improvement in his social condition. The answer of this reformer to social problems is "Be like us." This mode of reform is *assimilative*, holding out to the potentially reformed person the possibility of entry into the more dominant circles of the community. Conversely, the action of the reformer reinforces his own belief in his social supremacy.

The assumption that the norms-violator recognizes the legiti-

---

[13] National Education Association of the United States, *The Pasadena Story* (Washington, D.C.: National Education Association, 1951).

macy or domination, at any level of normative order, is contradicted when the norms-violator is perceived as an enemy. The question "Who dominates?" is now an open one. The norms-violator can no longer be dealt with as someone who can be converted and assimilated. If the culture of the reformer is repudiated, his exhortations fall on deaf and angry ears. The expected homage is not paid; the act of deference is absent. The reaction of the reformer must be *coercive* rather than assimilative. The object of reform is not someone to be helped but someone who is hostile and must be approached as an enemy; who must be forced to accept the dominance of the reformer. "The law-norms determine who . . . among the governing agents are the superior and the inferior, entitled to command and obliged to obey." [14]

ASSIMILATIVE REFORM

Two Types of Temperance Reform

By the advent of the Civil War both assimilative and coercive traditions were established in the Temperance movement. The assimilative strand was marked by sympathy of the righteous toward those too weak to help themselves. In a tone of missionizing humanitarianism, the assumption was made that the object of reform was suffering. He wished to be saved but could not help himself. The social welfare of the downtrodden was the aim of Temperance in this facet of its doctrines and action. In this complex of ideas and programs, the Temperance adherent assumed that his norms were dominant in the society. The drinker is given the opportunity to remake himself so as to fit in with the style of life of those who seek his reform. While legislation may be sought to aid the process, the major activities are efforts to persuade the sufferer and to remake his habits and customs. The orientation of the movement in this form is toward the welfare of the potential abstainer by his conversion to the habits of abstinence.

As long as Temperance is a dominant set of norms in the society, the Temperance adherent can feel himself functioning as the enunciator of a morality which both reformer and potentially reformed admit as legitimate. The attempt to persuade others operates within a common culture. When conflicts in culture emerge this

[14] Pitirim Sorokin, *Society, Culture and Personality* (New York: Harper and Bros., 1947), p. 79.

is no longer the case. When the Temperance movement faced populations, such as the Irish and German immigrants of the 1840's, the assumption of cultural continuity between classes was not sustained. The second strand within the movement is a response to such a situation. It is *coercive* rather than assimilative, hostile rather than missionizing.

Faced with the recalcitrance of the drinker as a deviant, the advocate of respectability can feel pity, sympathy, and love in his effort to win back a lost soul. Faced with sinners who refuse to define themselves as such, who perceive the reformers as cruel, immoral, and tyrannical, and deny the dominance of Temperance norms as ideals, the reformer is shocked and appalled. The object of his reform is a hostile enemy who must be coerced through legislation if Temperance values are to retain a dominant value position in his society and the temperate person retain his prestige. A challenge to the domination and legitimacy of his norms is a threat to his power and prestige, to his superior position vis-à-vis the drinker.

Social Workers and Slum Dwellers

The relation between the social worker and the slum dweller is an illustration of the assimilative orientation as a means of acting out status levels. The group with the higher prestige and power presents its system of conduct as worthy of emulation by those of lesser power and prestige. To possess greater prestige in a society implies precisely this kind of situation: prestige is connoted by the tacit agreement that the way of life of the dominant group is morally superior to that of the lowly.

Commentators on contemporary social welfare practices have pointed out the discrepancies between the values and norms of the social worker and the culture of residents in the slum community. Faced by the facts that crime, political corruption, limited motivation in school, high rates of desertion, and delinquency characterize an area, sociologists in past generations have pronounced the slum an "area of disorganization." [15] Recently sociologists have shown that this designation hides the fact of very real differences in values between one level of society and another. Slum life often is highly organized, although the values around

[15] For one such example see Clifford Shaw, *Delinquency Areas* (Chicago: University of Chicago Press, 1929).

which the organization of behavior occurs may seem immoral, unjust, or incredible to observers.[16] Here is William F. Whyte's description of the assimilative role of the settlement house in Cornerville, a north Boston slum area: "The social worker's conception of his functions was quite evident. He thought in terms of a one-way adaptation. Although in relation to the background of the community, the settlement was an alien institution, nevertheless the community was expected to adapt itself to the standards of the settlement house. Some people made this adjustment; most people did not." [17]

The assimilative orientation has played a significant role in the history of the Temperance movement in all its phases. It has not always been the central orientation of all wings and at all times. Some organizations and some periods have been more assimilative than others. Both assimilative and coercive reform have appeared in the movement at all times.

While coercive motifs and activities were part of the Temperance movement, a missionizing, assimilative tone was one major strand in the movement during the last half of the nineteenth century. Several factors of nineteenth-century religious and economic change produced problems of deep interest to a segment of middle-class Americans for whom abstinence was an accepted and honored part of their culture. Temperance activities were part of the ways in which they reacted to the development of a large number of underprivileged, low-status persons in the society. Within this context total abstinence was a doctrine of change and assimilation of the nonconformer into middle-class life, an expression of the terms by which social and economic success had been gained by the Temperance adherent and could be gained by the reformed drinker. In this fashion the total abstainer bolstered his feeling that his culture dominated the ideals of his society— through Temperance, he tried to incorporate alien cultures and deviant actions into his framework of values.

During much of the remainder of this book, our attention will

---

[16] This is a major point of William F. Whyte's study of a slum community, *Street-Corner Society* (Chicago: University of Chicago Press, 1943), p. 1. Also see Joseph D. Lohman, "Knowledge Needed for Redevelopment and the Control of Slums and Blighted Areas," in Donald Bogue (ed.), *Needed Urban and Metropolitan Research* (Oxford, Ohio: Scripps Foundation, 1953), pp. 28-37, at 28-29.

[17] Whyte, *op. cit.*, p. 99.

be given to the Woman's Christian Temperance Union, although by no means exclusively. The long life of the WCTU (1874-present) provides us with a consistent organization against which to assess changes from one historical period to another. During its years of continued activity, the WCTU has amassed a large number of state and national records in the form of journals, proceedings, and reports. It has published a weekly or biweekly magazine almost since its initial formation. Biographical and autobiographical material on its leaders has been available and it has published a great many tracts, pamphlets, and statements of Temperance doctrine. The length of its existence and its system of unit reporting have made it possible to compile data on changes in social composition and regional membership. Interviews with local, state, and national leaders during the 1950's have added to our knowledge. The use of the WCTU as a major source of data, however, has not meant that we have ignored other aspects of the movement. The relations and differences between parts of the movement are a basic theme in the remaining chapters as they were in the last one.

TEMPERANCE AND CHRISTIAN PROGRESSIVISM

At all times the Temperance movement in America has drawn its membership, its energies, and its moral code from organized religion. In the final quarter of the nineteenth century, when Temperance was again a significant social and political activity, much of its tone was permeated by the spirit of Christian concern for humanitarian justice and sympathy. Intemperance was part and cause of a complex of evils which the social Christian sought to eradicate. (Earlier Temperance activities had helped prepare a soil for this later humanitarianism by sensitizing men to the needs of those around them.[18]) The doctrines of Christian progressivism provided an ideological soil within which assimilative reform easily took root.

In analyzing the ideology of Temperance in this phase of Christian charity, we shall adopt the typology used by Henry May in his study of late nineteenth-century Protestant social thought.[19]

---

[18] This point is made by Timothy L. Smith, *Revivalism and Social Reform* (New York: Abingdon Press, 1957), pp. 167-168.

[19] Henry May, *Protestant Churches and Industrial America* (New York: Harper and Bros., 1949), pp. 167-271.

May depicted three forms of social Christianity. There was a *conservative social Christianity*, which fully accepted the principles of an individualistic, laissez-faire economy. The reform for which the conservative called was conducted on an individualistic, voluntary, and philanthropic basis. In no sense was he an advocate of institutional change. A *radical Christianity* utilized religious doctrine as a foundation for an attack on the existing social and economic order. This form of social action was a call to fashion a new social system. Christian Socialism was one manifestation of the radical Christian's approach.

Progressive social Christianity was an intermediate position between the two poles of conservatism and radicalism. The Christian progressivist sought to improve upon present institutions through specific and ameliorative reforms in the institutions. He was for collective bargaining in industry but not for the disappearance of private property; for equal rights for women but not for changes in sexual morality. He was for changes which insured that those now handicapped might get fairer play in the operation of the institutions. The progressive Christian might support the underdog in his struggles with dominant economic or political groups but he was not for fundamental changes in the structure which produced the conflicts. What he wanted was for institutions to be operated in a moral manner. He wanted to ameliorate their operation when they proved harsh and unChristian. He was not looking for a new model on which to build a new order of things.

All three of these religious doctrines were types of assimilative reform. Social Christianity was not a movement by the disinherited to improve their lot in life. It was a reaction of the educated and pious middle classes to the suffering of others.[20] The effort to bring religion to social action evoked the sentiments of an urban middle class which was disturbed by the slum, the factory, and the multiple problems of an expanding industrial economy. Insofar as Temperance organizations derived support from the ideology of social Christianity they also reflected the urban middle-class atmosphere of acceptance of the social order coupled with a disturbing sense that injustice and harm were being done to some unfortunate souls.

[20] *Ibid., passim.*

Conservatism in the WCTU

The three approaches of social Christianity were all represented in the Woman's Christian Temperance Union. It was the progressive position, however, which developed into the major force in doctrine and activity during the last two decades of the nineteenth century. This was allied to other movements which expressed a larger concern for the entire scope of problems of a nascent industrialism and urbanization.

The conservative implications of Temperance stem largely from the fact that, as an explanation of distributive results, it places attention on personal character rather than institutional arrangements. If sobriety were a matter of character and will and if abstinence would increase the economic and social position of the person, then the man who continued to use alcohol and to visit the saloon was the willing arm of his own victimization. As a statement of what is wrong with society, the doctrine of Temperance makes the creation of moral behavior—that is, the behavior of the Protestant Christian of middle-class respectability—a major goal of social reform.

Conservative social Christianity was dominant in the WCTU for only a short time following the organization's beginnings in 1874. After the Civil War one wing of the Temperance movement sought to restrict activities to moral suasion for total abstinence and to measures that might effect the religious conversion of the drinker. Being aimed solely at change in the hearts of men, WCTU members and leaders who shared this orientation resisted all attempts to ally the WCTU with other social questions. The first president of the WCTU, Annie Wittenmyer, held to this position. She rejected the demands of many members that the organization commit itself to woman's suffrage, to Prohibition, and to a set of other reforms. In opening the national convention of the WCTU in 1877 she said to the delegates:[21] "I trust the atmosphere of this meeting will be prayer. This society was born of prayer and must be nurtured and sustained by prayer. Prayer is the strongest weapon we can lay hold on." She repeated the theme in her presidential address of 1878 when she argued for "singleness of purpose" and

[21] *Annual Report of the National Woman's Christian Temperance Union* (1877), p. 143.

maintained that the Temperance movement should not put its faith "in princes or in the son of man, in whom there is no help." [22]

The conservative bent was also reflected in missionary efforts to convert sinners among the *lumpenproletariat*—criminals, unemployed, and bums of the big cities. During their first decade, and even into the 1880's, the WCTU held revivalistic services in major urban centers. Similar in spirit and form to the later activities of the Salvation Army, they were efforts to "rescue" the underprivileged and the indifferent outcasts of society. Reports of these activities are full of references to the criminal character of the men reached and the disreputable parts of the city in which the meetings were held.[23]

In this approach, the social problem of Temperance is defined as one of moral lapse. The reform must take place in the character and conduct of the individual, not in the institutions which make alcohol available. A great increase in drinking after the Civil War provided an impetus for the threat to Temperance habits.[24] The movement, however, was not directed at the social class from which its members were drawn, but rather at the downtrodden and the lowest rungs of the social ladder. The religious orientation is, through the familiarly assumed nexus between religious commitment and middle-class life style, again a means of controlling the existence of disturbing and nonconforming behavior. Without any location of the problems of the suffering sinners in an institutional setting this orientation is congruent with the optimistic complacency of a dominant social class. Though all may not be right in the world, we can set it right without conflict, pain, or cost.

[22] *Ibid.* (1878), pp. 12-13.

[23] An illustration is taken from a report of a gospel Temperance meeting conducted by the WCTU in Philadelphia in 1878: "The second such meeting has been started in the lower part of the city. Among converts at these meetings are freshly-released convicts, professional gamblers, and would-be suicides." This is taken from the WCTU weekly journal *Our Union* (May, 1878), p. 5.

[24] The per capita annual consumption of beer increased from 1⅓ gallons in 1840 to 5⅓ gallons in 1870. Daniel Dorchester, *The Liquor Problem in All Ages* (New York: Phillips and Hunt, 1887), p. 461. (These figures are not controlled for differences in the age composition of the population, nor do they reflect possible shifts from liquor to beer in American drinking habits.) The belief existed that drunkenness was less condemned in the decade after the Civil War than before. See the account of drinking in the Midwest in Henry C. Hubbart, *The Older Middle West, 1840-1880* (New York: Appleton-Century-Crofts, 1936), pp. 264-266.

Frances Willard and the "Do-Everything" Policy

The development of a wider set of objectives and a generalized response to industrialism in the Temperance movement is associated with the life and career of the second president of the WCTU, Frances Willard.[25] She was one of those reformers with a capital R who fill the pages of nineteenth-century histories. Her motto might well have been, "Nothing reformist shall be alien unto me." In her statements and activities she spanned all the major movements of conservative, progressive, and radical Christianity. Woman's suffrage, dress reform, cremation, vegetarianism, Christian Socialism, the Populist Party, and the Labor movement are among the movements in which she was an active and often a leading member. She led the WCTU in Temperance agitation from 1879 to her death in 1898. Without any doubt she was the leading Temperance advocate of the late nineteenth century and the most dominant person in the historical development of the Woman's Christian Temperance Union.

It was apparent that Frances Willard and Annie Wittenmyer represented two poles of opinion in the Temperance movement. Even at the first convention of the new organization, Willard (then National Corresponding Secretary of the WCTU) wrote a statement of principles (still in use in the WCTU) that flatly opposed the conservative and missionizing tone of the first president: "We believe in a living wage; in an eight-hour day; in courts of conciliation and arbitration in justice as opposed to greed in gain; in 'Peace on Earth and Good-Will to Men.'"[26] These were hardly the terms of a conservative approach to social problems or a narrow interpretation of WCTU aims. For the times in which they were written, the principles Miss Willard presented were a sharp criticism of in-

[25] In addition to WCTU journals and annual reports we have relied on Miss Willard's published books and several biographies of her. Most useful of Miss Willard's works have been *Glimpses of Fifty Years* (Chicago: Woman's Temperance Publication Association, 1889); *Women and Temperance* (Hartford, Conn.: no publisher listed, 1883); *A Wheel Within a Wheel, or How to Ride a Bicycle* (New York: F. H. Revell Co., 1895). Two detached biographies of Miss Willard are Mary Earhart, *Frances Willard: From Prayers to Politics* (Chicago: University of Chicago Press, 1944), and Ray Strachey, *Frances Willard: Her Life and Her Work* (New York: F. H. Revell Co., 1913).

[26] Attribution of this creed to the *first* WCTU convention is based on E. P. Gordon, *Women Torch Bearers* (Evanston, Ill.: National Woman's Christian Temperance Union, 1924), p. 13. It was certainly in use in WCTU reports by 1879.

dustrial practice in the 1870's in problem areas not directly connected with Temperance.

Within two years these diverse approaches collided in a struggle for power in the WCTU. In contrast to Wittenmyer's "singleness of purpose," Frances Willard stood for a "Do-Everything" policy: "We speak about the germ of a new church in which, as Christ declared, there shall be neither male nor female. . . . We speak, too, about the germ of a new political party. . . . We speak about a better Indian policy, wherein dwelleth righteousness and from which firewater is eliminated, about a wiser civil service reform. . . ." [27]

The struggle between Willard and Wittenmyer reflected the social bases and ideologies of conservatism and progressivism. Wittenmyer had made her reputation during the Civil War, as one of the leaders of the Sanitary Commission, the forerunner of the American Red Cross.[28] She had been active in church-related activities of the Methodist Church. Willard, on the other hand, was one of the first women in American life to achieve note as a feminist. She had been President of Evanston Female College and a professor at Northwestern University. As a lecturer on the topic of feminine equality, she was one of the respectable leaders of the then growing Feminist movement.

The support these women received from factions within the WCTU shows the relationship between the two strains in the Temperance movement in the 1870's. The Eastern wing supported the conservative and older Annie Wittenmyer while the Western wing was drawn to the suffragist views of Miss Willard.[29]

The Industrial Victim

After Willard's election to the presidency in 1879, the WCTU was

---

[27] *Annual Report of the NWCTU* (1877), p. 136.

[28] For material on Annie Wittenmyer see Ernest H. Cherrington (ed.), *Standard Encyclopedia of Alcohol Reform* (Westerville, Ohio: American Issue Publishing Co., 1930), pp. 2888-89. Also see Annie Wittenmyer, *History of the Woman's Temperance Crusade* (Philadelphia: Mrs. Annie Wittenmyer, 1878).

[29] This sectional interpretation appears in remarks of Miss Willard on the suffrage issue during the convention of 1878, reported in *Annual Report of the NWCTU* (1878), p. 30. She said that the suffrage issue was "a green persimmon in Maryland" but it was not so in the West. "It is a ripe one yonder on the prairies." This view is bolstered by our classification of the sectional membership of convention debaters on the suffrage issue in the conventions of 1877 and 1878. There were 13 prosuffrage speakers, 8 of them from the Midwest or West. There were 16 antisuffrage speakers, of whom 13 were from the Northeast or South.

pervaded by an interest in a number of allied movements which displayed sympathy for the victim of industrial expansion and which sought to ameliorate the lot of the unfortunate. One of these alliances was with the Labor movement. Willard was a friend of Terence Powderly, President of the Knights of Labor. She wrote for its journal and the two organizations helped each other in securing signatures for petitions on issues of the work week and on Temperance legislation. During the strikes of the 1880's and 1890's, even after the Knights ceased to be a significant movement, WCTU reports and journals were progressively sympathetic to the unionist's right to strike and to the demands of the strikers. Elsewhere in America the striker was severely upbraided by middle-class Americans, but within the WCTU the employer was more likely to be the target of disapproval. Employers were warned against arousing worker revolt by "kindling the spirit of animosity among those struggling under the iron heel of oppression." [30] Hardly the language of conservatism!

Elsewhere the ameliorative elements of the WCTU also displayed the attention given to the poor and the underprivileged. While the WCTU was aloof from the religiously inspired movement for Sabbatarian legislation, the six-day work week was a cause for which the WCTU worked hard. In the campaign for prison reform they showed an interest in bettering the conditions of imprisonment not as an instance of Temperance reform, as in the earlier prison gospel meetings, but as goals which were meritorious irrespective of the Temperance issue. "All over the land," wrote a committee chairman, "our jails cry out against us unto the God of Justice." [31]

The progressivism of the movement lay in part in its concern for the industrial and urban human refuse, the poor and the underprivileged whose very presence clashed with its view of a moral society. Even the work of religious conversion was pursued in special committees for evangelical activity among workers and laborers. There were special agencies set up for religious and Temperance agitation among miners, lumberjacks, railroad employees, streetcar conductors, policemen, expressmen, and train newsboys.

[30] *Ibid.* (1894), p. 447. In 1881 the WCTU organized a Department of the Relation of Intemperance to Labor and Capital. It was both ameliorative, sponsoring efforts to get laborers to abstain, and institutional, in supporting the right of laborers to organize and to strike.

[31] *Ibid.* (1879), p. 107. During the 1880's reports of this committee consistently reflected efforts to reform penal systems so as to have a rehabilitative function. There was constant criticism of the operations of jails and prisons.

Temperance, unalloyed with efforts at change, smacked of call-ing the poor responsible for their own misfortunes. But the WCTU went beyond that. They did perceive the urban, industrial poor as a problem and themselves as charged with duties toward them. In doing so, of course, they again held out their own way of life as the model of behavior and tried to solve the difficulties of the worker and the *lumpenproletariat* by the mirror technique of offer-ing themselves as sources of emulation. Thus the Kitchen Gardens department of the WCTU was founded so that through schools of cooking and household management girls might be saved from a life of sin. In this way they would not have to take jobs in saloons and other places where they might be exposed to evil. They could become housemaids and thus be saved from "eating the bread of idleness." [32] Here is the conservative bent appearing within the progressive orientation toward institutional change. The way to prevent the social problem of urban unemployment and immorality lies in developing middle-class habits of industry. This is both a moral duty upon the Temperance adherent and sound advice to the young woman on how to get ahead.

One common and unifying element of these various organizations and movements in which the WCTU was active was their interest in problems which were connected with the urban, industrial ex-pansion—crime, prostitution, unemployment, and labor unrest. In the concern displayed for social reform of institutions and for aid to the victims of urbanization and industrial development, the re-sponse was progressive and liberal.

TEMPERANCE AND THE ASSIMILATIVE INVITATION

The conversionist tone of the movement portrayed the drinker in the kindly images of a sufferer to be uplifted rather than the indig-nant tones of an enemy to be conquered. Drinking was pictured as a major cause of the misfortunes of the urban poor. Temperance was described as a way to copy middle-class habits.

Both the antipathy to industrial leadership and the sympathy toward the urban poor reflected the strains felt by an established

[32] The phrase appears in a WCTU committee report dealing with ways to save "fallen women." *Ibid.* (1884), pp. 47-51. The entire work of such com-mittees during the 1880's and 1890's was directed toward this assimilative goal. Women were to be rescued from sin by being taught good habits and moral character. There seemed little doubt that the women might resent such concern for their character and relish their sin.

class which was witnessing profound social changes. Between 1870 and 1900 the urban component of American population increased from 25.7 to 39.7 per cent. Much of this increase was a result of the growth of the larger cities.[33] At the same time, the agricultural segment of the labor force declined from approximately 52 to 38 per cent. Both immigration and migration swelled the growing populations of major cities. The resultant industrialized, urbanized society was a strange and frightening situation for a people who had been small-town and agricultural. The small businessman, the professional, and the farmer were understandably upset at the development of industrial communities.[34] They were uneasy with a community whose social problems were at variance with the small towns and farms in which they were raised. The existence of a large population with the problems of the urban poor was antithetical to their image of society. It threatened the social position of those who strongly identified their social status with dominance in the small-town image of the community. Religion bolstered this uneasiness and directed attention toward the ill effects of industrialism in a context which stressed both moral and economic betterment. The maintenance of the old norms of Temperance, as ideal or reality, was one way to insure their continued prestige.

This doctrine of Temperance was itself couched in a set of ideas in which intemperance was a source of moral suffering and a major impediment to middle-class status. The concern of the movement was with the underprivileged as victims. The middle classes were the sources of Temperance support and the models for emulation: "The class least touched by the evil thus far is that which here, as elsewhere in the land, forms its bone and sinew—the self-respecting and self-supporting class whose chief pleasures in life center in and about the home." [35]

The middle-class location of Temperance adherents is supported in data gathered on the occupations of husbands of WCTU leaders. At the local level the organization was led by wives of independent professional and small businessmen. The wives of physicians, lawyers, doctors, and ministers made up a large segment of the WCTU

[33] In 1870 there were 14 cities in the United States with a population of 100,000 or more. By 1900 there were 38 such cities. Wilbur Hallenbeck, *American Urban Communities* (New York: Harper and Bros., 1951), p. 55.

[34] See the discussion of the status revolution experienced by these groups in Richard Hofstadter, *The Age of Reform* (New York: A. A. Knopf, 1955), Ch. 4.

[35] *The Union Signal* (May 16, 1889), p. 3.

leadership. Retail storeowners, manufacturers in small plants, and wholesalers of varying sorts made up another major group. Together they accounted for about two-thirds of the leadership in the sample studied (see Table I).[36]

TABLE I. PER CENT OF WCTU LOCAL LEADERS, CLASSIFIED BY HUSBAND'S OCCUPATION FOR SELECTED STATES, IN 1885

| State | Husband's Occupation | | | | | | |
	Pro. & Semipro.	Prprtrs., Mgrs., & Officials	Clerical & Sales	Skilled Labor	Unskilled Labor	Farm	Total (per cent)
Connecticut	25.7	20.0	22.9	22.9	5.8	2.9	100
Michigan	17.8	33.3	6.7	28.9	8.9	4.4	100
Illinois	20.0	35.6	11.2	24.4	8.8	0.0	100
Minnesota	25.6	33.3	15.4	17.9	5.2	2.6	100
Maryland	22.2	44.4	27.8	5.6	0.0	0.0	100
Total	20.6	30.6	16.5	23.0	6.5	2.8	100

While these groups were dismayed at the development of industrial and urban communities, they were still a socially dominant part of American society. They could still enunciate a doctrine of assimilation in which sobriety and abstinence were tickets of admission into their social circles. Even so, they found both upper-class and lower-class life guilty of the sin of intemperance. "Poverty and suffering everywhere results to the lower classes (from alcohol); among the higher classes, usefulness and genius are quenched." [37]

Poverty, Mobility, and Temperance

The heart of the doctrine of Temperance lay in the manner in which it coupled economic and social success with moral virtue. The theme of uplifting the underdog through drinking reform is a major one in the Temperance literature of this period. The argument is addressed to the worker and not to the employer. The Temperance adherents were not interested in converting the employers to the possible recognition that abstinence was good business. In fact, they

[36] The list of officers, with home addresses, was taken from state WCTU reports. Occupations of the husbands were obtained from city directories. We were restricted to such states, and city units within them, for which reports during the 1880's were available and for which comparable city directories were available at the national WCTU Library and the Library of Congress.

[37] *Annual Report of the NWCTU* (1874), p. 23.

appeared to feel that the employer agreed with them. What they wanted to do was persuade the underprivileged that drinking was unrewarding.

The argument addressed to the worker went somewhat as follows: Economic success is a result of reputability and efficiency at work. Drinking destroys both reputation and ability. Abstinence assures the person of his reputation and also prevents the decrease in abilities brought on by chronic or episodic alcoholism. The man interested in his economic welfare has an interest in being abstinent.

Temperance fiction supported the argument in a vivid manner. Typical of this is the story "Just My Luck." Ned fails to receive a job for which he has made application. Puzzled by the rejection, Ned discovers that the potential employer was upset by the fact that Ned's uncle, Jack, is known for thriftlessness and drunkenness. No employer will risk hiring Jack. Ned might have avoided this "guilt by association" but he too has been seen smoking and drinking.[38] In another type of story, the lawyer or similar professional takes to drink and loses the love of his family and his lucrative practice. Through abstinence, however, he is reformed and recovers his family and his wealth. In a steady stream of stories, the German or Irish immigrant is converted to abstinence through the love of a child. He is rescued from his poverty by his own efforts, prospers, and becomes a respectable member of the society, usually as a small business owner. Interestingly, the child is usually led to Temperance through the dominant institutions of the society—church or school.

The implications of this doctrine of Temperance constitute an assimilationist approach to social differences. The dominant group is the tutor to the subordinates. As the social workers in Cornerville assumed that the inhabitants should be like the social workers, so the Temperance advocates assumed that the drinkers should be converted to the modes of life of the middle-class, respectable citizen. The assertion that Temperance is morally right and that it is a way to middle-class membership is taken for granted. Not only is Temperance legitimate to the abstainer, it is dominant in society and worthwhile for others to copy. It is in this way that the Temperance worker could see himself as bringing about a solution to social problems without fundamental changes in the economic or social arrangements. What could be done for the poor, the downtrodden, and the underprivileged was conceived in status terms, as

[38] *The Union Signal* (January 1, 1883), p. 6.

methods to improve his morality. This was the first stage in economic welfare. It was presented in terms which advocated a change in customs rather than a change in the distributional systems or in the political structure.

Temperance and Social Justice

This emphasis on moral perfection as a prelude to improvement of social or economic conditions is apparent in the argument that Temperance was a solution to national problems of economic distress. Temperance was also a program of social betterment as well as a doctrine of individual self-help.

Temperance literature and Temperance leaders stressed abstinence as a program through which prosperity might be achieved. While they were sympathetic to the claims of labor for a greater share of the common production, they were also critical of the amount of money which workers spent on beer and liquor. "The central question of labor reform is not how to get higher wages but how to turn present wages to better account." [39] This was the source of Powderly's interest in the Temperance movement as one aspect of the Labor movement. He wanted workers to use their money in a more "constructive" fashion. The less spent on beer, the more there is for bread.

A fictional story in the WCTU journal illustrates this aspect of the Temperance doctrine. "The Strike at Dennis Moriarity's" is a story about factory workers on strike. Dennis, the young son of one of the strikers, is asked to bring his father and other unionists a pail of beer from the nearby saloon. He refuses, saying that even though they are on strike the workers could pay their bills if they didn't drink. The strikers are impressed and one of them says: "It's the saloon that hurts and keeps us poor. I've been wondering all this while why Debs and the rest of the leaders didn't see it." [40]

Temperance as Symbol of Middle-Class Dominance

To be sure, the upper classes were not exempt from attack as targets of Temperance conversion. The idea that drinking is sophisticated and abstinence provincial was often mentioned as a dangerous part of the way of life in "high society." It was, however, not the major thrust of the movement in any of its facets during the

[39] Willard, *Glimpses of Fifty Years*, pp. 412-415.
[40] *The Union Signal* (October 11, 1894), pp. 2-3.

nineteenth century. The metropolitan elites who merited scorn as upholders of a cosmopolitan culture were few and irrelevant as competition in the status structures of the small town and middle-sized city. They had little impact on the school, the church, and the local community as the setters of style or the arbiters of morality. The WCTU made an attempt to reach the wealthy and the upper classes with a Committee on Drawing Room Conversions. It was short-lived.[41] The very name of the committee, with its image of the British aristocracy, is a commentary on the remoteness of the upper class from interaction with the abstainer. The man of wealth was also seen by the Temperance movement as a sufferer, who risked the loss of friends and family even if he survived the threat of economic ruin.

The assimilative approach to Temperance, then, emerged as the ideology of a group who occupied a position of relative social dominance in American life, although subject to the strains of industrial change. Only if they perceived their style of life as the institutionally dominant one could they have held it out to others as a route to economic and social well-being. There are many ways in which the world may appear as wicked and the evildoers called to repent and reform. The Amish see American life as wicked but they are too marginal to its culture to attempt to convert it.[42] Sects often excoriate the major norms of the society in which they have developed. In its assimilative spirit, the WCTU, as well as the Temperance movement of the late nineteenth century, was neither sectarian in this respect nor was it composed of persons who were marginal to American society. Its members belonged to major churches and were middle-class citizens of an economic and social status which spelled assurance and security.

The solutions which Temperance in its progressive phase provided for the problems of an expanding industrial society were predicated upon the belief in the dominance of middle-class styles of life as symbols of success and prestige in American life. In holding

[41] This committee was led by several WCTU women of upper-class urban background, such as Mary Hanchett Hunt. By holding exclusive meetings in parlors and as garden parties, they hoped to reach potential adherents who were repelled by the middle-class status of the movement. It was an unsuccessful venture. Committee reports of the 1890's expressed great disappointments.

[42] This is based on Walter Kollmorgen, "The Older Order Amish of Lancaster County, Pennsylvania," condensed in Joseph Gittler, *Social Dynamics* (New York: McGraw-Hill, 1952), pp. 110-129.

out that style of life as the legitimate and dominant definition of respectability, the propagators of Temperance doctrine had confidence that power, prestige, and even income were legitimately tied to the values of the sober, industrious, and steady middle-class citizen. Before the Civil War the Temperance movement was preoccupied with the establishment of abstinence as a norm of behavior. In the last half of the nineteenth century they operated with the conviction that such was indeed the case: that abstinence as an ideal was a mark of middle-class membership.

In using Temperance as a vehicle for dealing with urban social problems, the middle-class citizen attempted, whatever his motivations, to set the terms for mobility and justice by sponsoring the uplift of the lowly. Through the doctrine of total abstinence they issued an invitation to the poor, the immigrant, and the criminal to take on the symbols of middle-class membership by reforming their styles of consumption. Perhaps nowhere is this sense of middle-class values as the gate to happiness more apparent than in those young women who formed a special corps of WCTU members pledged to marry only total abstainers. Their motto has become a clichéd image of the Temperance movement: "Lips that have touched liquor shall never touch mine." [43]

This assumption of middle-class dominance of the socially dominant values is the source of the symbolic import of Temperance. The failure of Temperance norms to elicit approving responses indicates the weakness of those norms in the society. Every effort to enforce or promote a set of values has consequences for the status of its promoters. It indicates in concrete terms of imitation and repulsion the attractiveness, hence prestige, of its style of life. The social workers assume that not only are their modes of life superior to the slum dwellers, but also that the slum dwellers agree with them.

Assimilation and Politics

The major accomplishments of the WCTU lay in the fields of persuasion and education. While Frances Willard attempted to swing the organization behind the Prohibition Party, efforts toward direct legislation of drinking were overshadowed by the intensity of the

[43] For a news account of how feminine charm was enlisted in the cause of abstinence see the story of this corps in *The New York Tribune* (August 20, 1896), p. 16.

work in the schools. The Department of Scientific Temperance Instruction was the major aim of the WCTU through which this work was performed. In the 20-year period between 1882 and 1902 the WCTU succeeded in establishing laws in every state compelling some form of Temperance instruction in the public schools.[44]

The laws compelling Temperance instruction were, of course, one form of indirect use of coercion. They were not, however, attempts to change the institutions of the society so as to prohibit liquor or beer sales or drinking. They fell within the framework of conversion because they attempted to persuade the drinker and the child of the drinking family that such conduct was harmful and immoral. In doing this, the schools were only making explicit the codes of conduct which a middle-class orientation presupposed. Even without Temperance instruction laws, the McGuffey Readers had been special pleaders for temperance, sobriety, and the Protestant ethic in all its attributes.[45]

Despite this affinity between the schools and Temperance, the demand for such legislation was itself evidence that the schools could not be depended upon to complete the process of socializing children to total abstinence as the moral code of the dominant segments of the society. Either teachers were not trusted to enunciate the doctrine or the cultural supports of church and family were declining in their function of socializing the next generation to the legitimacy of abstinence. The appearance of political demands was indeed a sign of the weakened position of Temperance forces in the prestige structure of American life. In depicting the changing orientations of the movements, it is now necessary to turn to orientations which made coercion through politics increasingly salient in the Temperance movement.

[44] This was the work of the Department of Scientific Temperance Instruction of the WCTU. Led by Mary Hanchett Hunt, its members not ony obtained legislation compelling Temperance study but also wrote or influenced the content and choice of textbooks. WCTU domination of text content in this area continued until the 1940's, when the Yale Center of Alcohol Studies provided the first major competition. For analysis of the scope and possible effects of this work see Anna Roe, *A Survey of Alcohol Education* (New Haven, Conn.: Quarterly Journal of Studies on Alcohol, 1943), and Norton Mezvinsky, "Scientific Temperance Education in the Schools," *History of Education Quarterly,* 1 (March, 1961), 48-56.

[45] The McGuffey Readers introduced a Temperance ethic as part of the general model of character. For an analysis of the content of McGuffey Readers see Richard Mosier, *The Making of the American Mind* (New York: King's Crown Press, 1947).

4

Coercive Reform and Cultural Conflict

The coercive reformer does not perceive the subjects of his reform with sympathy or warmth. They are not victims who can be assimilated into his communities or converted to his culture. Coercive reform is a reaction to a sense of declining dominance. The violators of norms are now enemies, who have repudiated the validity of the reformer's culture. They are beyond repentance or redemption. Coercive reform is nurtured by a context in which groups hold contrasting norms. In this context each group challenges the power and prestige of the other. The coercive reformer has begun to feel that his norms may not be as respected as he has thought. He is less at home and somewhat more alien to his own society.

There is a similarity between the orientation of political radicalism and the orientation of coercive moral reform. Both stem from a polarized society in which the radical and the coercive reformer are both alienated from social and political dominance. By *polarization* we mean a process in which groups within the society are sharply separated from each other. They hold different values, live in different areas, are affiliated with different organizations, and hold different political orientations. There is little cross membership. As a result the lines of group differentiation are clearly drawn. Cultural polarization refers to the process in which cultural groups—ethnic communities, religious groups, status groups of other kinds—are sharply separated. Polarization implies a situation of conflict rather than one of dominant and subordinated groups. In a polarized society there is little middle ground. Each class or status group feels alien to the other. In this sense, the radical, like the coercive reformer, cannot see his problems solvable within the frame of existent institutions. The middle ground of common agreement or of accepted domination between political or economic groups has disappeared. Both types are in a critical posture toward the existent situation.

These orientations of both political radicalism and coercive reform existed in the Temperance movement during the late nineteenth century in both the WCTU and in the Prohibitionist wing of the movement. The politically radical elements in Temperance contributed to the growing polarization of cultural forces in the United States which culminated in the drive for constitutional Prohibition. That drive for political enforcement was an attempt to defend the position of social superiority which had been stabilized during the nineteenth century but was threatened during the first two decades of the twentieth.

SOCIAL CRITICISM IN THE WCTU

The WCTU demonstrated its criticism of American institutions in two major aspects of its activities and program in the late nineteenth century: in its support of the Feminist movement and in Frances Willard's attempt to ally the organization to the Populist Party and to Christian Socialism.

The Feminist Movement and the WCTU

An affinity between Temperance and the movement for female equality was evident even before the Civil War. Most of the great figures in the history of the Woman's movement were active in the Temperance movement,[1] at some time or other. It was one of the few organizational activities open to women in the mid-1800's. The formation of the WCTU was in itself an important event in the history of women in the United States. During the winter of 1873-74 church women in Ohio and other Midwestern states led a "crusade"

---

[1] Susan B. Anthony, Elizabeth Cady Stanton, and Lucy Stone, the leaders of the Suffrage movement, were first active in Temperance organizations. We have already referred to Frances Willard's Suffragette commitment. Mary Livermore, one of the foremost feminists of the late nineteenth century, was President of the Massachusetts WCTU. The role of women in both the Feminist and the Temperance movements is treated in Arthur Schlesinger, "The Role of Women in American History," in his New Viewpoints in American History (New York: Macmillan, 1922), p. 136; Gilbert Seldes, The Stammering Century (New York: John Day, 1928), Ch. 17; Inez Haynes, Angels and Amazons (Garden City, N.Y.: Doubleday, Doran and Co., 1933), pp. 80-90.

into saloons, praying and pleading for their closing. Such conduct was shocking by the rules of middle-class female conduct of the time. The direct action by women, and the subsequent formation of the WCTU as a result of it, was a unique activity for the women of the 1870's.[2]

Despite the feminist significance of its origins, neither Feminism nor the more radical Suffrage movement received immediate support from the WCTU. Suffrage carried the onus of secularism and sexual immorality. The conservative forces of the WCTU were deeply against any action which might suggest WCTU approval of Suffrage. The progressive wing of the organization was deeply committed to working for Suffrage. Frances Willard's ascent to the presidency in 1879 settled the issue in favor of the drive for the women's vote. The issue was so intense a matter that continued WCTU support of Suffrage led to the resignation of Mrs. Wittenmyer and her followers from the organization.

Frances Willard became one of the leading figures in the Feminist movement and in the Suffrage organization, the Woman's Party. Both during her administration and later, the WCTU was active in a number of movements which attempted to gain greater equality for women. Many of its conservative activities were oriented toward the demands of Feminism. In prison reform work, for example, the WCTU led a move to hire policewomen and to segregate male and female prisoners. It championed the appearance of women as delegates to ecclesiastical conferences and as ministers. Even in an attack on prostitution and in its aid to destitute women there was a harsh criticism of men and the double standard of morality which allowed the client to go free.[3] Since drinking had been largely a male activity, the concern of the woman for Temperance was itself an act of controlling the relations between the sexes.

The support the WCTU gave to the Woman's movement had two

[2] Accounts of the Temperance crusade by observers and participants can be found in Annie Wittenmyer, *History of the Woman's Temperance Crusade* (Philadelphia: Mrs. Annie Wittenmyer, 1878); Elizabeth Jane Thompson, *Hilsboro Crusade Sketches* (Cincinnati, Ohio: Jennings and Graham, 1906); Eliza Steward, *Memories of the Crusades* (Columbus, Ohio: William G. Hubbard Co., 1888); J. H. Beadle, *Women's War on Whiskey* (Cincinnati, Ohio: Wilstach, Baldwin and Co., 1874). The crusaders spread across the country, similar actions being reported for more than 300 communities. Most occurred in Ohio, Indiana, Illinois, Michigan, and western New York.

[3] For reports of the committee for work with fallen women see the *Annual Report of the NWCTU* (1878), pp. 104-111; (1884), p. 40; (1894), p. 47.

important consequences. It established a critical posture toward the status quo and it identified the organization as one dedicated to progress and the future, rather than upholding traditions of the past. In both ways it increased the sense of opposition to the status quo. The present relations between men and women, so went the argument, were enslaving. The future would be less oppressive. Dress reform and physical exercise were turned into symbolic acts of rebellion and liberation. With their multiple folds of undergarments and with the use of tight corsets, the female fashions of the 1880's and 1890's made work and movement difficult.[4] Taboos of modesty made it immoral to dress in ways which enabled the woman to exercise. The WCTU offered prizes for the design of freer garments and its journals carried advertisements for dress reform shops and for less restrictive corsets.[5] A Department of Physical Culture was formed and young Temperance women demonstrated the use of the dumbbell at WCTU conventions. Frances Willard, with her characteristic flamboyance, did the daring thing of riding a bicycle in public and then wrote a book about it.[6] There was even a move to persuade the women of the WCTU to use their first names in formal address even though they were married. "We dislike," wrote a *Union Signal* editor, "to see the good wives losing their identity and individuality." [7]

These actions were a step away from the customs of the day. They not only provided one anchor of critical orientation toward the prevailing social patterns, but also bolstered the identification of Temperance itself with a favorable attitude to change. Whatever was new, modern, and part of the future carried a ring of acceptance with it. Speakers were eulogistic in referring to the WCTU as "radical" and derogatory in calling opponents "conservative." [8] The pos-

[4] This was a theme used by Veblen throughout *Theory of the Leisure Class.* Veblen's point was that female garments made labor impossible, hence displaying the ability of the husband or father to support such abstention from work.

[5] In her presidential address of 1884, Willard said: "Niggardly waists and niggardly brains go together . . . the emancipation of one would always keep pace with the other. . . . Bonnetted [sic] women are not in the normal condition for thought; high-heeled women are not in the normal condition for motion; corseted women are not in the normal condition for motherhood." *Annual Report of the NWCTU* (1889), pp. 133-134.

[6] Frances Willard, *A Wheel Within a Wheel, or How to Ride a Bicycle* (New York: F. H. Revell Co., 1895).

[7] *The Union Signal* (October 11, 1894), p. 1.

[8] *Annual Report of the NWCTU* (1877), p. 190; (1878), p. 183.

ture of radicalism was, in the WCTU, allied to an optimistic sense of growing success. "Caterers should look forward and not backward," wrote a WCTU editor in criticizing the use of alcohol at a public affair.[9]

Political Radicalism and the WCTU

Under the leadership of Frances Willard, a determined attempt was made to ally the WCTU to a wide range of radical movements. Woman's suffrage was only one of the unpopular causes which gained Miss Willard's attention. While it was an unsuccessful attempt, it had two effects upon the organization: (1) it laid the basis for the critical attitude toward American institutions which united the Populistic and the more conservative wings of the movement in the Prohibition campaigns of the early twentieth century, and (2) it united political forces of conservatism, progressivism, and radicalism in the same movement.

Criticism of American Institutions

Before the late 1880's, Willard's speeches were characterized by a general tone of assimilative welfare, couched in a concern for the underdog and the underprivileged. During the 1880's, however, she was deeply influenced by the criticism of the capitalistic industrial economy expressed in agrarian and Christian Socialism. During visits to England and the Temperance leaders there she had formed a number of friendships among the British Fabians. She was an associate editor of the American journal of the Society of Christian Socialists, to which she frequently contributed.[10]

These associations led her to try to commit the WCTU to a program of radical economic and political reconstruction. The program which she advocated was one version of the then common Socialist proposals to utilize government as the vehicle of economic justice and moral reform. In speeches to the WCTU national conventions she demanded the triumph of Christ's law and the abolition of competition in industry; a minimum wage for labor and an equiva-

[9] *The Union Signal* (May 16, 1889), p. 16.

[10] In 1889 she joined the staff of *The Dawn*, the journal of the Nationalists, as the Society of Christian Socialists were also called. The motif of this group was that of the Socialist utopia inspired by Edward Bellamy's *Looking Backward* (Boston: Houghton Mifflin Co., 1889). A lengthy stay in England led to a close friendship with Lady Somerset, leader of the British Temperance movement and a member of the Fabian Society. Through her, Willard was influenced by Fabian Socialism.

lent of a guaranteed wage; collective ownership of the means of production; public ownership of newspapers as a way to end obscenity; and the nationalization of amusements as a way to insure standards of decency.[11] She was all for ending the rule of "Capitalists in control." Henry George and the Single Tax, Samuel Gompers and the Universal Federation of Labor, Sidney Webb and the Fabians, Keir Hardie and Tom Mann were all subjects of her great approval. She told audiences that in some future day humanity will declare itself one huge monopoly, the New Testament will be the basis for regulating human behavior, and "all men's weal is made each man's care *by the very construction of society and the constitution of government.*" [12]

This explicit support for the tenets of Christian Socialism contradicted the ameliorative conservative and progressive strands in the movement. Although it was still an assimilative perspective, marked by sympathy toward the urban, immigrant worker, it placed Temperance in a framework of multiple social problems, rather than visualizing it as the cornerstone of all social reform. In placing her stress on institutional reforms of a wide character, Willard implied that Temperance was itself a consequence of the economic and social structure. An immoral society produced immoral people. In her addresses between 1892 and 1898 she was quite clear that individual moral imperfection was not the root of social evils. It was institutions that brought about imperfect human beings. Crime and prostitution, she declared, are not only matters of human choice; they are also matters of the low wages paid to men and women. She took a most heretical step for the advocate of Temperance; she maintained that intemperance is itself a result of social conditions: "We are coming to the conclusion—at least I am—that we have not assigned to poverty at one end of the social scale and idleness at the other those places of prominence in the enumeration of the causes of intemperance to which they are entitled." [13]

Willard's views were never the "official" doctrine of the WCTU or of any other Temperance organization. Some members were shocked by her Socialism. For many reasons, as well as ideology, there was a brief movement to unseat her. Nevertheless Willard's radicalism succeeded in drawing into the WCTU many women who

[11] See the *Annual Reports of the NWCTU* for 1892-94.
[12] *Ibid.* (1889), p. 117.
[13] *Ibid.* (1894), p. 334.

were attracted by its identification with the new and the daring.[14] She was moderately successful in developing a Department of the Relation of Temperance to Labor and Capital which sought to aid the development of the Labor movement.

Union of Conservative, Progressive, and Radical Christianity

What is so outstanding about the WCTU in this period (1870-1900) is the union of the diverse strands in social Christianity. Populists and anti-Populists, Suffragists and non-Suffragists, pro-Labor and anti-Labor views were all represented in the WCTU.[15]

Despite the generally Republican support which Temperance people displayed in national politics, the WCTU did develop backing for Prohibitionist candidates. Although legislative measures were not as dominant as education in their arsenal of weapons against alcohol, the organization did provide an audience for Prohibitionist speakers and a source of actual workers in local and state campaigns. In 1884 Willard even claimed that the Prohibitionists, and with them the WCTU, were responsible for the balance of power. By withholding potential Blaine votes they permitted Cleveland to become President.[16]

During the 1890's Willard also tried to forge an alliance with the Populist Party, especially in its formative stage. She was chairman of the first Populist Party convention. During the campaigns of 1892 and 1894 she used the WCTU committee system as a device for gathering Populist petition names. This attempt to place the WCTU in the orbit of sponsors of Populism failed, partly because the urban orientation of the organization was indifferent to the rural problems of Populism and partly because the Populists were unwilling to risk the loss of immigrant votes which Temperance support would have endangered.

[14] Thus Josephine Goldmark, looking for some vehicle through which to press her concerns for social welfare work, turned to "Frances Willard's WCTU."

[15] Again and again, one finds in accounts of reformers a display of a syndrome of movements including Temperance. People in Temperance were not likely to make it their sole outlet for reform. In Boston, for example, Vita Scudder and Mary Livermore were active in Feminism and Temperance. Often a special committee of the WCTU was headed by some women who had a prior and continued interest in another reform. In 1881, Wendell Phillips listed among the great social questions of the age feminism, temperance, and prison reform, a very common WCTU "package." Arthur Mann, *Yankee Reformers in an Urban Age* (Cambridge, Mass.: Harvard University Press, 1954), p. 105.

[16] *Annual Report of the NWCTU* (1884), pp. 65-69.

Relationships to political radicalism were merely one element in the WCTU. They were an important part of the total Temperance movement and make up the ideological and social basis of the coercive strain in Temperance.

POPULISM AND COERCIVE TEMPERANCE REFORM

All forms of radicalism have at least one element in common: they are united by their critical posture toward the existing social order. Whether they are trying to resurrect an earlier form or to fashion a new plan, radical movements see the present as distasteful and preach the necessity of deep and fundamental changes. It is just this lack of identification with present social and political dominance which marks the coercive strain in Temperance doctrine. The Populist component in Temperance contributed to coercive reform in two respects. It provided a general expression of alienation from the urban and industrial culture and it directed attention toward the institutions of business as targets of reform. Its orientation to social problems was clearly not assimilative. The goal of Temperance through direct prohibition of sales was more in common with Populism and radical social Christianity than it was with conservative and progressive reforms.

Agrarianism and Temperance

Some historians have suggested that the Prohibition Party of the nineteenth century was one arm of the leftist movements elsewhere manifested by the Greenbackers, the Non-Partisan League, the Populist Party, and the agrarian elements of the Socialist Party.[17] There is some truth in this assertion but it must be carefully qualified.

The emergence of an organized political party dedicated to national Prohibition occurred in 1869, in response to the reawakened Temperance movement which produced the WCTU. The 1872 and 1876 platforms of the Prohibition Party read like many manifestoes of the agrarian radicalism of the time. The Prohibitionists advocated a federal income tax, woman's suffrage, the regulation of railroad rates, the direct election of United States senators, free schools, and an inflationary monetary policy.[18] Their platforms also contained

[17] Paul Carter, *Decline and Revival of the Social Gospel: Social and Political Liberalism in American Protestant Churches, 1920-1940* (Ithaca, N.Y.: Cornell University Press, 1956), pp. 32-33.

[18] D. L. Colvin, *The Prohibition Party in the United States* (New York: George H. Doran Co., 1926), Chs. 5-6.

planks which advocated the use of the Bible in public schools and the national observance of restrictions on Sunday business and amusements. The economic and political measures were similar to those of the Greenbackers and the National Grange. They were the sentiments of farmers who saw themselves oppressed by urban financial institutions, manufacturing interests, and the political machines.

We would be misled, however, if we interpreted Temperance as a logical outcome of agrarian economic discontents. The union between Populistic, agrarian sentiment and Prohibitionist doctrine was more adventitious than that. During the 1880's, when the state Dry campaigns were most intense and agrarian movements less striking, these planks were dropped from the Prohibitionist platforms or replaced by general statements of an antimonopolist nature. In 1892, in the wave of Populist state elections, the platform again reflected agrarian economic ideas. In 1896 we would have expected the most forceful statement of Populist sentiments, both because such sentiments were at their height and because they would have been politically necessary to counteract the appeals of the Bryanites. Indeed, within the party the "broad gaugers" sought just such a platform. They were defeated by the "narrow gaugers," who restricted the party to the single issue of Prohibition.[19] At no time from 1872 to 1896 were non-Prohibition issues given much attention in the speeches of the Prohibitionist leaders.

The platform inclusions and exclusions of the Prohibition Party suggest that party leaders saw Populist territory as a major center of Prohibitionist support. They felt it necessary to counteract the possible appeals of other third parties and of the major parties to the economic and political interests of this social base. These were neither dominant nor significant appeals to Prohibitionists, however. There was no concern with the range of urban social problems which we have encountered in the WCTU. Labor, for example, was treated in very general terms or exhorted to follow abstinent standards.[20] While Prohibition was not a part of the economic and political response of the farmer to his conflicts with industrialism,

[19] *Ibid.*, Chs. 7-9, 14.

[20] For example, the 1884 platform of the Prohibition Party contained a plank addressed to Labor and Capital. It called attention to "the baneful effect upon labor and industry of the needless liquor business." No position was taken toward unions or strikes. It was claimed that Prohibition was the greatest thing that could be done to insure the welfare of laborers, mechanics, and capitalists. *Ibid.*, p. 160.

it did have a special appeal to the rural segment of the population, where Populist sentiments were also strong.

Agrarian discontent was at its height in the same parts of society where Prohibition made its greatest state gains in the 1880's— Kansas, Iowa, and Ohio. The Grange lent active support to the Woman's crusades in 1874 and often helped the WCTU in its local and state campaigns for liquor restrictions. At the state levels, the Populist Party often included Prohibition as one of its aims, although it balked at including it in the national platform. The immigrant vote was considered too important to be alienated. The affinity between Prohibitionist sentiment and Populist support was close enough so that a delegate to the People's convention in 1892 could remark that a "logical Populist" was one who had been a Granger, then successively a Greenbacker, a Prohibitionist, and a Populist.[21]

The Prohibitionist appeal was not based on any effort to convert the sufferers, as was the conversionist doctrine of the WCTU. Prohibition, both in the usage of the party and as an element in the other Temperance organizations, assumed that its views represented moral righteousness and that the drinkers could not be converted by means other than legislation and force. It is just this that Prohibition had in common with Populism. Both movements were nourished by a sense of conflict with the urban, industrial communities of the United States. What Populism contributed to the Prohibitionist spirit was the confrontation of one part of the society with another. On one side were the manufacturer, the banker, the director of railroads, with their urban culture from which homey virtues of church and family were absent. On the other side were the farmer and the small-town businessman, in debt to the monopolies of transport, finance, and manufacture but committed to the culture of Protestant, temperate America. In this cultural confrontation, unlike the urban progressivism of the WCTU, the native American, Protestant, sober man was the underdog. The assimilative appeal tried to redeem the urban alienated. The coercive appeal was an attempt of the alienated rural population to strike back against the urban powers.

[21] Fred Haynes, *Third Party Movements* (Iowa City: State Historical Society of Iowa, 1916); Solon Buck, *The Granger Movement* (Cambridge, Mass: Harvard University Press, 1933), pp. 121-168.

Prohibition and the Rhetoric of Alienation

What this contributed to the coercive strain in Temperance was a sense of economic and political powerlessness which formed the ideological justification for Prohibitionist doctrine. Richard Hofstadter has detailed the manner in which Populist appeals were based on a theory of conspiracy.[22] That theory held that evil men of the commercial cities of the East manipulated currency, tariffs, and national policy for their selfish advantage. Politics, too, was suspect as the area in which the monopolist bribed legislatures and rigged elections. The "people" were cheated and preyed upon by the business interests that rendered them powerless to use their constitutionally developed political institutions. The primary, the referenda, and the direct election of senators were devices to return government to "the people."

This bridge between Populist and Prohibitionist ideology is crucial for the later development of the Prohibitionist cause. In assimilative doctrines, the drinker is the subject of Temperance reform. He must be persuaded to take on Temperance habits. The Populist assumption of business malevolence is a very different point of view with distinct consequences. It leads quite easily to the assertion that institutional forces of the business quest for profits are at the root of intemperance. It was logical to link together, as Prohibition orators did, the forces of "grogshops and monopolies" as the prime enemies of total abstinence.

Populist sentiment and rhetoric made it easy to focus attention on the liquor industry as the dominant cause of drinking. The leading Prohibitionists of the 1880's manifested a Populist commitment. John B. Finch called his collected speeches *The People versus the Liquor Traffic*. John P. St. John, 1884 presidential candidate of the Prohibition Party, was the former Populist governor of Kansas. Both men spoke of the enemies of Temperance largely as "the organized liquor interests."[23]

If the liquor "trusts" were opposed to Temperance, it was difficult to see that anything short of coercion could appeal to them to stop their immoral trade. The liquor lords were seen as absolute political autocrats who tried to dictate the nominations of both

---

[22] Richard Hofstadter, *The Age of Reform* (New York: A. A. Knopf, 1955), pp. 70-81.

[23] For the speeches of St. John see Colvin, *op. cit.*, Ch. 8.

Democratic and Republican parties. This sense of malevolence and power put the liquor interests outside the moral norms through which men might persuade each other, and outside the middle-class appeals to social mobility by which the dominant might impress the subjugated.

The coercive strain in Temperance orientations was thus a response to cultural confrontations which took place in an atmosphere of conflict and threatened alienation. As the economic and political dominance of agrarian society was undermined by the urban, industrial capitalism of the late nineteenth century, the cultural differentiation between rural and urban, native and immigrant, sacred and secular was given an added dimension of meaning. The failure of Temperance forces to have brought about a sober, temperate, and well-behaved society was more than the failure of a dominant culture to have implanted its style of life as the ruling style. It was tantamount to the failure of that culture to continue as the dominant source of values.

Nevertheless the Temperance issue remained in the orbit of a general stream of conservative, progressive, and radical movements expressive of dominance or alienation in the American social structure. Only as the cultural confrontations widened and the economic struggle lost some of its politically separating tendencies did Prohibition emerge as a vital and politically dominant issue.

POLARIZATION AND THE PROHIBITION CAMPAIGNS

By the turn of the century Temperance was a movement which combined both assimilative and coercive appeals within and among the various wings. Because of this mix of appeals and subsidiary movements Temperance had a pluralistic rather than a super-imposed following. These terms—pluralistic and superimposed—refer to the degree of political diversity and isolation which characterize social groups. Groups that differ in political outlook on almost all questions with little overlapping are in a posture of superimposition. The situation is pluralistic when the opposite is the case, when outlooks are not sharply related to group affiliation. When the rural, Protestant, native American is almost always in favor of Prohibition, and the urban, Catholic, immigrant almost always opposed, the situation is one of superimposition. Each element of group identity reinforces the other. The more an issue represents a constellation of superimposed social forces, the more likely is it that the issue becomes one of sharpened group loyalties and compromise is less feasible. In a pluralistic structure there is a middle ground, pulled in both directions by the competing forces. Under conditions of superimposition the political sides are more sharply polarized.

The campaign for national Prohibition had a polarizing effect on the Temperance movement. It maximized the cultural differences between pro- and anti-Temperance forces while minimizing the class differences. In this fashion it promoted an atmosphere in which the meaning of Prohibition as a symbol of Protestant, middle-class, rural supremacy was enhanced. This process was a necessary stage in the development of Prohibition as a test of the prestige of the old middle classes in a period of industrial growth, urban development, and Catholic immigration.

The polarizing effects of the campaign for national Prohibition were unwittingly expressed in an editorial of the Anti-Saloon League journal:[24] "The liquor issue," wrote the editor of *The American Issue,* "is no longer one of 'wet' and 'dry' arguments. Henceforth it is to be a question of 'wet men' and 'dry men.'" In effect, the issue of Prohibition posed a question of cultural loyalties in explicit terms. Attack on the saloon, rather than the drinker, located the problem of drinking in contexts which accentuated the conflict of cultures represented by the divergent sides.

The formation of the Anti-Saloon League, in 1896, has a symbolic importance for the Temperance movement. Tactically, the organization led the fight to gain state and national Prohibition. Symbolically, the very title of the League suggests the movement away from the assimilative approaches of the WCTU or the political party approaches of the Prohibition Party. Both the singleness of purpose represented in the idea of the League and the sense of opposition suggested by the "anti" character of its name are dominant features of the Temperance movement in the period between 1900 and the passage of the Prohibition Amendment in 1920.

The saloon was pre-eminently an urban institution, a substitute for the less anonymous entertaining of the *salon,* from which it derived its name. For the small-town native American Protestant, it epitomized the social habits of the immigrant population. To the follower of the Progressive movement, the saloon was a source of the corruption which he saw as the bane of political life. Ac-

---

[24] *The American Issue,* 20 (January, 1912), 4.

customed to moralizing about politics, the Progressive reacted against the ethics of personal reciprocity on which machine politics was built. Increasingly alienated from political power, the native American, urban middle class found a partial solution to its problems in the Progressive movement. It made common union with the already fixed alienation of the Populist. The growth of urban communities, so ran this argument, would wreck the Republic. It would lead to the segregation of an element responsible for corruption, "which gathers its ideas of patriotism and citizenship from the low grog shop." [25]

Within the context of Populist antipathy to urban and Catholic communities, the saloon appeared as the symbol of a culture which was alien to the ascetic character of American values. Anything which supported one culture necessarily threatened the other. "The Anglo-Saxon stock is the best improved, hardiest and fittest . . . if we are to preserve this nation and the Anglo-Saxon type we must abolish [saloons]." [26]

Agrarian Sentiments and the Prohibition Drives

A new wave of Prohibition campaigns broke out in the United States after 1906. As a result of it, national Prohibition was achieved. During its spread, the rural nature of Temperance was enhanced and it became a dominant political issue, separated from the wider net of movements current at the same time. The agrarian nature of the movement and the isolation of the movement from other political issues are major characteristics affecting its symbolic appearance.

Between 1843 and 1893, 15 states had passed legislation prohibiting statewide sale of intoxicants. Only in three states, Iowa, Kansas, and Maine, was Prohibition still in force. Between 1906 and 1912 seven states passed Prohibition laws. By 1919, before the passage of the Eighteenth Amendment, an additional 19 states had passed restrictive legislation, some through referenda. Most of these shifts into the Dry column had occurred by 1917, before the amendment seemed possible or probable in the near future. [27]

The active work of the Anti-Saloon League and the Methodist Board of Morals of course had a great deal of influence on such

[25] *Ibid.*, 21 (June, 1913), 4.
[26] *Ibid.*, 20 (April, 1912), 1.
[27] For a year-by-year chronology of the Prohibition movement see Ernest H. Cherrington, *The Evolution of Prohibition in the United States* (Westerville, Ohio: American Issue Publishing Co., 1920).

victories. They did bring to bear the power and influence of the Protestant churches behind candidates and legislation of Dry aims. But the churches had long ago taken a staunch Temperance stand. Temperance sentiment had existed for a long time.

Several changes appeared in drinking habits during the first 20 years of the twentieth century which reflected the decrease in the legitimacy and dominance of Temperance norms in the American society. For one thing, the consumption of alcohol was higher than at any time since 1850.[28] After 1900 it began to rise and reached its peak in the period 1911-15. Also, the increase in consumption appears to have involved more persons as drinkers. The rise in alcohol consumption was accompanied by a decrease in consumption of distilled spirits but a large increase in beer drinking, a situation which suggests both a rise in moderate rather than excessive drinking, and immigrant populations as a source of a large percentage of the rise.[29]

That the cities were probably the source of much of the increase is also suggested by two other facts. First, local option appeared to have been evaded in the cities but in the small towns and rural areas it was well enforced.[30] Second, despite the fact that by 1914

[28] See the statistics on consumption of alcoholic beverages, corrected for age composition of population, collected by Mark Keller and Vera Efron and printed in Raymond McCarthy (ed.), *Drinking and Intoxication* (Glencoe, Ill.: The Free Press, and New Haven, Conn.: Yale Center of Alcohol Studies, 1959), p. 180.

[29] This interpretation is consistent with recent studies of the drinking habits of ethnic and religious groups in the United States. Such studies show that a bimodal drinking pattern is more typical of native American Protestants than of first- and second-generation Americans, both Catholics and Jews. The bimodality implies that both abstainers and hard drinkers are more numerous among Protestants than among non-Protestants, where the moderate drinker is the more frequent case. In studies of college drinking, for example, the Mormons had the highest percentage of abstainers of any religious group and Jews the lowest percentage. Mormons who did drink, however, showed patterns of excessive drinking more frequently than did Jews. Robert Straus and Selden Bacon, *Drinking in College* (New Haven, Conn.: Yale University Press, 1953), p. 143. Other studies with supportive findings are Robert Bale, "Cultural Differences in Rates of Alcoholism," *Quarterly Journal of Studies on Alcohol,* 6 (March, 1946), 480-498, and Charles Snyder, *Alcohol and the Jews* (Glencoe, Ill.: The Free Press, and New Haven, Conn.: Yale Center of Alcohol Studies, 1958).

[30] Joseph Rowntree and Arthur Sherwell, *State Prohibition and Local Option* (London: Hodden and Stoughton, 1900), using both systematic observations of small towns and cities and the payment of federal liquor sale licenses, concluded in 1899: "Local prohibition has succeeded [in the United States] precisely where state prohibition has succeeded, in *Rural and thinly peopled districts* and in certain small towns . . . local veto in America has only been found operative outside the larger towns and cities" (p. 253).

there were 14 Prohibitionist states, all predominantly rural, the national drinking rates, based on legal sales, were at their all-time high in 1915. A change was taking place in American drinking norms.

The rise of Prohibition strength owed a great deal to the sense of cultural change and prestige loss which accompanied both the defeat of the Populist movement and the increased urbanization and immigration of the early twentieth century. During the initial decade of the twentieth century, the domination of American life, thought, and morality by the ethics of Protestant theology was waning. It was far from a period of serenity, despite the lack of the flamboyant issues of 1896. Assimilative tactics had not succeeded in curtailing the drinking habits of the cultures nor in winning assent to ascetic norms.[31] The assimilative response made little sense when the dominant culture felt its dominance slipping away.

The radicalism of the coercive approach to drinking bears a remarkable resemblance to the geographical distribution of agrarian radicalism. Areas of the country which demonstrated state support for Populist candidates in the 1892 or 1894 elections were prone to adopt state Prohibition in the 1906-19 period. Table II provides the data to support this.

TABLE II. PROHIBITIONIST STATUS (NUMBER OF STATES) IN 1919 AND POPULIST VOTE (1892-94)[32]

Populist Vote (1892-94)	Dry (statewide Prohibition)	Wet (no statewide Prohibition)	Total
Above 30 Per Cent	13	4	17
15-30 Per Cent	4	3	7
Below 15 Per Cent	7	14	21
Total	24	21	45

By no means do we imply that Prohibition is explainable as an extension of Populism. Both, however, express increased tension between parts of the social structure and between divergent cul-

[31] Norton Mezvinsky, "Scientific Temperance Education in the Schools," *History of Education Quarterly*, 1 (March, 1961), 48-56.

[32] Populist vote based on data reported in *The World Almanac and Encyclopedia—1894* (New York: The Press Publishing Co., 1894), pp. 377 ff.

tures. The centralization of opposition to Prohibition within the Eastern, urban, states, where large percentages of Catholics and immigrants were to be found, is a fact which a great many observers and analysts have noted. Major urban and industrial areas like Illinois, New York, and Pennsylvania were the last to ratify the Eighteenth Amendment. Table III indicates that there was a very close relation between rural status and Prohibitionist sentiment. It shows that where the ratio of rural to urban population was high, the likelihood that the state had gone Prohibitionist in areas affecting more than 50 per cent of its population was also high. Rural states were more likely to support Prohibitionist sentiment than were urban states.

TABLE III. URBAN-RURAL POPULATION RATIO AND PERCENTAGE OF STATE POPULATION UNDER PROHIBITION BY STATE OR LOCAL LAWS IN 1913 [33]

Ratio of Urban to Rural Population	Number of States		Total
	More than 50 Per Cent of Population Under Prohibition	Less than 50 Per Cent of Population Under Prohibition	
Less than 50 Per Cent	19	5	24
More than 50 Per Cent	6	18	24
Total	25	23	48

The areas of national Prohibition sentiment were thus Protestant, rural, and nativist. They were more likely to be found in the South and the Midwest, although New Hampshire, Maine, and Vermont were strong supporters of Prohibition. While states with high percentages of foreign-born were likely to oppose Prohibition, this was less true where the foreign population was Protestant and rural. In South Dakota, where 22 per cent of the population were foreign-born, 68 per cent lived under Dry conditions. In Illinois, where 20.1 per cent of the population were foreign-born, only 33 per cent were in Dry areas.[34]

More significant, perhaps, was the fact that within the individual state it was the urban areas that provided the greatest opposition to Dry laws. Here was the greatest source of votes against Dry legislation and for the repeal of such laws as did exist. Even in

[33] Compiled from data in *Anti-Saloon League Yearbook, 1913* (Westerville, Ohio: American Issue Publishing Co., 1913), p. 10.
[34] Based on data in *ibid., passim.*

rural states, it was in the cities that the state or local laws were most often and openly evaded. In Alabama, where Prohibitionist sentiment was strong, the ten strong Wet counties were the dominant political, industrial, and financial centers of the state. The same was true in North Carolina and the other Southern states, where the Catholic population was small and the percentage of foreign-born almost nil.[35]

The polarization of population into distinct cultural and geographical areas was a salient aspect of the Prohibition campaigns. The campaign for Prohibition in California is a striking example of polarities around which the issue was drawn. Here the cultural distinctions were formed around regional differences, to an even greater degree than was true of urban-rural differentiation. Northern California was cosmopolitan, secular, Catholic, and Wet. Southern California was fundamentalist, Protestant, and provincial in its loyalty to the ideals of rural America. Although Los Angeles County was the second largest county in California in 1892, it polled approximately 14 per cent of its presidential vote for the Populist candidate (Weaver) and 4 per cent for the Prohibitionist (Bidwell). At the same time, San Francisco County, largest in California, polled 5 per cent of its vote for the Populists and 1 per cent for the Prohibitionists. The state returns were below those of the Los Angeles vote: approximately 9 per cent for the Populists and 3 per cent for the Prohibitionists.[36] The Populist campaign in California in 1894 displayed a marked Prohibitionist strain. This continued during the Anti-Saloon League and Progressive campaigns of 1909-13.[37] The League placed its organization at the use of the California Progressives. Temperance, nativism, and Progressivism were linked. It was the North that represented the greatest opposition to this triad, rather than the city per se. Southern California was Protestant and Progressive. "Los Angeles is overrun with militant moralists, connoisseurs of sin, experts on biological purity."[38] The saloon was identified as the

---

[35] James Sellers, *The Prohibition Movement in Alabama, 1702-1943,* James Sprint Studies in History and Political Science, 26 (1943); Daniel Whitener, *Prohibition in North Carolina, 1715-1945, ibid.,* 27 (1945). (Both published at Chapel Hill by the University of North Carolina Press.)

[36] *The World Almanac and Encyclopedia—1894, loc. cit.*

[37] This account is based on Gilman Ostrander, *The Prohibition Movement in California, 1848-1933,* University of California Publications in History, 57 (1957).

[38] A statement by Willard Huntington Wright, quoted in *ibid.,* p. 65.

major deterrent to the good government sought by the political reformers. In the Populist vein, it was against railroads and railroad control that the Southern Californians directed their political animosities. In all these issues, the lines of political opposition were drawn along cultural attributes even though the urban-rural dimension was subordinated. The North-South distinction had cultural as well as geographical implications.

The cultural distinction between Dry and Wet areas was even revealed in the period following Repeal in the South. In Alabama, South Carolina, and Mississippi in the 1930's the Dry vote was strongest in those areas which had been Populist in the late 1890's, were fundamentalist in religion, and where the farmholdings and the percentage of Negroes were small.[39] It was not a simple urban-rural split that Prohibition touched off in these essentially rural states.

The polarities were also related to the cultural distinctions between the plantation areas of the delta and the poor white farmer of the inland regions.[40] Some writers have interpreted the rise of state Prohibition campaigns in the South after 1906 as an effort to control the Negro.[41] Our interpretation is quite different. After 1900 whatever political power the Negro had had was broken by effective legal disenfranchisement.[42] As long as the Negro had been anti-Prohibitionist and had voting influence, there was fear among Southern politicians that Prohibition questions were likely to bring about appeals by the Wets for Negro votes. It was the disenfranchisement of the Negro which made the political movement for Prohibition feasible in the South.

The Prohibitionists understood and were conscious of the con-

[39] In Alabama, Mississippi, and South Carolina, the counties most likely to have voted Dry in the post-Repeal period were those which were rural but where the percentage of Negroes was well below the state average. These were generally counties which had also been the basis of support for Populist candidates in the 1890's. This analysis is derived from county voting data in *The World Almanac and Encyclopedia—1894, loc. cit.,* and Alexander Heard and Donald Strong, *Southern Primaries and Elections* (University: University of Alabama Press, 1950).

[40] C. Vann Woodward, *Origins of the New South, 1877-1913* (Baton Rouge: Louisiana State University Press, 1951), Ch. 9; V. O. Key and Alexander Heard, *Southern Politics* (New York: A. A. Knopf, 1949), Ch. 11.

[41] Sellers, *op. cit.,* pp. 46-48; Preston Slosson, *The Great Crusade and After, 1914-1928,* Vol. 12 in Arthur Schlesinger and Dixon Ryan Fox (eds.), *A History of American Life* (New York: Macmillan, 1931), Ch. 4.

[42] C. Vann Woodward, *The Strange Career of Jim Crow* (New York: Oxford University Press, 1955), Chs. 1-2.

flict of cultures which both produced the issue and characterized the opponents. Dry men were native Americans; they were Protestants who took their religion with seriousness; they were the farmers, the small-town professionals; and their sons and daughters, while they had migrated to the big city, kept alive the validity of their agrarian morals. Wet men were the newcomers to the United States; the populations that supported the political machines of Boston, New York, and Chicago; the infidels and heathen who didn't keep the Sabbatarian laws of Protestantism; and the sophisticated Eastern "society people." All these were perpetuating and expanding the modes of life which the Dry had been taught to see as the mark of disrepute in his own local social structure. The outnumbering of the rural population by the urban, wrote an Anti-Saloon League editor, has been the cause of the wreckage of republics. "The vices of the cities have been the undoing of past empires and civilizations." [43]

The attack on the saloon emerged in urban areas as a link between elements of Progressivism and the Temperance movement. It made it easier to depict Prohibition as a move toward good government and the end of political corruption. In the same fashion, nativism carried with it connotations of positive progressive reform. It guaranteed the end of machine politics by limiting the power of groups who were felt to have no respect for American political principles. The sources of this reform were as much religious in origin as they were political. The California Voters League could declare that its objective was "a management of public offices worthy of an enlightened, progressive and Christian country." [44]

Before the Prohibition drives of the early twentieth century, the Temperance movement had played an important role in local, state, and national politics. Often the Temperance vote had been a decisive balance of power. Nevertheless, state Prohibition was usually not enacted and usually repealed when it had been in force for several years. It is true that the organized movement led by the Anti-Saloon League and the Methodists was more efficient in rallying and focusing Temperance sentiment than previous organizations had been. It is true, however, that after 1906 Temperance forces in the United States made a more concerted politi-

---

[43] *The American Issue*, 21 (June, 1913), 4.
[44] Ostrander, *op. cit.*, p. 105.

cal effort than they had ever done before, that this effort was largely the activity of rural populations, and that it occurred in a period when the United States was more urbanized than it had ever been. The strength and vibrancy of Temperance as a political force is the dominant attribute of the movement in the period between 1906 and the passage of the Prohibition Amendment.

The great movement toward national Prohibition was not the long-awaited outcropping of a slowly developing movement over 90 years of agitation. It was the result of a relatively short wave of political organization supported by the new enthusiasm of church members in the Presbyterian, Methodist, Baptist, and other "evangelical" Protestant congregations. It is certainly true, as Virginius Dabney has pointed out, that "when the movement for nation-wide Prohibition was approaching its climax in 1917, the political center of gravity of the country was not in New York or Chicago or San Francisco but in Junction City and Smith's Store and Brown's Hollow." [45] But this was not a new feature of American state politics. If anything it was changing as urban populations grew larger by the addition of immigrants and rural migrants.

In striving to obtain Temperance by legislative controls of liquor and beer sales, one part of the American population was trying to coerce another part. The areas of the country where Temperance norms were most respected, where alcohol sales were most easily controlled, and where the Prohibition vote was strongest were demanding that the other areas be subject to the ways of life which were most legitimate to the total abstainer. The opponents of Prohibition were no longer sufferers to be helped but enemies to be conquered. "This battle is not a rose-water conflict. It is war—continued, relentless war." [46]

Another consequence of the movement toward political solutions to the drinking problem was the isolation of the Temperance movement from other movements of reform. In the struggle to pass legislation, Temperance people devoted all their strength and perceived of most of their efforts as part of the political campaigns. Assimilationist reform diminished and past activities took on a political bent. For example, the work of the WCTU with laborers and with the Labor movement became single-mindedly oriented to gathering votes for the support of Prohibitionist meas-

[45] Virginius Dabney, *Dry Messiah* (New York: A. A. Knopf, 1949), p. 128.
[46] *Anti-Saloon League Yearbook, 1911*, p. 4.

ures. A 1909 committee report even argues that the alleviation of poverty is commendable because well-housed and well-fed people are more likely to vote for "civic righteousness" than are those of lesser wealth and comforts. The work of the WCTU lost much of its social welfare and religious evangelical character as the Prohibitionist cause dominated the Temperance movement. This move away from assimilative reform is striking when we consider that the Social Gospel movement gained in influence and importance in American churches during the first decade of the century.[47]

In this single-minded pursuit of legislative victories, the Temperance movement became isolated from other movements whose political and social doctrines Temperance people had supported in earlier periods. Woman's suffrage, Abolition, Labor, Populism, and even the Kindergarten movement were past lines of alliance which served to blunt the specific meaning of Temperance as a vehicle of cultural conflicts. Even the Prohibition Party, as we have seen, had to find a political ideology to which it tried to attach itself. The Anti-Saloon League, however, operated as a "pressure group," with no formal attachment to any political or social system of ideas other than evangelical Protestantism. The League followed the policy of "rewarding our friends and punishing our enemies." [48] Unlike the Temperance leaders of the nineteenth century, like Frances Willard, John St. John, and Lyman Beecher, the Anti-Saloon League officials had little past or later experiences with a wide gamut of reform activities or political programs.[49]

Neither did the linkage to Progressivism provide a major source of liaison between urban, nonnativist, and non-Populist groups and the spirit of coercive reform. For one thing, Prohibition was still largely rural, strongest in rural states, and couched in the language of Populist aggression against the city. While a number of Progressives were drawn into it, it was always an uneasy alliance between the urban, upper middle classes and the small-town farmer or businessman. Second, the elements of Progressivism which formed the appeal to the coercive side of Temperance were

[47] Henry May, *Protestant Churches and Industrial America* (New York: Harper and Bros., 1949).

[48] Peter Odegard, *Pressure Politics* (New York: Columbia University Press, 1928), esp. Chs. 3-5.

[49] While some of the Dry leaders, such as Bishop Cannon, had been sympathetic to other reform movements, they can hardly be said to have played an important role in them at any point in their lives.

largely the hostile, antinativist aspects rather than the assimilationist elements of the progressive parts of social Christianity.[50] In these assimilative aspects the immigrant was a victim of a source of suffering. For the coercive reformer the liquor evil was sinful but it had to be attacked institutionally rather than individually. This is the source of its radicalism. Here, for example, is a statement by Daniel Gandier, Director of the Anti-Saloon League in California and a staunch supporter of Hiram Johnson and the California Progressive movement. In 1910 he wrote:

The fight is just begun. The selfish forces of the landowner—Big business and its ally, commercialized vice—are preparing for the death struggle. I believe the spirit of our age is against them. Everything which lives by injuring society, or which enriches the few at the expense of the many, is doomed to go. The spirit of brotherhood, which means a square deal for all and that those of superior cunning shall not be allowed to rob their less cunning fellows any more than the physically strong shall rob the weak, is abroad and is going to triumph.[51]

From a number of standpoints the drive for national Prohibition, which began in 1913, was an inexpedient movement. The Dry areas appeared to have been fairly successful in restricting liquor sales in the areas where Dry sentiment was strongest. In many urban areas, to be sure, the laws against sale were openly evaded. In the areas where sentiment was strongest against prohibitive legislation, urban parts of rural states and the urban states, laws had not been passed. By 1913 an equable arrangement appeared to have developed. Temperance sentiment was recognized where it was strong by both law and behavior. Where such sentiments were weak, the populace continued to act in accordance with their sense of what was culturally legitimate. Enforcement in urban areas where cultural support was small had been tried and had been shown to be at best a doubtful possibility. Contemplated in areas such as New York and Boston, it should have seemed an impossible task to the reformer. Instead of deepening the enforcement of the law in areas already dry, the movement aimed at expanding its status as a recognized legal norm, as an ideal if not a behavioral reality.

[50] The organized Temperance movement among Catholics was greatly weakened by the turn of the Temperance movement toward Prohibition. The Catholic Temperance Union did not support Prohibition at any time. See Sister Joan Bland, *Hibernian Crusade* (Washington, D.C.: Catholic University Press, 1951).

[51] Ostrander, *op. cit.*, p. 104.

It is in this characteristic of cultural conflict that the disinterested nature of coercive Temperance reform is manifest. Assimilative reform diminished as the Temperance advocates sought to coerce the nonbeliever to accept an institutional framework in which drinking was no longer socially dominant. What we have shown in this chapter is that this facet, the coercive side of Temperance, emerged in a context in which the bearer of Temperance culture felt that he was threatened by the increasing strength of institutions and groups whose interests and ideals differed from his. He took a radical stand toward his society when he began to feel that he was no longer as dominant, as culturally prestigeful as he had been in an earlier period.

The development of Prohibition as a political measure focused these cultural conflicts in a form which maximized struggle. Elections and legislative contests are fights; somebody opposes somebody else. One group tries to bring force to effectuate what another group detests, even though the force may be more potential than actual. The unwillingness of the potentially assimilable to follow the lead of the assimilative reformer is not a blow to the reformer's domination. The political victory of the norm-violator is, however, a blow to belief in one's domination, in his right to be followed in cultural and moral matters. It is the threat to domination which the existence of drinking on a wide scale implied, both as a moral and legal norm and as a norm of recurrent behavior. It became necessary to settle the issue by establishing social dominance through political measures, even if unenforceable.

Prohibition was an effort to establish the legal norm against drinking in the United States. It was an attempt to succeed in coercive reform. But in what sense can a legal norm, which is probably unenforceable, be the goal of a reform movement? If the drinking behavior which the movement sought to end occurred in communities in which the Temperance advocates were unlikely to live and the laws were not likely to be enforced, what was the rationale for the movement? We have shown that Prohibition had become a symbol of cultural domination or loss. If the Prohibitionists won, it was also a victory of the rural, Protestant American over the secular, urban, and non-Protestant immigrant. It was the triumph of respectability over its opposite. It quieted the fear that the abstainer's culture was not really the criterion by which respectability was judged in the dominant areas of the total society.

5

Moral Indignation
and
Status Conflict

The coercive reformer reacts to nonconformity with anger and indignation. Sympathy and pity toward the victim have no place in his emotional orientation. The coercive response came to dominate the Temperance movement during the first 30 years of this century. In Prohibition and its enforcement, hostility, hatred, and anger toward the enemy were the major feelings which nurtured the movement. Armed with the response of indignation at their declining social position, the adherents of Temperance sought a symbolic victory through legislation which, even if it failed to regulate drinking, did indicate whose morality was publicly dominant.

The analysis of the Prohibition and post-Repeal periods provides an opportunity for understanding the relation between moral indignation and social structure. We are able to observe both the process of symbolic solutions to conflict and the indignant response to loss of status.

Indignation implies a righteous hostility. Webster defines "indignant" as "wrathful because of unjust or unworthy treatment." [1] Durkheim speaks of crime as leading to reactions of a passionate nature among the law-abiding and directed toward the punishment of the criminal.[2] Svend Ranulf sees indignation as the disposition to inflict punishment.[3] Max Scheler uses a somewhat similar concept of *ressentiment*, a psychological disposition involving

[1] *Webster's Collegiate Dictionary*, 5th ed., p. 510.
[2] Emile Durkheim, *The Division of Labor in Society*, tr. George Simpson (Glencoe, Ill.: The Free Press, 1947), p. 96.
[3] Svend Ranulf, *Moral Indignation and Middle Class Psychology* (Copenhagen: Levin and Munksgaard, 1938), p. 1.

the free use of emotions of spite, vengeance, hatred, wickedness, jealousy, malice, and envy.[4] All these definitions have in common the conception of an affective state in which the indignant person feels a just or rightful hostility toward the subject of his indignation and seeks to punish him in some fashion.

Moral indignation brings into play the quality of disinterested anger. The morally indignant person directs his hostility at one whose transgression is solely moral. The action does not impinge upon the life or behavior of the morally indignant judge.[5] Moral indignation is the hostile response of the norm-upholder to the norm-violator where no direct, personal advantage to the norm-upholder is at stake. It is exemplified in the reactions of conventional citizens to those who lead unconventional lives. The intensity of hatred and persecution which the homosexual, the Bohemian, and the drug addict meet in American society today is illustrative of moral indignation. We will exempt attitudes toward political radicalism or delinquency since these are interpretable as affecting the direct interests of the conventional person in his institutions. The radical desires change in the institutions within whose framework the conventional person lives. The delinquent poses a threat to property or person.

INDIGNATION AND PATTERNED EVASION OF NORMS

Two major theories have been advanced to explain the sources and functions of moral indignation. One is the functional theory of Emile Durkheim. In his analysis of legal norms, Durkheim interpreted the disposition to punish criminals as a response which maintains the respect for law and morality on which social order depends. Since norms derive their force from their sacredness and uncontested nature, crime shows that this respect is not universal. "Crime thus damages this unanimity which is the source of their authority. If, then, when it is committed the consciences it offends do not unite themselves to give mutual evidence of their communion and recognize that the case is anomalous, they would

---

[4] Max Scheler, *L'Homme du Ressentiment*, tr. unknown (Paris: Gallimard, n.d.), p. 14. The original was published in German in 1912. As Scheler acknowledges, the idea was developed in an earlier form by Nietzsche in his *The Geneology of Morals*.

[5] Robert K. Merton's discussion of "disinterested" reaction to norm-violation was mentioned above (Chapter 3, p. 61) and is found in *Social Theory and Social Structure*, rev. ed. (Glencoe, Ill.: The Free Press, 1957), pp. 357-368.

be permanently unsettled. They must re-inforce themselves by mutual assurances that they are always agreed." [6]

This functional theory is partially supported by our analysis of the two forms of reform reaction, assimilative and coercive. The assimilative reaction is not one of indignation and thus contradicts the Durkheimian assumption that the response to norms-violation is always a punishing attitude. However, our analysis concluded that assimilative reform occurred where the validity of the norms were not threatened. Where they were threatened, coercive reform was more likely, with its hostile and angry tones. Durkheim's view of the punishment orientation as functioning to uphold the validity of the norm is strengthened by this conclusion.

A second theory is the psychological one advanced, in different forms, by Svend Ranulf and also by Max Scheler. Both interpreted laws attempting to enforce sexual, sumptuary, and other moralities as one form of envy directed by less privileged classes toward more privileged classes: "The disinterested tendency to inflict punishment is a distinctive characteristic of the lower middle class, that is a social class living under conditions which force its members to an extraordinarily high degree of self-restraint and subject them to much frustration of natural desires . . . moral indignation is a kind of resentment caused by the repression of instincts." [7] Like Ranulf, Scheler also sees the reaction of *ressentiment* as one in which the authors of moral condemnation themselves wish to engage in the condemned behavior. Unable to satisfy the desires as others can, they end by condemning the satisfied. "In *ressentiment* one condemns what one secretly craves; in rebellion one condemns the craving itself." [8]

It is difficult to explain coercive reform in the Temperance movement in accordance with this theory. If we argue that hostility, anger, and indignation are reactions to behavior which we, ourselves, would like to follow, this reasoning is inconsistent with the fact of assimilative reform. We have shown that norms-violation is not necessarily responded to with anger. The same norm can be violated in different situations of status designation. Not the behavior but the implied threat which the behavior held for the status of the norm was the crucial variable. If the Temperance adherent

[6] Durkheim, *op. cit.*, p. 103.
[7] Ranulf, *op. cit.*, p. 200.
[8] Merton, *op. cit.*, p. 156.

secretly craved drink, he should have responded the same way to all violations of the norm. He didn't.

The assertion that the abstainer unconsciously admires and envies the behavior of the drinker assumes a "natural" craving for the joys of impulse gratification and drinking. The norms-violators are then threats to the tenuous system of internal controls which the Temperance adherent has constructed. This viewpoint also fails as an explanation of the Temperance movement. That movement was seldom directed, as we have shown, against members of the same class or even the same community as the Temperance supporter. In its most coercive form, it was directed outward, at the Catholic, urban, lower classes or the urban, high-status church member of the upper classes.

Both the functional theory of the need for norms unanimity and the social-psychological theory of reaction-formation present further difficulties in application to modern societies, and to the United States in particular. To speak of "the norms of a society" is a vast abstraction when we refer to the complex of divergent classes, ethnic groups, cultures, and regions that are part of the United States. "Within a given political entity such as a nation the differentiation of groups may proceed to a degree that we have to be quite cautious in speaking of a culture at all. . . ." [9] Divergent cultures, subcultures, and contracultures have shown a remarkable ability to persist in American society.[10] Rather than the unanimity which Durkheim thought essential, norms of tolerance appear functionally necessary to modern society. In many areas, such as religious tolerance, such norms have been developed and a pluralistic social organization made a major value in American life.

Quite evidently the movement to reform drinking habits and to prohibit liquor and beer sales is not a movement to tolerate differences. The adage that one man's moral turpitude is another man's innocent pleasure has no place in the attitude of the Temperance adherent. On the other hand, the difficulties in enforcing Prohibition in communities where it is anathema seemed, and were, almost unbeatable. To understand what is at stake in the movement, we need to analyze the existence at the same time of both official, legal norms and illegal but recurrent patterns of behavior. This is a char-

[9] Robin Williams, *American Society* (New York: A. A. Knopf, 1960), p. 374.
[10] J. Milton Yinger has analyzed a wide range of such subgroups in his "Culture, Subculture, and Contraculture," *American Sociological Review,* 25 (October, 1960), 625-635.

acteristic situation in modern societies. Robin Williams has called this mode of organization the "patterned evasion of norms."[11] This was the case during Prohibition.

The evasion of normative patterns occurs when a pattern of behavior regularly expected in the society is performed and is unpunished although the written, publicly stated norms of the society call for punishment and proscribe the behavior. Two examples of institutionalized evasion are the methods of obtaining divorce and the abortion "racket." The legal grounds for divorce proscribe collusion between plaintiff and defendant, but most divorces are mutually agreed upon by the parties. The form of the trial as a battle between two parties is a fiction. The grounds for divorce are usually narrow, and the parties, including witnesses, frequently perjure themselves. The legal fictions are accepted and no one is called to legal account for such collusion or perjury. The abortion case shows a similar pattern of accepted evasion. Abortions, except for a few specific reasons, are illegal in all states. Nevertheless abortions are obtainable, through illegal action or through the willingness of physicians granting medical diagnoses which, while false, will sustain "legal" abortions.

Williams has interpreted institutional evasion as functional in a society of great cultural inconsistencies. Those groups who adhere to the public norm see it upheld at a public level while those whose cultural norms are offended are able to pursue the behavior they find legitimate. Conflict between the two groups is thus minimized. The existence of divergent and potentially conflicting cultures "does not necessarily constitute any particular problem for the society as a whole so long as the two groups are not in direct interaction and do not directly confront one another's differing orientations."[12]

This formulation of the systematic evasion of public norms does not help us understand why groups struggle to define public norms in one way rather than another. If tolerance is the fact of social organization, why struggle over the legal and moral norms at the public level? The public level, of mass communications, community and nationwide institutions, government and legal action is precisely an area in which the divergent groups do interact and in which the public definition of a norm has consequences. Doctors cannot make their support of abortion visible to all nor can wit-

[11] Williams, *op. cit.*, pp. 372-396.
[12] *Ibid.*, p. 375.

nesses admit to strangers that they have perjured themselves in a divorce suit. Institutionalized evasions are covert; public, overt evasion is likely to result in punishment.

While systematic evasion of rules may be functional in minimizing conflict between subcultures, it does not remove the significance of public affirmation. For the cultural group that shares the normative pattern which is evaded, public affirmation has several important consequences.

1. It prevents the perception of the large extent of norms-violation. The violator of the public norms is not observed by those who do not directly interact with his cultural groups. He sees the norm-violator being punished and hence assumes that the norm is being reasonably obeyed.

2. It directs the major institutions of the society to the support of its norms. The covert nature of abortions in the United States is affirmed by the fact that schools (including medical schools), churches, newspapers, and government neither sanction abortions nor provide information on how to obtain them.

3. The fact of affirmation is a positive statement of the worth or value of the particular subculture vis-à-vis other subcultures in the society. It is in this sense that public affirmation is significant for the status of a group. It demonstrates their dominance in the power structure and the prestige accorded them in the total society.

This last point is crucial. Prestige in the total, national society is not the same as prestige in the small, local group. Social status is not simply a matter of where one stands in relation to those with whom he comes in contact. It is also a matter of where he stands vis-à-vis other groups in the total society. His perception of his status in the society comes either from acts of deference performed toward him as he interacts directly or from the public acts in which his norms have power and prestige. Status is reciprocal. It must be bestowed by both subordinates and peers.

The public affirmation of norms is thus a sign of their societal dominance. It is a symbol of the social status and prestige accorded to those who are identified with the public norms. Moral indignation, in this case, arises when that status is threatened. The object of indignation has not only violated *my* norm; he has violated the socially dominant norm and I have a legitimate right to indignation. Scheler partially recognized this. He wrote that moral indignation was a quality more likely to be found among lower-class white-collar workers and other *petite bourgeoisie* in egalitarian rather than in nonegalitarian cultures. In an egalitarian culture the powerlessness of the *petite bourgeoisie* belied the norm of equality.[13] It is the discrepancy between the expected public deference and the actual injury to prestige and power that generates the hostility of indignation—the feeling that one has been *unjustly* treated.

These ideas receive confirmation in two respects in the history of Temperance. In the period of Prohibition, the legal status of abstinence produced a strong sense of societal dominance among Temperance adherents. It was as important to maintain the legal affirmation of Prohibition as it was to enforce it. Repeal was thus more than a political defeat. It represented the loss of societal validity and the decline of social status of the Protestant, rural, native upholders of Prohibition.

PROHIBITION: SYMBOL OF MIDDLE-CLASS DOMINATION

During the 1920's critics of Prohibition often maintained that passage of the Eighteenth Amendment was a political fluke, unrepresentative of any widespread sentiment in American life. They held that it had been passed during wartime while an energetic nation was looking the other way. This interpretation is decidedly belied by the Prohibition agitations of the early twentieth century. In the period 1906-17, 26 states passed prohibitionary legislation, although of diverse scope. In 18 of these states, the proposal had been adopted at state elections. In 1914 the House of Representatives had voted in favor of a constitutional amendment. When the Eighteenth Amendment was ratified on January 20, 1919, it was the fruition of a wave of successful Temperance agitation and legislation in the preceding 20 years.

As critics claimed, the structure of state and national legislatures was most favorable to rural constituencies. The pressure politics of the Anti-Saloon League, backed by the organized influence of the Protestant churches, was probably an essential element in the victory. The electoral victories at the state level were close, an average of less than 4 per cent differences between Wets and Drys.[14] These facts lessen the validity of assertions that Prohibition represented the enthusiastic endorsement of most Americans. Nevertheless, the

[13] Scheler, *op. cit.*, pp. 42-45.
[14] Charles Merz, *The Dry Decade* (Garden City, N.Y.: Doubleday, Doran and Co., 1937), p. 22.

electoral and legislative victories, the movement toward state Prohibition, and the successful power of the Anti-Saloon League do
show that, within the structure of American politics, the Temperance forces were strong. While the Anti-Saloon League may have
been unscrupulous at times, its power rested on the genuine sentiment of the Protestant church member. That sentiment might be
mobilized by effective organization. It was not manufactured by it.

The passage of the Eighteenth Amendment did not produce a
drastic decline in anti-Temperance sentiment. In most communities
and at most times before Prohibition, this was a significant segment
of opinion. If by the victory of the Temperance movement we mean
a change in the cultural legitimacy of drinking, there is little evidence that this occurred. Neither is there much evidence that the
sale of liquor disappeared. The bootlegging and systematic evasion
of the Volstead Act, especially in urban centers, was evident even
to the most loyal and enthusiastic Prohibitionist.[15] The conflict between cultures that had generated the pre-Prohibition hostilities
continued and intensified throughout the Prohibition years.

The Prohibition period is often used as a striking instance of
institutional evasion. Even during Prohibition, however, there is
much to suggest that the number of drinkers and the frequency of
drinking greatly declined. Since consumption figures based on tax
receipts are lacking, estimates of actual drinking conditions remain
most inexact. Jellinek estimates that the rate of alcohol consumption per capita of population of drinking age during Prohibition was
about one-half of that for the average of the four years preceding
Prohibition.[16] If we assume that moderate drinkers were more
likely to have abstained entirely, perhaps the heavy drinkers were
not greatly affected by the law. A more telling indication of drink-

[15] Almost every historical account of the 1920's makes this point. For an
account of drinking during this period which is consistent, even though heavily
favorable to Prohibition, read Preston Slosson, *The Great Crusade and After,
1914-1928*, Vol. 12 in Arthur Schlesinger and Dixon Ryan Fox (eds.), *A
History of American Life* (New York: Macmillan, 1931), Ch. 4. We have
found no convincing data which could give any accurate estimate of the amount
of drinking which occurred during the Prohibition years. On the basis of Jellinek's evidence and reasoning, cited and discussed below, it would seem most
accurate to say that during the Prohibition era less alcohol was consumed by
the nation than was consumed in the 14 years before or after. This provides
no statement about quantitative drop nor does it answer questions about drinking in those areas where Prohibition was most strongly resisted.

[16] E. M. Jellinek, "Recent Trends in Alcoholism and in Alcohol Consumption,"
Quarterly Journal of Studies on Alcohol, 8 (July, 1947), 1-43, at 9.

ing quantity is given by the rates of alcoholism during the decade of the 1930's. The rates from 1920 to 1945, as studied by Jellinek, show a decided drop in alcoholism as compared to the 1910 and 1915 rates. Since chronic alcoholism is a reflection of past drinking habits (approximately 10-15 years) and indicated by deaths from cirrhosis of the liver, it is good evidence of the changed habits brought about during state and national Prohibition in the early twentieth century. Heavy drinking *was* less frequent.

Whether or not the law was evaded in those areas where it was least supported by cultural beliefs, the doctrine of Prohibition was given a position as the officially sanctioned policy of the nation. No public official could openly evade it. Whatever his covert habits, the President of the United States lent it his sanction in his public behavior. It was endorsed by legislative majorities and given mythical support by the Constitution. Temperance materials of this period stressed the "unAmerican" connotations of Wet opinion and depicted the violator of the Dry law as unpatriotic, a nihilist without respect for law, and an opponent of constitutional government. Speaking before the annual convention of the National Woman's Christian Temperance Union in 1927, Senator Capper said that refusal to obey a law is equivalent to treason.[17]

In two respects the passage of the Eighteenth Amendment made the Temperance position dominant. First, it actually did restrict the ability of the person to take a drink. It was a fact of life that liquor, beer, and wine were sold covertly and not openly; that public exposure of evasion might force fines or jail or both. People *were* sentenced to prison and punishment *did* exist, even though on a scale well below that of less evaded norms, such as those against stealing.[18] Second, the official status of a law lent it a sanction which made it the societal behavior at the level of public visibility. In any argument over the recognition of one culture as of greater worth or respect than another the public definition supported the abstaining, dry proclivities of the Protestant middle classes and denigrated the less ascetic habits of the metropolitan Catholic, the secularist, and others who "struck a blow for liberty."

Enforcement and Symbol Protection

Faced by the systematic evasion of a legal norm, the upholders of

---

[17] *The Union Signal* (March 5, 1927), p. 5.
[18] Merz, *op. cit.*, Chs. 3, 6.

the norm can press their power and authority further and attempt eradication, even at the price of social conflict. They can also accept the compromise between legal acceptance and rejection which a system of institutionalized evasion represents, taking comfort from the small crumbs of enforcement and the symbolic satisfactions of being the chosen in the contest for societal dominance. The action of Temperance forces during the Prohibition decade strongly suggests that they did not utilize their political power to demand as much enforcement as they might have obtained. The passage of the legislation itself presented satisfactions which could not be endangered by too zealous an effort to enforce it.

Whether or not the Volstead Act and the various state laws supporting it could have been totally enforced is a moot question, although it is doubtful that evasion could have been totally stopped. What does stand out, however, is that the Volstead Act, which contained the legal sanctions to enforce the Eighteenth Amendment, never received appropriations adequate to the attempt. New personnel and new methods of prohibition organization were tried. Repeatedly they floundered on the unwillingness of federal and state legislatures to grant the necessary funds that would have made possible a large legal and police organization to cope with bootlegging.

The power of the Anti-Saloon League and the organized Drys was sometimes astounding. From the passage of the Webb-Kenyon Act in 1913, forbidding the importation of alcohol from Wet to Dry states, to the passage of the Eighteenth Amendment the Drys constituted one of the most effective pressure groups in the history of American politics.[19] With the passage of the Prohibition Amendment they were at the height of power. In the elections of 1920 and 1922 they surpassed this and showed even greater power by defeating a number of incumbents who had dared to oppose Dry legislation. Despite this strength little was done to provide effective enforcement. A policy of "nullification by inaction" was set by Congress. The Dry forces possessed considerable power to multiply the appropriations but they made no major efforts to raise the sums needed. "The law limped on. It was scarcely the business of the prohibition Bureau to quarrel with its peers." [20]

[19] Peter Odegard, *Pressure Politics* (New York: Columbia University Press, 1928); Justin Steward, *Dry Boss* (New York: F. H. Revell Co., 1928), Ch. 9.
[20] Merz, *op. cit.*, p. 129.

The Drys were in the common dilemma of those who support a law which a significant minority oppose and which is illegitimate to them. The Temperance forces had claimed that they represented the legitimate position of most citizens. To maintain that the law was not enforceable without great sums of money and much police action was to deny the legitimacy claimed for it. Furthermore, increased appropriations might stimulate the opposition of those who were rallied by fears of high taxation.[21] In the final analysis, a system of institutionalized evasion persists because the upholders of the official norm fear that thorough enforcement will so enrage the objects of coercive reform they they will threaten the official status of the norm itself. Some Temperance personnel argued that time would lead to a new generation who would accept Prohibition more adequately than had the old.

The self-imposed limitations on the use of their political power suggests that the Prohibitionists were at least content to settle for the public validity of Temperance even though the factual situation was a long way from the utopia of a Dry society. It was evident to a number of Drys, however, that this could not be sustained without greater effort. The domination of the rural powers in politics was threatened by the rise in urban population and the higher birth rate of first and second generation immigrants. By 1924 it was apparent that Catholic, urban power was now a major factor in the Democratic Party.[22] If Prohibition were to be enforced, appropriations and greater use of Dry power were needed than had been used in gaining the Eighteenth Amendment. The entire episode reinforces the belief in the importance of the passage of the legislation as itself granting great satisfactions to its adherents, sufficient enough to cushion the blows of a widely publicized evasion of the Prohibition norm in just those areas where the original movement sought to expand control.

In another way, the corruption and inadequacies in Prohibition enforcement served as a convenient device to hide the extent to which the norms of Temperance were not shared by a great many citizens. A more thorough enforcement effort might well have displayed the intensity of opposition and hatred the law incurred

[21] *Ibid.*, p. 82.
[22] See the account of developing Catholic voting power at the 1924 Democratic convention in Samuel Lubell, *The Future of American Politics* (New York: Doubleday and Co., Inc., 1956).

in subcultures where drinking had been part of the accepted way of life. It is still Temperance doctrine that Prohibition was never really tried, was foiled in practice by its enemies and cannot be said to have been rejected by the American people.[23] Here, again, what is protected is the claim to legitimacy and social dominance.

Murray Edelman has shown that interest groups are frequently rendered politically quiescent by the mere passage of legislation which has their support.[24] The citizen is satisfied that his interests are being championed and fails to perceive that enforcement is lax and that the substantive results of enactment are not at all what he had expected and are sometimes contradictory. The failure of the Anti-Trust Act to control business price regulation has not diminished the feeling of economic security derived by many from the existence of such legislation. The attitude of the Temperance movement to Prohibition contained much that is similar. Having already attained symbolic victory, the Prohibitionist was unwilling to press too hard for a more tangible kind of change. The good citizens of small towns, hamlets, and farms of rural America saw less of drunkenness than they had before the Volstead Act had hallowed a sober world. If Prohibition was systematically evaded in the cities, the urban Temperance adherent did not come into contact with its covert operations. The Dry knew that somewhere in the evil jungles of urban society Law and Morality were being mocked, but there was little question about whose law and whose morality they were. It was *his* culture that had to be evaded and *his* morality that was transgressed.

Cultural Conflict and Symbolic Victory

What Prohibition symbolized was the superior power and prestige of the old middle class in American society. The threat of decline in that position had made explicit actions of government necessary to defend it. Legislation did this in two ways. It demonstrated the power of the old middle classes by showing that they could mobilize sufficient political strength to bring it about and it gave dominance to the character and style of old middle-class life in contrast to that of the urban lower and middle classes.

[23] Typical of this material are Fletcher Dobyns, *The Amazing Story of Repeal* (Chicago: Willett, Clark, and Co., 1940), and Ernest Gordon, *The Wrecking of the 18th Amendment* (Francestown, N.H.: The Alcohol Information Press, 1943).

[24] Murray Edelman, "Symbols and Political Quiescence," *American Political Science Review*, 54 (September, 1960), 695-704.

The power of the Protestant, rural, native American was greater than that of the Eastern upper classes, the Catholic and Jewish immigrants, and the urbanized middle class. This was the lineup of the electoral struggle. In this struggle the champions of drinking represented cultural enemies and they had lost. James Cannon, the Methodist bishop who was among the handful of major leaders of the Prohibition movement during its decade of power, expressed this side of the conflict: "In any discussion of 'why' the Eighteenth Amendment was ratified, it cannot be too strongly emphasized that the Prohibition movement in the United States has been Christian in its inspiration and has been dependent for its persistent vitality and victorious leadership upon the active and, finally, the undivided support of American Protestantism, with support from some Roman Catholics." [25]

The Temperance movement had utilized the theme of alien support of drinking in its campaign for wartime Prohibition. At that time they had attacked the brewing industry as German in leadership and pro-Kaiser in the war.[26] It was more than effective propaganda, however. It was one aspect of a conflict of cultures which was rooted in divergent values. Anna Gordon, then President of the WCTU, hailed wartime Prohibition as a patriotic victory over "the Un-American liquor traffic." From the beginning, she said, the liquor traffic in America has been "of alien and autocratic origin." [27] Even the assimilative reform of work with immigrants took on this tone of hostility and concern for dominance. In 1929 Athena Marmaroff, Director of Ellis Island Work for the WCTU (a program of Americanization of immigrants), complained that the laws, especially the Eighteenth Amendment, were broken frequently by foreigners. "Let us see that the laws are obeyed and those who do not like them or obey them should be sent back to the country from which they came. Prohibition is here to stay and let us work to see that it is enforced." [28]

In legitimating the character and style of the old middle class, Prohibition stood as a symbol of the general system of ascetic behavior with which the Protestant middle classes had been identified. Not only was Temperance at stake but so too was the Tem-

---

[25] Virginius Dabney, *Dry Messiah* (New York: A. A. Knopf, 1949), p. 136.
[26] Hearings of the Senate Committee on the Judiciary, 65th Congress, 2nd and 3rd Sessions, *Brewing and Liquor Interests and German Propaganda* (1919).
[27] *Annual Report of the NWCTU* (1919), p. 68.
[28] *Ibid.* (1929), p. 73.

perance ethic which provided its rationale and its moral energy. Supporters of Prohibition identified the struggle to dry up American society as part of the defense of a "way of life" against groups who subscribed to other cultures. Prohibition was not seen as an isolated issue but as one which pitted cultures against each other. Speaking to a WCTU national convention in 1928, Ella Boole (then President of the WCTU) said:

This is the United States of America, my country and I love it. From the towering Statue of Liberty to the sun-kissed Golden Gate, this is my country. It is all I have. It is the foundation and security for my property, home and God.

As my forefathers worked and struggled to build it, so will I work and struggle to maintain it unsoiled by foreign influences, uncontaminated by vicious mind poison. Its people are my people, its institutions are my institutions, its strength is my strength, its traditions are my traditions, its enemies are my enemies and its enemies shall not prevail.[29]

Mrs. Boole made it clear to her listeners that the enemies she had in mind were those who opposed Prohibition and evaded its laws. She had equated Prohibition with the total American culture.

The victory of the Prohibitionists and the later fight against Repeal only intensified the cultural conflict and further polarized the forces of urban and rural, Catholic and Protestant, immigrant and native. The disposition to assimilate the nonconformer was even further minimized, as anti-Prohibition forces became organized for Repeal. The Temperance movement became an active supporter of legislation to curtail immigration drastically.

Increasingly the problem of liquor control became the central issue around which was posed the conflict between new and old cultural forces in American society. On the one side were the Wets—a union of cultural sophistication and secularism with Catholic, lower-class traditionalism. These represented the new additions to the American population that made up the increasingly powerful political forces of urban politics. On the other were the defenders of fundamental religion, of old moral virtues, of the ascetic, cautious, and sober middle class that had been the ideal of Americans in the nineteenth century.

In Alfred E. Smith the Wets found a perfect symbol of their ways of life—a champion of progressive liberalism through social welfare, an urban type whose speech and sentiments manifested the "sidewalks of New York" where he had been reared. He was in

[29] *The Union Signal* (December 15, 1928), p. 12.

many ways the best of the machine politicians, loyal to his friends, a genial good fellow, and a deep defender of that urban underdog who worked in factories, spoke broken English, and wanted a good time on Sundays.

If Smith was the symbol of the Wets, then William Jennings Bryan was the epitome of the Drys. He was born in a small town in rural Illinois and raised in the farmland of Nebraska. The Scopes trial dramatized again Bryan's religious fundamentalism, which his Biblical references had already made a part of American oratorical history. More than any other political figure it was Bryan who had been the champion of the rural underdog, who depended on the land, the railroads, and the banks for his livelihood, whose roots were several generations in America, and who treasured the quiet and peace of a Protestant Sunday.

These cultural dichotomies became increasingly sharpened in the Prohibition issue. The pluralism of political life which had made possible a union of urban and rural social welfare concerns in the Populist-Progressivist alliance and in assimilative Temperance reform was difficult to sustain as Prohibition ranged one culture against another. The Dry, the Protestant, the fundamentalist, the neo-Populist, the nativist were increasingly the same person. It was difficult to take one position and avoid the others. This tended to push the moderate elements out of the movement and to emphasize the others. The Federal Council of Churches of Christ, a moderate, welfare-oriented group, had been enthusiastic contributors to the campaign for legislative Prohibition. Antipathy to nativism and fundamentalism made them cool to the defense of the amendment. Bryan, in his struggle against Smith's potential nomination in 1924, came to the defense of the Ku Klux Klan and the attitude of nativist hostility to immigration. While the intellectual, the political liberal, and the assimilative reformer might have seen Temperance as an ally to other causes, this was less and less possible as the Prohibition decade continued and the Prohibitionists turned their cause increasingly into a crusade against urbanism, immigration, and Catholicism.

What was more than ever at stake in the symbol of Prohibition was the status of the old middle classes in America. The threat of Repeal carried with it the fear of status decline which had been offset by the Prohibition victory itself. A spokesman for the Anti-Saloon League responded to proposals for referenda on repeal of

the Eighteenth Amendment by an attack on the cities and identification of American civilization with rural America: "When the
great cities of America actually come to dominate the states and
dictate the policies of the nation, the process of decay in our
boasted American civilization will have begun." [30] Here was the
same appeal to rural virtue and anti-urbanism that had characterized Bryan's Cross of Gold speech in 1896. The neo-Populism of
Prohibition was a political philosophy devoid of economic content
but filled with the cultural tones of an attacked status group.

REPEAL AND STATUS LOSS

When the Eighteenth Amendment was repealed it meant the repudiation of old middle-class virtues and the end of rural, Protestant dominance. This is what was at issue in the clash between the
Wets and the Drys. Victory had bolstered the prestige of the old
middle classes. Defeat meant decline. Temperance norms were
now officially illegitimate and rejected as socially valid ways of
behaving.

The repeal of the Eighteenth Amendment has never been subject
to a scholarly analysis. In the absence of definitive research, ex-
planations of Repeal have reflected the pros and cons of Wet and
Dry convictions. Wets have chosen to consider the Dry decade as
an experiment that failed when its unenforceability was obvious
to all but the bigoted and the fanatical. Drys have resorted to cries
of trickery or, in more directly Populist spirit, held the wealthy
and the powerful accountable for an effort to increase sources of
tax revenue through beer and liquor sales.

It seems likely that the failure to enforce Prohibition in urban
areas need not have destroyed its status as a legal pattern. The
Prohibition episode is constantly used as evidence that law cannot
effect social change. The bootlegging industry is depicted as the
disorganizing consequence of Prohibition. It is true, however, that
institutionalized systems of evasion have often been maintained
over very long periods of time without damaging the symbolic
status and social validity of the legal norms. This has been the
case in prostitution, gambling, drug addiction, political corruption,
abortion, and the other nonconformist actions called "business
crimes." This might well have happened in the case of Prohibition.
The ability of the underworld, the politician, and the police to

[30] *Anti-Saloon League Yearbook, 1931* (Westerville, Ohio: American Issue
Publishing Co., 1931), p. 9.

regulate such institutions in concert is a major finding of criminologists and students of urban communities.[31] Bootlegging in its early stages, like most American industries, displayed the disorder of individualistic competition. By the late 1920's it was beginning to move into the stage of monopolistic competition which has since characterized the regulation of much crime in America.

Of course, the rising power of urban political forces might well have doomed even an orderly system of institutionalized evasion. In the early thirties this was not yet the case. Alfred E. Smith had been defeated by a wide majority in an election in which the Prohibition Amendment was a major issue. When Herbert Hoover was elected President, Temperance forces were powerful supports to his victory.

The most significant element in the repeal of the Eighteenth Amendment was not directly related to the cultural conflicts and struggle for status that had precipitated the Prohibition issue. It was the change in the tone of political life brought about by the Great Depression that killed the Eighteenth Amendment. In 1929 the amendment was safely in the Constitution, having survived the attack of the 1928 election. By 1932 neither major political party made its support a part of their platform. Two things had happened. The Depression had enormously strengthened the demand for increased employment and tax revenues which a reopened beer and liquor industry would bring, and it had made issues of status secondary to economic and class issues.

Congressional hearings on bills to modify or repeal Prohibition show the effect of economic arguments against Prohibition. In 1926 there were few witnesses in opposition. The argument against the Drys was couched in the logic of personal liberty.[32] In 1930 many unions appeared and took a strong stand against the amendment on the grounds that Repeal would put men back to work. The same was true of the 1932 hearings.[33] They contain pleas for

[31] William F. Whyte, *Street-Corner Society* (Chicago: University of Chicago Press, 1943), Ch. 4; Daniel Bell, "Crime as an American Way of Life," in his *The End of Ideology* (Glencoe, Ill.: The Free Press, 1960), Ch. 7.

[32] See the Hearings of the Senate Committee on the Judiciary, 69th Congress, 1st Session, *Bills to Amend the National Prohibition Act* (1926).

[33] See the Hearings of the House Committee on the Judiciary, 71st Congress, 2nd Session, *On the Prohibition Amendment* (1930), and the Senate Committee on the Judiciary, 72nd Congress, 1st Session, *Modification or Repeal of National Prohibition* (1932). Unions had appeared in opposition to Prohibition at the 1926 hearings but in the 1930's there were many more and they used economic rather than ethical arguments.

Repeal by the Lithographers' Union (makers of bottle labels), the Glass Blowers' Union, and the Allied Association of Hotel and Stewards' Associations, as well as other unions with a direct interest in the alcoholic beverage industries. By 1930 both the American Federation of Labor and the National Association of Manufacturers had come out for Repeal.

The economic argument was twofold: put men back to work and provide another source for tax revenues. With the large decline in national prosperity, the question of tax relief seemed most important to businessmen who had championed Prohibition as the way to a sober and reliable work force.[34] In 1926 the DuPonts swung over to active opposition to the Drys. Even such stalwarts of moral reform as John D. Rockefeller and S. S. Kresge left the movement in 1932. Shrinking federal revenues were an enormous detriment to the Drys.[35]

More important, perhaps, was the tendency for the Depression to minimize the importance of status politics. Tangible economic needs were paramount. Whatever the cultural differences between the lower-class urban workers and the rural farmers they were both in desperate financial straits. Not status groups but economic classes were now the salient axes of political movement. In 1929 *The Christian Advocate* listed enforcement of the Volstead Act as the most serious problem facing America.[36] In 1932, with 15 million men out of work, this statement would have been more tragic than ludicrous.

Despite the decline in status issues, Repeal was nevertheless experienced as a loss of status for the old middle classes. In 1915 Anna Gordon, President of the WCTU, had described the growing dominance of Temperance in national life in terms of increasing prestige: "Total abstinence is no longer a ridiculed fanaticism. It sits in regal state on the throne of empires and of kingdoms and in

[34] In North Carolina, for instance, the manufacturers proved strong supporters of state Prohibition. Daniel Whitener, *Prohibition in North Carolina*, James Sprint Studies in History and Political Science, 27 (1945), p. 155. The argument of an efficient work force was always of some importance in Temperance, although seldom dominant. Irenee DuPont had used it when he had championed the Prohibition Amendment.

[35] Dabney, *op. cit.*, pp. 210-211.

[36] Cited in Paul Carter, *Decline and Revival of the Social Gospel: Social and Political Liberalism in American Protestant Churches, 1920-1940* (Ithaca, N.Y.: Cornell University Press, 1956), p. 129.

republics sways, in ever increasing measure, the voting citizen-ship."[37] After Repeal this was clearly not the case. Of the 37 states holding referenda on Repeal, only in five (North Carolina, Mississippi, Kansas, Oklahoma, and South Carolina) was there a majority vote against Repeal.[38] In 1911, midway in the movement for state and national Prohibition, 50 per cent of the American population lived in Dry areas.[39] In 1940 18.3 per cent were living in Dry areas.[40]

Status Decline in the Temperance Movement

The symbolic decline has also been accompanied by an actual shift in the status of the Temperance adherent. This has meant that Temperance adherence is no longer prestigeful even in the communities which used to be sources of strong Temperance support. "People don't like us," said one WCTU local leader in a metropolitan city. An articulate and committed WCTU member stated the same result in terms of historical change. She described her experience in a small rural New York state town: ". . . this isn't the organization it used to be. It isn't popular you know. The public thinks of us—let's face it—as a bunch of old women, as frowzy fanatics. I've been viewed as queer, as an old fogey, for belonging to the WCTU. . . . This attitude was not true thirty years ago."

Between 1925 and 1950 the local leadership of the WCTU changed in its social characteristics. The percentage of women from upper middle-class background declined while the percentage from lower middle- and lower-class backgrounds increased. Data on the occupations of the husbands of WCTU local leaders is presented in Table IV (for sources see Chapter 3, p. 81, n. 36).

Table IV indicates the lessened prestige of the movement. Over the 65 years of WCTU membership surveyed there has been a steady decrease in the representation from high-status occupations and a steady increase in the representation from lower-status occupational groups. In 1885 the professionals and businessmen made up more than 50 per cent of the occupations represented among WCTU local presidents studied. (This also lends credence to our

---

[37] *Annual Report of the NWCTU* (1915), p. 93.
[38] Jellinek, *op. cit.*, p. 30.
[39] *Anti-Saloon League Yearbook, 1911*, p. 30.
[40] *Annual Report of the Distilled Spirits Institute* (1940), Appendix E.

view of the upper middle-class nature of assimilative reform.) By 1950 this group had declined to almost one-fourth. The decline in status after Repeal is even more pronounced than is indicated by the table. In 1925, the two relatively low-status professional categories of clergymen and teachers accounted for 32.1 per cent of all the professionals in the sample. In 1950 they accounted for 61.4 per cent of the professionals.

These conclusions of a diminished status are further reinforced by the statements of WCTU people themselves. Many of the local

TABLE IV. PER CENT OF WCTU LOCAL LEADERS, CLASSIFIED BY HUSBAND'S OCCUPATION FOR STATE AND YEAR

State and Year	Husband's Occupation						Totals (per cent)	N
	Pro. & Semipro.	Prprtrs., Mgrs., & Officials	Clerical & Sales	Skilled Labor	Unskilled & Semiskilled Labor	Farm		
Connecticut								
1885	25.7	20.0	22.9	22.9	5.8	2.9	100	68
1910	21.0	31.6	13.2	21.0	10.6	2.6	100	34
1925	3.8	15.4	21.2	36.6	21.1	1.9	100	51
1950	12.4	18.6	25.0	29.2	14.8	0.0	100	52
Michigan								
1885	17.8	33.3	6.7	28.9	8.9	4.4	100	42
1910	15.3	19.4	19.4	26.4	15.3	4.1	100	72
1925	13.0	14.6	18.8	24.6	27.6	1.4	100	66
1950	13.2	7.1	16.6	26.2	36.9	0.0	100	77
Illinois								
1885	20.0	35.6	11.2	24.4	8.8	0.0	100	50
1910	14.5	22.0	20.4	25.4	15.2	2.5	100	136
1925	11.8	19.3	23.5	19.3	24.4	1.7	100	124
1950	12.4	14.2	16.8	25.6	31.0	0.0	100	127
Minnesota								
1885	25.6	33.3	15.4	17.9	5.2	2.6	100	38
1910	14.0	19.3	27.3	28.9	9.6	0.9	100	116
1925	12.7	22.8	20.1	28.9	15.5	0.0	100	151
1950	10.3	17.6	23.6	31.5	17.0	0.0	100	164
Maryland								
1885	22.2	44.4	27.8	5.6	0.0	0.0	100	15
1910	13.6	36.4	40.9	9.1	0.0	0.0	100	22
1925	16.7	35.2	20.4	18.4	9.3	0.0	100	57
1950	21.4	33.3	21.4	16.8	7.1	0.0	100	41
Totals								
1885	20.6	30.6	16.5	23.0	6.5	2.8	100	213
1910	14.8	24.4	22.4	25.0	11.4	2.1	100	380
1925	12.6	22.4	20.8	27.1	16.2	0.9	100	449
1950	12.9	15.3	22.4	27.8	21.2	0.5	100	451

leaders whom we talked to said that it is more difficult to recruit people with local prestige today than it was during Prohibition. Wives of doctors and lawyers and women who are teachers were reported as much harder to interest in the cause. "I remember," said one woman in New York State, "when the ——— family lived in that house. They were the finest people in the town and they were Temperance people." Upper middle-class, Protestant, small-town people are less prone to be active in Temperance work than they were two and three decades ago. As a number of WCTU members have themselves mentioned, the attitude has emerged that "we ladies who are against taking a cocktail are a little queer."

MORAL INDIGNATION AND THE CRISIS OF LEGITIMACY
The decline in the status of the active worker in Temperance is probably less significant than the decline in the legitimacy and dominance of Temperance norms. Since the repeal of Prohibition, a crisis has developed in the relation between Temperance and social status. Where once the abstainer could identify himself with the publicly dominant norms of his own community and reference group, today he is more likely to find that Temperance ideals are deviant even within the Protestant middle-class society to which he has felt affiliated. Temperance norms are increasingly illegitimate or invalid. As one minister has put it: "Once you were a queer if you imbibed; now you are a queer if you don't." [41]

American Alcohol Consumption
In order to understand the shift that has taken place in American attitudes toward drinking it is necessary to analyze the changes in the composition of American drinking. In the period between 1850 and 1915 there was a drastic change in the use of distilled spirits and beer. Table V shows that while we were once primarily a nation of liquor drinkers we have now become a nation of beer drinkers as well.

While the total amount of all alcoholic beverages consumed per capita of population of drinking age (14 and over) is much higher than it was in the periods before World War I, the per capita amount of alcohol consumed is much less. This is a result of

[41] Arthur W. Anderson, "Is There a Positive Equivalent to Drink?" *The Union Signal* (December 14, 1957), p. 10.

TABLE V.   PERCENTAGE CONTRIBUTION OF DISTILLED SPIRITS, WINE, AND BEER TO THE AP-
PARENT CONSUMPTION OF TOTAL ABSOLUTE ALCOHOL IN THE UNITED STATES, 1850-1957 [42]

Total Absolute Alcohol [a]		Per Cent Alcohol Contributed by		
Year	Gallons	Distilled Spirits	Wine	Beer
1850	2.07	89.6	3.7	6.7
1911-15 (ave.)	2.56	36.7	5.9	57.4
1940	1.56	42.9	10.3	46.8
1957	1.91	40.3	11.0	48.7

[a] Gallons per capita population of drinking age, 14 and over.

a shift from liquor to beer in the drinking patterns of the society.
The change toward greater beer drinking and less distilled spirits
indicates a change from a pattern of extremes to one of moderation. A heavy consumption of distilled spirits and a low consumption of beer suggests there are few drinkers but that those who
are drink heavily. A high consumption of beer indicates many
users of alcohol but relatively few heavy drinkers. "The early Temperance societies thus had a strong case and their contention that
3 out of every 10 users became chronic alcoholics dates from experience in the nineteenth century. Under present-day drinking
habits approximately 3 drinkers out of every 200 become chronic
alcoholics." [43]

The period before World War I and during the wave of state
prohibitory legislation marks the high point in American drinking.
During no year since then have rates of alcohol consumption been
higher. The pattern of drinking in contemporary American society
is thus one of moderate drinking rather than either abstention or
excessive use.

Abstinence as Deviant Behavior

The general decrease in alcohol use and increase in number of
consumers has been most clearly revealed since Prohibition, although it would be gratuitous to ascribe its cause to Prohibition
alone. The implications of this pattern for the legitimacy of total
abstinence are great. The object of change for the Temperance

---

[42] Based on data compiled by Mark Keller and Vera Efron, *Selected Statistics
on Alcoholic Beverages (1850-1957) and on Alcoholism (1910-1956)* (New
Haven, Conn.: Quarterly Journal of Studies on Alcohol, 1958).

[43] Jellinek, *op. cit.,* p. 9.

movement has been the act of drinking in any quantity. Any pattern of drinking, even though moderate, violates Temperance norms. The decline in the social status of WCTU women reflects a decline in the status of the Temperance norms. Not only have the Wet forces achieved political supremacy but now the Protestant middle classes have come to define abstinence as a deviant set of norms. As one informant put it: "There has been a breakdown in the middle classes. The upper classes have always used liquor. The lower classes have always used liquor. Now the middle class has taken it over. The thing is slopping over from both sides."

Within the adherents of the Temperance movement there is a clear perception that abstinence is not a recognized and respected position, that abstinent behavior is no longer a symbol of prestigeful social position. There is a realization of the increased dominance of new middle-class norms in which the abstainer appears as an object of ridicule, contempt, and inferior status. One of the leading Temperance writers, Albion Roy King, has expressed the changed value of abstinence as a symbol of status:

There was a time when the rural pattern dominated the colleges, especially in the West. . . . Parents who have migrated from farming to urban vocations, with some nostalgia, still send the children to the rural colleges. But if they have climbed the ladder to a $10,000 a year status it is fairly certain that they have turned their backs on the rural mores and nothing symbolizes this more dramatically than the cocktail bar in the home.[44]

The crisis for the abstainer is a crisis of legitimacy. Before Prohibition the status of the drinker was clear. He was at best a tolerated person within the circles of respectability which made up the reference groups of the abstainer. The people who thoroughly rejected Temperance norms were below him in social class or so far above him and so few as to be relatively unimportant for his sense of status in his community. The upper-class culture in which drinking was wholly accepted was a cosmopolitan one, not to be found in the small towns and rural areas. The lower-class culture in which drinking was unambiguously accepted was outside the pale of the abstainer's society—the ne'er-do-wells of his town or the foreigners of the big cities. This is no longer true and the change threatens to reverse the position of abstainer and drinker. It is the norms of

[44] Albion Roy King, "Drinking and College Discipline," *Christian Century* (July 25, 1951), pp. 864-866.

abstinence which, increasingly, lack social dominance and are less and less legitimate in the middle class than was the case a generation ago. It is bitter for the abstainer to taste the truth of the advertiser's assertion that "Beer belongs."

In the nineteenth century an attitude of contempt toward alcohol was a positive sign of membership in respectable, middle-class life. In the mid-twentieth century an acceptance of pleasant vices on a moderate scale is a mark of the tolerance and fellowship in which leisure and comfort are prized. As drinking becomes a sign of membership in the upper middle classes, even the churchgoer is less steadfast in support of the legitimacy of abstinence. Not only are official church pronouncements less severe in their denunciation of drinking, but the ministry is seen as more protective and less condemnatory of the member who drinks. The abstainer feels less sure that his usual circles of church, family, and neighborhood support his own belief. ". . . drinking has become so prevalent that one who would cry out against it is regarded as a fanatic." [45]

The ambiguity of Temperance as the legitimate doctrine of Protestant, native, middle-class society is reflected in the failure of the Temperance advocate to associate abstinence with people of prestige and the act of drinking with lowered prestige. Moderation is the prevailing norm which young people are likely to meet in school and in church, as well as in the mass communications media. "The greatest difficulty to be found today among youth, in anti-alcohol education, is the fact that 'good people' are using liquor." [46]

The crisis stems from the openness with which drinking occurs, the acceptance of the pattern of moderation rather than abstinence, and the ambiguous, even deviant position of the abstainer in relation to figures of prestige in his own local communities as well as in the larger national society. It is less a matter of the statistical regularity with which abstinence is followed than its symbolic import in fixing and validating social status.

Actually, there is little indication that less people uphold abstaining sentiments than they did shortly after Repeal. For the past 20 years, the Gallup Poll has consistently shown that about one-third to two-fifths of the American adult public claim that

[45] *The Union Signal* (February 21, 1953), p. 9.
[46] Roy L. Smith, *Young Mothers Must Enlist* (Evanston, Ill.: NWCTU Publishing House, 1953), p. 3.

they are abstainers.[47] If there has been any change, it has been seen in a slight increase in the proportion of those claiming to be abstainers. Temperance sentiment, as indicated by political activity, has changed remarkably little since 1939. In that year 18.3 per cent of the American population lived in areas that had voted to become Dry. In 1959 the percentage had declined to only 14.1 per cent.[48]

Abstinence is less prestigeful than it was a generation ago. The college-educated male and female have shown greater change toward increased drinking than any other proportion of the American population.[49] The public acceptance of the moderate drinking pattern as prestigeful is the backdrop to contemporary Temperance sentiments. As one writer complains, in discussing the use of liquor at weddings of church people, "Liquor is safely and securely in . . . because so many of the very best people of the community are not refusing it." [50]

Moral Indignation and Dominant Renegadism

The relation of the Protestant, upper middle-class moderate drinker to the Temperance movement is much like that of the renegade to the troops in which he was once a soldier. He has turned his back on their rules and committed an act of disloyalty. The moderate drinker has disavowed Temperance norms and has expressed his disaffection for the rules which once were standard guides to

---

[47] In 1945 67 per cent of the national sample said they were users of alcohol; in 1950 it was 60 per cent; in 1958 it was 55 per cent. News release of March 5, 1958, American Institute of Public Opinion, Princeton, N.J. While the precision of the Gallup Poll is open to much debate, an estimate of 30-40 per cent abstainers appears reasonable since it is also supported by other studies during the past 15 years. Riley and Marden found 35 per cent of a national sample were abstainers in 1947. John W. Riley, Jr., and Charles F. Marden, "The Social Pattern of Alcoholic Drinking," *Quarterly Journal of Studies on Alcohol,* 8 (September, 1947), 265-273. Maxwell found approximately 37 per cent of a Washington state sample were abstainers in 1951. Milton Maxwell, "Drinking Behavior in the State of Washington," *ibid.,* 13 (June, 1952), 219-239. Mulford and Miller found 40 per cent abstained in their 1958 sample of Iowa residents. Harold Mulford and Donald Miller, "Drinking in Iowa," *ibid.,* 20 (December, 1959), 704-726.

[48] *Annual Reports of the Distilled Spirits Institute* for 1939 and 1959.

[49] See Mulford and Miller, *op. cit.,* p. 72. Gallup has found the same trend. As college becomes a source of cosmopolitan values it widens the population among whom drinking is respectable. See my "Structural Context of College Drinking," *Quarterly Journal of Studies on Alcohol,* 22 (September, 1961), pp. 428-443.

[50] *The Union Signal* (October 18, 1952), p. 8.

his action. From the standpoint of the total abstainer, this moderate drinker is a traitor to his status group. He has taken on the norms of the enemy.

There is, of course, one major difference between the renegade and the middle-class, moderate drinker. The drinker has succeeded in universalizing his renegadism. He has not gone from one camp to another. Instead his action has become the new standard and those from whom he defects are now the aberrant followers of a past doctrine. His rebellion has succeeded. The similarity to renegadism, however, lies in the defection from a previously fixed standard. The Catholic, urban, immigrant could not be expected to live up to norms of what is to him an alien culture. The middle-class moderate drinker could be expected to do so.

The renegade is often a figure of greater hostility than is the member of the deviant or culturally opposing group. ". . . the behavior of the repudiated membership group toward the former member tends to be more hostile and bitter than that directed toward people who have always been members of an out-group." [51]

In the case of the attack on the legitimacy of Temperance norms the threat to the normative system and the status of the abstainer is even greater than in simpler instances of renegadism. The moderate drinker not only represents the fear that his example may be catching. His prestige and his behavior are actually diminishing the value of abstinence in the hierarchy of actions by which prestige can be increased or maintained. Furthermore, the prestige-deflating action occurs at the hands of people from whom the abstainer had greater expectations. They have let him down.

These considerations help us to understand both the bitterness and indignation of the Temperance movement toward moderate drinking and the concentration which the movement has shown since Repeal on the moderate drinker as the focus of reform. As the object of the movement's concern and anger is no longer socially subordinate, assimilative reform has very greatly diminished. The hostility, bitterness, and aggression of the movement is less that of Protestant-Catholic, urban-rural, or foreign-American conflict than it was before and during Prohibition. Both of these past strains exist. They are overshadowed by conflicts of an internal nature and of indignation directed at the defectors from the past standards. These are the people who are most responsible for the

[51] Robert Merton, op. cit., p. 296.

decline of the status of the abstainer and the rejection of Temperance as a legitimate and dominant system of behavior.

An illustration of the indignant response can be seen in one of the many similar stories in Temperance journals since Repeal in which the source of Temperance alienation is within the ingroup of one's fellow church members. In this story, "Today's Daughter," a 16-year-old girl goes to a party at the home of a new boy whose family has just moved into the neighborhood. Aunt Liz is suspicious when the boy tells Ruth's family that his new house has a game room in the basement. She knows that many of the new houses in the area now have bars in the game room. Ruth's mother tries to calm her sister's fears by telling her that this family is "alright. They joined the church last Sunday." Aunt Liz's reply upsets the mother and expresses the indignation of the Temperance advocate at the changed culture in which he now lives: "As if that meant respectability *these days!* Many's the church member who drinks and smokes and thinks nothing about it." [52]

Temperance, in this aspect of its doctrine, becomes a censure of the new habits of middle-class Americans. Wherever he looks the abstainer finds his expectations of respect for Temperance norms contradicted by the new doctrines of socially acceptable moderation. The Temperance advocate becomes the upholder of the past to this segment of the middle class, rather than the enunciator and defender of its norms at the level of moral ideals.

A great deal of Temperance denunciation is of moderate drinking and of the role of social acceptance in middle-class circles. A suburban woman, local officer in her WCTU, was typical of those we talked to in holding the churches partly responsible for the decline in Temperance morality. "The churches aren't helping some of them. We went to the home of a professor for a church meeting and his wife served sherry."

In terms of activities this has meant a great concentration on issues of church acceptance, of testimonials from prestigeful people, and on counteracting the implications of the fashionableness of drinking. The National Temperance League has even condemned the fashion of "cocktail gowns" because it establishes and supports the status symbol of drinking as prestigeful. [53] Great attention has

---

[52] *The Union Signal* (December 25, 1937), pp. 5-6.

[53] "Cigarettes and fashion, cocktail hours and cocktail dresses, tie women into drinking . . . the pressure of cocktail fashions on women has subtly led them to feel that ours is a cocktail culture." "Women Now, Children Next?" *The American Issue,* 67 (June, 1960), p. 4.

been given to maintenance of restrictions against liquor and beer advertising and on establishing the validity of social dissent, that is, the ability of the person to say "No" when offered a drink.[54] In all these ways the abstainer has concentrated on convincing his own membership groups to accept him even though he is an abstainer and to reaffirm their own past norms. Perhaps nothing illustrates better the need for the movement to again identify its norms as dominant than the slogan which the WCTU tried to popularize in the middle 1950's—"It's Smart Not to Drink."

The embittered sense of rejection and antipathy to the defectors from the Temperance standards represent a decided change from past tendencies to place Temperance in a context of religious and ethnic conflict. The wrath of the abstainer is now placed in a cultural conflict, divorced, to a large extent, from this framework and implicated in another conflict in which the declining status has new political consequences. In discussing these in the next chapter, we must keep in mind the decline in the norms and values of Temperance which has generated the specific direction of contemporary Temperance hostility. The position of the abstainer and of abstinence in the status hierarchy is not as significant as the sense of loss from a past place of legitimacy in the middle class and dominance in the society. A woman in upstate New York gave us an intellectualized statement of this sense of status decline: "We were once an accepted group. The leading people would be members. Not exactly the leading people, but upper-middle class people and sometimes the leaders. Today they'd be ashamed to belong to the WCTU. . . . Today it's kind of lower-bourgeois. It's not fashionable any longer to belong."

[54] In 1959 the WCTU organized a Committee on Social Freedom to help develop norms of hospitality which would enable abstainers to take part in many social activities. The pamphlets and reports of this committee remind hostesses to present guests with the option of fruit juices, as well as alcohol. Here, again, is clear recognition of the decline in the social dominance of Temperance within the social circles constituting their own membership groups.

6

Status Politics and Middle-Class Protest

The polarization of the middle classes into abstainers and moderate drinkers is part of a wider process of cultural change in which traditional values of the old middle class are under attack by new components of the middle stratum. In this process of change, Temperance is coming to take on new symbolic properties as a vehicle of status protest. In the current arena of American cultural conflicts a potential affinity exists between the Temperance movement and other forces whose political identities take shape from status issues which symbolize the revival of old middle-class values.

For much of the nineteenth century and in the early twentieth the conflicts between cultures over consumption patterns and the uses of leisure took place in an institutional context of classes, churches, regions, and ethnic identities. Most of the conflicts between pro-Temperance and anti-Temperance forces which we have described in the earlier chapters were of this kind: Protestant versus Catholic, "native" versus "ethnic," rural versus urban, middle class versus lower and upper class. In recent decades, the development of a more homogeneous and nationalized society, coupled with extensive social mobility, has diminished the close relation between institutional and cultural commitment. As we have seen in the previous chapter, the conflicts about drinking within the Protestant churches and churchgoing groups today are as great as those between Protestant and non-Protestant or between the religious and the secular. The terms "fundamentalism" and "modernism," which we shall use to characterize two different sets of values in present-day American life, are applicable to groups at the same class level in the society, and within the same institutions. The two middle-class groups are no longer poles apart. They live in the same cities or towns, share the same neighborhoods, belong to the same churches, and even send their children to the same schools and universities.

THE FUNDAMENTALIST RESPONSE TO MASS SOCIETY

In the past two or three decades cultural polarities in American life have been deeply influenced by new sources of ideas, techniques of operation, and associational commitments beyond the level of the local community. These have resulted in a split within communities dividing the society into two major cultural groups. One group reasserts older, traditional values which have been identified with the old middle class of the nineteenth century. The other group identifies the modern as the normative order to be followed. It sees its model in the values of new middle classes of salaried professionals, employed managers, and skilled workers in the basic industries.

The cultural fundamentalist is the defender of tradition. Although he is identified with rural doctrines, he is found in both city and country. The fundamentalist is attuned to the traditional patterns as they are transmitted within family, neighborhood, and local organizations. His stance is inward, toward his immediate environment. The cultural modernist looks outward, to the media of mass communications, the national organizations, the colleges and universities, and the influences which originate outside of the local community. Each sees the other as a contrast. The modernist reveres the future and change as good. The fundamentalist reveres the past and sees change as damaging and upsetting.

Sources of Cultural Conflict

In recent years a number of writers have pointed out that a major change in American values has made the cultural truths of the nineteenth century less certain and less honored in the twentieth. In the now classic statement of this view, David Riesman refers to "the characterological struggle" between inner-directed and other-directed personality types. These persons find their values in opposition. Feeling themselves as losers in the historical process, the champions of the older forms are deeply upset: "Inner-directed types, for instance, in the urban environment may be forced into resentment or rebellion. . . . I think that there are millions of inner-directed Americans who reject the values that emanate from the growing dominance of the other-directed types." [1]

The sources of these changes are many and their analysis beyond the scope of this work. They represent, however, two major axes of conflict in American life: the struggle between local and mass society and the struggle between a production-oriented and a consumption-oriented culture.

The conflict between local and mass society is that of divergent sources of power and influence. Where the locality, the immediate community, is the source, the orientation is local. Where the nation, the region, and the metropolis are sources, the orientation is toward mass society. As American society is increasingly dominated by national rather than local structures, the mass society assumes great significance as the source of cultural ideas while local power and status are undermined. The local banker manages a branch of a larger system whose basic framework is determined by policies in Washington and in the major cities. The local grocery store competes with the chain outlet of a national firm. The local teacher is torn between the values disseminated by her professional, national codes and those of the community in which she teaches and may have been raised. [2] The local social lion looks like "small potatoes" when measured against the national status system.

These national and extralocal structures carry to the local community the content of a national, homogeneous culture. The media of mass communications, the professionally trained experts, and the migrant middle class carry the culture of the mass society into all communities. "The new society is a mass society precisely in the sense that the mass of the population has become incorporated into society." [3] The older, traditional patterns are enunciated by the status claimants within the local structure; the newer patterns are carried by those who are oriented toward the mass society.

[1] David Riesman, *The Lonely Crowd* (New Haven, Conn.: Yale University Press, 1950), p. 32.

[2] This distinction between local and cosmopolitan values and between local and mass society is discussed by several recent writers. See Arthur Vidich and Joseph Bensman, *Small Town in Mass Society* (New York: Doubleday Anchor Books, 1960); C. Wright Mills, *The Power Elite* (New York: Oxford University Press, 1961), Ch. 2; Alvin W. Gouldner, "Cosmopolitans and Locals," *Administrative Science Quarterly*, 2 (December, 1957, March, 1958), 281-306, 444-480.

[3] Edward Shils, "Mass Society and Its Culture," *Daedalus*, 89 (Spring, 1960), 288-314, at 288.

A significant aspect of the conflict in cultures represented in the fundamentalist-modernist struggle is in the area of production and consumption. The shifts in drinking patterns described in the last chapter are manifestations of general changes in American attitudes toward work, play, and impulse gratification. The culture of the mass society is increasingly a culture of compulsive consumption, of how to spend and enjoy, rather than a culture of compulsive production, of how to work and achieve.[4] Vidich and Bensman, in a study of small-town life, found a sharp distinction between the life styles of the farmers and businessmen as contrasted to the life styles of professionals and skilled workers: "The greatest shift in the dimensions of class is an increasing emphasis on stylized consumption and social activities as a substitute for economic mobility . . . the underlying secular trend indicates a shift from production to consumption values in the community."[5]

The gradual transition from a society of small enterprisers, of whom many were farmers, to one of employees of large-scale organizations has placed less importance on the direction of life through an ethics of work. Great increases in productivity and technological progress have introduced leisure time on a large scale. The result is a decreased emphasis in national culture on the importance of restriction, saving, and the core of work-oriented values represented in the Protestant ethic and the values of the Temperance ethic.

In their study of a small Michigan city, Gregory Stone and William Form have produced a clear picture of the cleavages within middle-class life to which we are referring. With the location of national corporations in Vansburg, a large number of managerial personnel and salaried professionals became residents of the city. These people rejected the existing symbols of status and styles of life held by the upper middle-class people who had been living in Vansburg. They did not attempt to emulate the patterns of the established social elites. Instead they utilized the habits and customs of the sophisticated metropolitan resident. They developed

---

[4] Riesman, *op. cit.*, esp. Ch. 6; Leo Lowenthal, "Biographies in Popular Magazines," in Paul Lazarsfeld and Frank N. Stanton (eds.), *Radio Research: 1942-43* (New York: Duell, Sloan and Pearce, 1944), pp. 507-548. This corresponds to what Rostow refers to as the postindustrial stage of economic growth. W. W. Rostow, *Stages of Economic Growth* (Cambridge, Eng.: Cambridge University Press, 1960).

[5] Vidich and Bensman, *op. cit.*, p. 79.

their own communal forms and challenged the previous status of the "old" elites:

> They appeared publicly in casual sport clothes, exploited images of "bigness" in their conversations with local business men, retired late and slept late. They "took over" the clubs and associations. . . . The Country Club, for example, has undergone a complete alteration of character. Once the scene of relatively staid dinners, polite drinking and occasional dignified balls, the Country Club is now the setting for the "business-man's lunch," intimate drinking, and frequent parties where the former standards of moral propriety are often somewhat relaxed for the evening. Most "old families" have let their membership lapse.[6]

Stone and Form found that the matter of drinking was the major symbol by which these two contestants in a status contest were differentiated, by themselves and by other residents of the city. The split in the middle class was characterized by interviewees as one between "drinkers and nondrinkers." Unlike our descriptions of these terms in late nineteenth-century Temperance accounts, this was seen as a horizontal cleavage, within the middle class, and not a vertical one, between middle and lower orders. It is also note-worthy that the examples of areas in which these two groups were in conflict were largely those of leisure-time behavior, with the "cosmopolitans" rejecting the restrictions on impulse release so central in the life styles of the "old families."

The effect of the cosmopolitan ethic of mass society is to debunk the older values of the middle classes in which a production orientation to life was bolstered by religious institutions. "There is the moral emancipation of 'Society,' with its partial permeation of the upper middle class, the adoption of manners and folkways not in keeping with various traditional canons of respectability." [7]

The Fundamentalist Reaction

These processes are more than upsetting to the person who, from his period of early socialization, has internalized traditional values and has made these the core of his claim to status and respectability. The fundamentalist reaction is a reassertion of those values and a condemnation of the modern values as illegitimate and unentitled to cultural domination.

[6] Gregory Stone and William Form, "Instabilities in Status," *American Sociological Review*, 18 (April, 1953), 149-162, at 155.

[7] Talcott Parsons, "Some Sociological Aspects of the Fascist Movements," in his *Essays in Sociological Theory* (Glencoe, Ill.: The Free Press, 1954), pp. 124-141, at 136.

We have spoken of the fundamentalist culture as an aspect of social structure, locating it in the old middle classes. Actually we are dealing with a cultural group, united by their common commitment to a set of values and norms. While the shared set of commitments may be historically associated with the old middle classes, at the present point in history the fundamentalist may be found in other structural contexts as well. Social change, because it does not involve patterns of socialization and internalization, often takes place more rapidly than does cultural change. During the past 40 years America has witnessed a great decline in percentage of farmers and rural non–farm dwellers. Migration has brought into urban places and into industrial occupations large segments of the society that have been socialized in different contexts. The cultural values laid down in early youth and passed onto children via familial training may contradict the structural position. This means that we should not assume that cultural categories, which we are here using in a framework of status hierarchies, are equivalent to structural categories, which we are here using in a framework of economic class. The term "old middle class" has both a structural and a cultural connotation. We are asserting that "old middle class" dies harder than the "old middle classes."

There are two aspects to the fundamentalist reaction, one defensive and the other aggressive. After Repeal both are common themes in Temperance materials. There is a revivalistic tone and a preoccupation with the regeneration of values in many areas—family life, child training, swearing, religion, and many others. In all these areas American life is depicted as having degenerated from an earlier position of virtue. There is a call for restoration of "those homely virtues of truth, honesty, recognition of authority, morality and respect for age." [8]

The defensive side of fundamentalism expresses a sense of estrangement from the dominant values and the belief that a return to the dominant values of the past, based on religion, economic morality, and familial authority, will solve social problems. One respondent remarked that conditions in the United States are similar to those at the time of the fall of Rome, that "there is a complete moral and spiritual degradation. The corruption and the spending and the drinking are the worst of it . . . . We need a regeneration."

Increasing secularism and the assumed decline in evangelical,

[8] From an address by Ida B. Wise Smith, President of the NWCTU, to the 1934 annual convention. *Annual Report of the NWCTU* (1934), p. 81.

fundamentalist religion is suggested as the cause of everything from juvenile delinquency to the threat of nuclear war. "Deepening the spiritual life of the nation" is seen as an essential prerequisite to national economic, moral, and political success. "Religion, in terms of weekly church-going, sincerity, and grace before meals, is the best form of juvenile protection." [9]

The detrimental consequences of the decline in middle-class dominance are expressed in this way by attention to the symbols connected with that dominance. Religious ritual, thrift, parental discipline, and individualism are contrasted with a contemporary society that applauds secular rationality, indulgence, equalitarian family relations, and economic dependence upon public agencies. Any change in the direction of the "old-fashioned virtues" enhances the social status of the Temperance followers. It is the decline in the general cultural standards which they bemoan.

The aggressive aspect of the fundamentalist reaction is its hostility to whatever smacks of the modern. If the values which manifested old middle-class superiority are undergoing decline, the responsibility for this loss of prestige is located in the modernist. As the fundamentalist has developed his institutional expectations around symbols which now appear less prestigeful, "aggression has turned toward symbols of the rationalizing and emancipated areas which are felt to be 'subversive' of the values."[10]

The central target of this hostility is the content of the mass society as contrasted with the local community. Sophistication, science, psychiatry, modern child rearing, contemporary educational methods are among the complex of patterns and institutions which are attacked as immoral and responsible for present-day ills. Cultural values that emanate from the national institutions of school, entertainment media, and even the major churches are depicted as sources for the decay in the status of the old middle class:

> The battle on the side of right used to be a shout; now it is a whisper. . . . No evil walks alone. Drinking is not the only wrong accepted by a society that would have been shocked at it yesterday. Sex crimes are common. . . . Honesty is no longer enthroned. . . . There is a tendency to tear down everything that the past has struggled to build. Personal hygiene no sooner attains the goal of common decency than some publicity seeker cries out against too frequent washing of hands. The college graduate shies away from the use of correct English for fear

[9] A statement by Mrs. D. L. Colvin, President of the NWCTU. Quoted in *The Chicago Daily News* (September 10, 1951).

[10] Parsons, *op. cit.*, p. 125.

of being classed with highbrows. The world is waiting for a return to some of the old virtues.[11]

Temperance as Fundamentalist Symbol

Moderate drinking itself symbolizes the loss of status incurred by followers of fundamentalist belief. Drinking is a matter of great significance in the fundamentalist complex of values. Because abstinence is a major fundamentalist virtue the increased acceptance of consumption-oriented styles of life in the United States constitutes a distinct threat to the old middle-class culture. It diminishes the socializing agencies committed to production-centered values and minimizes the institutional pressures supporting abstinence.

As the new middle class has developed cultural patterns distinctive to it and opposed to nineteenth-century values, the place of impulse gratification in work and leisure has been redefined. Self-control, reserve, industriousness, and abstemiousness are replaced as virtues by demands for relaxation, tolerance, and moderate indulgence. Not one's ability to produce but one's ability to function as an appropriate consumer is the mark of prestige.

The shift has a decided bearing on the status connotations of drinking. In the nineteenth century there was much fear that if the restrictions on impulsive action were even slightly lowered, the individual would go to the extremes of evil and social ruin. Temperance propaganda was often shocking in the detailed accounts of excessive actions brought about by one fatal sip. If there is a philosophy of leisure today it is not evoked by the fear of temptations but by the problem of capacity for enjoyment. The fear is one of inability to have fun, to relax, and to play. Liquor can become a social facilitator in a culture which is afraid that people are unable to "let loose" sufficiently.

In the recent past there has been an increased tendency to attempt by drinking to reduce constraint sufficiently so that we can have fun. . . . From having dreaded impulses and worrying about whether conscience was adequate to cope with them, we have come around to finding conscience a nuisance and worrying about the adequacy of our impulses. . . . While gratification of forbidden impulses traditionally aroused guilt, failure to have fun currently occasions lowered self-esteem.[12]

[11] From an editorial in *The Union Signal* (May 16, 1953), p. 8.
[12] Martha Wolfenstein, "The Emergence of Fun Morality," in Eric Larrabee and Rolf Meyersohn (eds.), *Mass Leisure* (Glencoe, Ill.: The Free Press, 1958), pp. 86-96, at 92.

This description of American culture today is all too real to the Temperance adherent. He agrees with Miss Wolfenstein's characterization of the current cultural atmosphere but he feels apart from it, estranged and a defender of the past. The rise of moderate drinking is a sign of this change and of the status loss which he has suffered. In reasserting the legitimacy of total abstinence he is also affirming the validity of the larger fundamentalist patterns.

POLITICAL FUNDAMENTALISM AND TEMPERANCE

The tenets of cultural fundamentalism have political corollaries which can lead to conservative, right-wing positions in American politics. The political significance of fundamentalism lies in the tendency of the fundamentalist reaction to produce a political perspective which converts issues of class politics into issues of status politics and which interjects issues of status into politics. In this section we are interested in the relation between the Temperance movement and the general orientation of the fundamentalist toward politics. We have already examined the Prohibition issue as a case of status politics. If the political effects of the fundamentalist reaction stem from the same sense of estrangement and search for status recoupment as has the Temperance issue, we can anticipate a close alliance between the Temperance movement and the forces of conservative and right-wing politics.

Political Fundamentalism and Status Politics

American attitudes toward politics often fluctuate between a cynical, compromising spirit and a hortatory moralism. As a "broker of interests" the politician is exhorted to handle all issues as matters of bargaining, adjusting one set of interests and values to another with little concern for anything but a solution acceptable to the parties involved. The moralizer in politics,[13] however, cannot adopt such an air of efficient search for compromise. For him, political issues are tests of virtue and vice in which those on the opposite side are immoral. Politics is a matter of possible sin and of hoped-for salvation. When issues are structured in moral terms they become tests of status. In the context of cultural conflicts, the moralization of issues places the prestige of each status-bearing group at stake.

[13] The term is used by David Riesman in his characterization of the inner-directed orientation to politics. *Op. cit.*, pp. 190-199.

A political issue becomes one of status when its tangible, instrumental consequences are subordinated to its significance for the conferral of prestige. With specific reference to the fundamentalist-modernist schism in culture, political issues which derive importance from their use as symbols of this conflict function in the orbit of status politics. The argument is less over the effect of the proposed measures on concrete actions than it is over the question of whose culture is to be granted legitimacy by the public action of government.

The issue of debt management is illustrative of one issue in American politics which has strong overtones of status conflict. As is true of many issues, there are those who stand to gain or lose materially by increased governmental deficit spending. The trauma induced in bankers and creditors by the fear of inflation is clearly understandable as a reflection of economic interests. The similar trauma induced in the professional, the businessman, the farmer, or the white-collar worker is not understandable on the same basis. Economists have pointed out the complexity of the problem of national debt and they do not see increasing debt as dangerous per se.[14] The reaction of the noncreditor can be understood as a response to the moral connotations of debt as evil and spending as vice. If the society is to applaud action which violates the norms of his style of life, then the abstemious, thrifty, saving businessman, professional, farmer, or white-collar worker has received a blow to his sense of esteem. He has found that his society does not support his claim to prestige based on his adherence to such norms. Whether he has personally suffered or gained by inflation, the changed attitude of public officials toward debt represents a status deprivation, and the old middle-class citizen responds with fear and hostility.[15]

In another form, the fundamentalist sees specific issues as con-

[14] For a leading, middle-of-the-road economist's view see Paul Samuelson, *Economics*, 3rd ed. (New York: McGraw-Hill, 1955).

[15] Keynes was quite aware of the implications of this change for the sense of psychological security of the old middle classes. ". . . this experience must modify social psychology toward the practice of saving and investment. What was deemed most secure has proved least so. He who neither spent nor 'speculated,' who made proper provision for his family; who sang hymns to security and observed most straitly the morals of the edified and the respectable injunctions of the worldly-wise—he, indeed, who gave fewest pledges to fortune has yet suffered her heaviest visitations." John Maynard Keynes, *Essays in Persuasion* (New York: Harcourt, Brace and Co., 1932), p. 91.

flicts between one cultural commitment and another. The fluoridation movement is a good example of how an issue of health has been turned into one of conflict between fundamentalists and modernists. Opponents of fluoridation reject the symbols of science, welfare, and governmental officialdom and assert the values of religion, natural environment, and individual action. "The imagery associated with a negative vote on fluoridation suggests that it was in large measure a revolt against authority, scientific as well as political." [16] The issue of health was subordinated to one of local versus mass culture, of one status group against another.

Conservatism and Temperance

Since the repeal of the Eighteenth Amendment there has been an underlying tone of political conservatism expressed on many issues in the Temperance movement. Although the issues of liquor legislation and education have been paramount, the materials of the WCTU and of the Prohibition Party display concern for more general political questions. They show a tendency to uphold fundamentalist ideologies by asserting conservative political positions which emphasize status elements.

The emphasis on style of political action is the dominant note in the criticism of the New Deal which was often voiced by Ida B. Wise Smith, the WCTU president during the 1930's. She left little doubt that she abhorred the legislative activities of the New Deal. The logic of her position was couched in terms critical of departures from past principle. In 1934, for example, she devoted one section of her annual address to warnings against departures from the Constitution. In the same year the WCTU passed a resolution deploring the legislative grants of power to the executive. In 1936 she referred to the evils that have come upon us in recent years, not in reference to Repeal, but as a general trend in the society. She called for preservation of the Constitution and election of persons who "will utterly rout the social evils that have come upon us in recent

---

[16] Here again is an instance of the negative reference group discussed in connection with contrast conceptions and drinking as a symbol of lower-class status (see Chapter 1). Whatever stems from scientific authority is immediately resisted by those who see science as an attack on their traditional symbols and sources of their authority. The quotation in the text is from James Rorty, in F. B. Exner and G. L. Woldblatt, *The American Fluoridation Experiment*, quoted in Kurt and Gladys Lang, *Collective Dynamics* (New York: Crowell and Co., 1960), p. 426.

years."[17] While not naming names, Smith implied that Roosevelt must be defeated.

The affront of the New Deal and of Roosevelt to the Temperance fundamentalist was only in part a result of the Repeal Amendment. In fact there is very little specific criticism of the Democrats as the authors of Repeal in the post-Repeal years. It is the morality of their general policies that is under fire. One of Smith's frequent complaints was that the President and other public leaders did not show enough religious commitment, especially by public acts of prayer: ". . . in past years when great emergencies arose, leaders like Washington and Lincoln called upon the people by proclamation to set apart a day for fasting and prayer and repentence in hope that the nation would come to that condition of mind and heart wherein God heals the land. There is no indication that this is so in the thinking of the nation now."[18]

The antipathy of the WCTU leaders to the New Deal was, of course, not necessarily shared by all fundamentalists, nor do we attribute it to all Temperance followers or WCTU members.[19] Nevertheless it was sufficiently widespread so that the president of the organization could express it openly in national meetings and in resolutions. It represents the growing separation between the liberal politics of assimilative reform and the Temperance movement. During the same period of the 1930's the Social Gospel went through a resurgence in American life which left little impression on the policies of the Temperance groups.

For the Temperance movement the fundamentalist reaction in politics has been heightened by two facts. First, Repeal was a major setback, reinforcing the alienation of the fundamentalist from domination and enhancing his sense of status decline. Second, the fact of Prohibition reinforced the identity of the Temperance adherent with the 1920's and Herbert Hoover. The WCTU all but ignored the Depression as a significant part of the experience of the 1930's. They did not address themselves to it. In a sense, the fact of the Depression severely damaged the prestige of the old order, the shining light of Herbert Hoover, and the claims of Prohibition to have brought about prosperity.

[17] *Annual Report of the NWCTU* (1936), p. 97.
[18] *Ibid.* (1934), p. 51.
[19] In 1934 one Baptist leader said to Franklin Roosevelt, "We are for you 96.8%. We cannot go the other 3.2." Quoted in Paul Carter, *Decline and Revival of the Social Gospel: Social and Political Liberalism in American Protestant Churches, 1920-1940* (Ithaca, N.Y.: Cornell University Press, 1956), p. 167.

The election of 1928 was a profoundly significant one for Temperance. In that election the movement supported Hoover and also openly allied itself with an anti-alien and anti-Catholic tradition. Not only did it repulse a number of liberal Temperance followers, such as William Allen White, but it strengthened the identification of the movement with the Republican Party and against the Northern Democrats. It was a decidedly bitter election, with much shifting of traditional party lines. For the first time in its history the WCTU openly endorsed a presidential candidate. The Prohibition Party openly opposed one major party candidate, favored another, and almost retired from the ballot entirely.[20] When Repeal occurred in 1933 it was with an administration whose pro-immigrant and urban character had been defeated in 1928 but rose to power in 1932. What could seem secure in such a topsy-turvy world? The symbols in which the abstainer had heavily invested were repudiated.

In assessing the policies of political figures in the 1930's, the Temperance follower looked for actions which might restore his sense of dominance. Emphasis on character and morality is a reflection of this. The political platforms of the Prohibition Party reveal this same concern with the decline in morality and plea for actions which bring about "spiritual awakening." [21] The assessment of economic issues carries with it the same recourse to the fundamentalist spirit. It sees new and unfamiliar actions as immoral. They disturb the certainty of belief in established, traditional solutions to national problems. In 1925 the editor of a conservative Baptist journal answered a writer who doubted the truth of Resurrection by saying: "It is like saying that the bank in which you have put all the money you have in the world is insolvent." [22] Of course, in 1931 and 1932 the banks did prove to be insolvent.

Rightist Reaction in the Postwar Period

Writing in 1952, in the journal of the WCTU, Mrs. D. L. Colvin, then national President of the organization, recounted her experiences as an observer at the Republican convention. There was need

[20] The 1928 platform implied that the party would retire if it were proved that Smith was close to victory. See Kirk Porter and Donald Johnson, *National Party Platforms*, 2nd ed. (Urbana: University of Illinois Press, 1961), p. 279.

[21] See the platforms of the Prohibition Party for 1932, 1936, and 1940 in *ibid.*, pp. 337, 363, 388.

[22] Quoted in Norman Furniss, *The Fundamentalist Controversy, 1918-1931* (New Haven, Conn.: Yale University Press, 1954), p. 16.

for a new party, she maintained, "which would bring together the level-headed Southerners and Northerners, with a middle of the road attitude, neither leftist nor extreme rightist but loyal Americans with the desire to do what is best for America and the world without destroying America while doing it." [23] Colvin was expressing two themes which appear in varying degree in the organizational literature of the Temperance movement during the 1950's. One theme is the alienation from major parties on general political issues, not solely Temperance. The other is the rightist political philosophy which is manifest in her implicit criticism of American foreign policy. At the time she wrote, political forces which attempted to use General Douglas MacArthur as a rallying point were the major political elements fitting her description of a new political party for the disaffected. To some extent, however, the Prohibitionists were moving in the same direction.

Colvin used the same argument in her efforts to persuade her followers to vote the Prohibition Party ticket in the 1952 elections. The Prohibitionists, she said, could appeal to voters dissatisfied with both parties and who see little between them on foreign policy matters. "Both claim to be conservative but both support New Deal policies." [24] *The Union Signal* reprinted an editorial from another journal which made even plainer the criticism of the Truman government on grounds of "coddling the Communists, against the 'leftwing' conduct of our domestic economy . . . against the tragedy and imbecility of war in Korea . . . the general incompetence of our leadership in our national affairs." [25]

As an organizational commitment the conservatism of the WCTU has remained diffuse, more a matter of tone than of definitive actions. A persistent antiwelfare orientation has emerged, but this too is more diffuse than concerted. In the area of general disaffection from current political positions, the WCTU has remained neutral, although expressing a political fundamentalism.

The Prohibition Party, on the other hand, has moved toward an

[23] *The Union Signal* (August 9, 1952), p. 12. At this time there was a large portrait-photo of General MacArthur displayed behind the librarian's desk in the WCTU Library.
[24] *Ibid.* (September 13, 1952), p. 2. Colvin's remarks may be taken to represent Prohibition Party official sentiment. She was a staunch supporter of the party and her husband was one of its leading officials.
[25] *Ibid.* (September 27, 1952), p. 8.

open appeal to right-wing elements of both major parties. They appear to be attempting to convert the Prohibition Party to one of extreme right-wing protest. They have accordingly emphasized the multiple issues of the party and the right-wing conservative position on a wide number of issues. *The National Prohibitionist,* organ of the party, is less concerned with liquor questions than it is with political issues instrumentally unconnected with Temperance, such as Communism, foreign policy, fluoridation, education, and governmental economy.

Reading the platforms of the Prohibition Party over the past 90 years one can see how Populism has turned into a neo-Populism which often contradicts its original instrumental tenets. For example, the early platforms of the party, as we have seen, were Populist in calling for government to aid the farmer in his struggles with big business and with finance. This theme continues during the early twentieth century. During the Depression it is again a basis for an attack on the banks and a demand for inflationary policies. By the 1950's, however, the actions of government in past eras have begun to take on hallowed characteristics. Political disaffection is less oriented toward increasing demands for governmental action than toward decrease. If there is a sense of not being part of the governing groups, then it is better to curtail governmental actions. If inflation as a major policy is threatening to the sense of moral fitness, and hence of prestige, of its adherents, then the opposite policy becomes virtuous. During the 1950's the Prohibitionists have built an appeal based on distrust of government, calling for decentralization, states' rights, limited taxation, and an end to restraints on free enterprise. "We believe that good government ought not to attempt to do for people what they can do for themselves." "We deplore the current trend toward development of a socialistic state." [26]

This orientation occurs in the context of status politics in two ways. First, it appeals to people to whom the symbol of Prohibition is evocative of cultural fundamentalism. Second, it expresses a demand for a government which will "restore" past conditions. It is this theme of regeneration and restoration which unites the Populism of the past with the neo-Populism of today.

[26] Porter and Johnson, *op. cit.,* p. 601.

THE EXTREMIST RESPONSE: LIMITED AND EXPRESSED

The concept of a "radical right" has assumed considerable usage both in social science and popular writing in recent years.[27] It expresses the phenomenon of radicalism as an orientation toward institutions and groups which may be identified with opposite sides of political struggles. It is possible to be radically anti-Communist, laissez-faire, pronationalist, and on a number of other issues to be identified with conservative positions in such a fashion as to be extremist and in opposition to the status quo. The right-wing extremist attacks the political institutions themselves, impugns the motives of officials, and repudiates the norms of political tolerance between opponents. The demands he makes for change are radical in that they represent sweeping alterations. Right-wing radicalism utilizes the fundamentalist culture as a source of its values but seeks to defend it as a holy war against enemies. "Its hostility is incompatible with that freedom from intense emotion which pluralistic politics needs for its prosperity . . . [the extremist] is worlds apart from the compromising moderates." [28]

In American politics right-wing extremists have demonstrated a search for status equality in attacks on the symbols of mass society and cultural groups whom they perceive as having become socially and politically dominant. As a consequence, the contents of rightist radicalism have been nativistic, jingoistic, and xenophobic. The extremist has sought to increase the value of his membership in native American culture by strident nationalism. He has sought to condemn his enemies by associating them with national enemies. Through it all, the extremist has expressed a deep mistrust of official, public institutions of church, government, communications, and school. It is in this latter sense that right-wing radicalism has been neo-Populist in its ideology.

Within the Temperance movement, the right-wing extremist has appeared as one possible direction in which the movement might have gone and in which some aspects of it have been going. In part a harsh anti-alienism and nationalism exist as a diffuse strain in some parts of the movement, unorganized and unchanneled. In part, an open rightist radicalism exists in the shape of Prohibition Party doctrine.

[27] See the collection of essays edited by Daniel Bell, *The New American Right* (New York: Criterion Books, 1955).

[28] Edward Shils, *The Torment of Secrecy* (Glencoe, Ill.: The Free Press, 1956), p. 231.

The Decreasing Attack on the Alien

Protestant-Catholic conflict was a basic part of the Prohibition movement and of the issues during the Dry decade. While different wings of the movement represented assimilative and coercive attitudes toward immigration, the alien was seen as an opponent of Temperance and of middle-class life styles. The status position that the Temperance adherent was defending had its origins in his identity as an ethnic and religious member. As the relevant cultural polarities in American life have come to overlap ethnic and religious diversities, anti-alienism has decreased its centrality in American politics, although it has by no means disappeared.[29]

A comparison of the role of Temperance forces in the 1928 and 1960 presidential elections is instructive in this regard. Alfred E. Smith was anathema to the Temperance forces and they committed themselves openly and intensely in the campaign to elect Hoover. Even here there were distinct differences within the movement. The WCTU, in their characteristically less coercive orientation, muted their aggressive tones. They supported Hoover and campaigned against Smith, but they presented a more restrained public face, less extremist in tone and less openly anti-Catholic and anti-alien than did the Anti-Saloon League and the Methodist Board of Temperance, Prohibition, and Public Morals. The prominent Prohibitionist leader, Methodist Bishop James Cannon, led the mobilization of Protestants against Smith as a holy war to maintain the social supremacy of the native American: "Governor Smith wants the Italians, the Sicilians, the Poles and the Russian Jews. That kind has given us a stomachache. We have been unable to assimilate such people in our national life. . . . He wants the kind of dirty people that you find today on the sidewalks of New York."[30]

The election of 1960 re-created the Protestant-Catholic issue on the plane of presidential politics. Despite the existence of a large amount of anti-Catholic sentiment generated in the campaign, the Temperance movement remained aloof from both the campaign and

[29] The wave of rightist sentiment during the period of McCarthyism (1950-54) lacked strong anti-Semitic or anti-Catholic sentiments. Both Jews and Catholics were among leading McCarthy supporters. It testified to the diminution of these tensions as central to contemporary antiforeign sentiments. See the essay by Seymour Lipset, "The Sources of the Radical Right," in Bell (ed.), *op. cit.*, pp. 166-234, at 201-206.

[30] From a speech by Cannon, given at Cambridge, Maryland, during the 1928 campaign. Quoted from *The Baltimore Sun* in Virginius Dabney, *Dry Messiah* (New York: A. A. Knopf, 1949), p. 188.

the nativist expressions which were current in many Protestant circles. Neither the WCTU nor the National Temperance League endorsed either candidate. In their journal *The American Issue,* the Temperance League, offshoot of the former Anti-Saloon League, ignored the campaign entirely. The WCTU was less indifferent but they took no position, despite some diffuse anti-Kennedy sentiment.

The attitude of the Prohibition Party is even more instructive. In 1928 they broke with their long-standing doctrinal position that the differences between the two parties were insignificant. They were on the ballot but had also endorsed Hoover, promised not to run in areas where he might be politically hurt by loss of Prohibitionist votes, and were pledged to withdraw entirely if this seemed necessary to Hoover's victory.[31] In 1960, while expressing considerable right-wing extremism, they did not serve as a vehicle of intensive anti-Catholic sentiment. While there appears to have been support for a pro-Nixon stand by the Prohibitionists, it was not dominant. The position of the party, as expressed by Earl Dodge, Editor of *The National Prohibitionist,* was that the Republicans were no more defenders of church-state separation than were the Democrats, that Kennedy would probably be less subservient to Catholic church influence on school aid questions than would Nixon, and that both candidates were socialistic.[32]

It appears that neither major party is sufficiently associated with Temperance or with cultural fundamentalism to have made the 1960 election as crucial for the movement as the 1928 one had been. This is a reflection of the alienation of the Temperance adherent from the major organized parties.

It is certainly not true that anti-Catholic and anti-alien sentiments have disappeared from the Temperance movement. They can be found in the literature of the movement in isolated passages[33] and expressed by some followers in congressional hearings.[34] The or-

[31] See the 1928 platform of the Prohibition Party in Porter and Johnson, *op. cit.,* p. 279.

[32] *The National Prohibitionist* (November, 1960), p. 2; (April, 1961), p. 3.

[33] The works of the late Ernest Gordon contained many references to the role of Jews and Catholics in the liquor industry. See *The Wrecking of the 18th Amendment* (Francestown, N.H.: The Alcohol Information Press, 1943), pp. 147, 158.

[34] Gerald Winrod, head of the Defenders of the Christian Faith, and the

ganized and patterned open expression is not as significant as it was in the earlier periods of Prohibitionist zeal. This facet of right-wing radicalism is less a part of Temperance doctrine than it has been in the past.

Nationalism and the Cultural Struggle

The opposite is evident in issues that touch upon foreign affairs, militarism, and domestic Communism. Here there has been drift in the direction of nationalist sentiments which express a defense of fundamentalist culture.

The Prohibition Party has shown an explicitly right-wing radical doctrine on a number of issues. They have expressed a fear that American policy is operated by groups and by criteria whose cultural commitments give no recognition to the fundamentalism the Temperance adherent stands for. An intense mistrust of science, of government, and of education runs through the pages of *The National Prohibitionist*. In February, 1961, for example, Rollin Severance, Prohibition Party candidate for U.S. Senator from Michigan, wrote an article opposing repeal of the Connally Amendment. In it he attacked the United Nations as having been organized by "Alger Hiss, Harry Dexter White and Russia's Molotov." He warned that if the Connally Amendment were repealed, the UN would have the power to ship Americans anywhere in the world to where "they" (the UN) wanted. He opposed the Genocide Treaty and warned about "China-betraying judges like Jessup." In the course of the article he also attacked fluoridationists and the mental health programs.[35]

This coupling of mental health, the UN, the American foreign policy, and fluoridation is also contained in the platform of the party, a document marked by its extreme defense of laissez-faire economics, states' rights, and opposition to governmental action in welfare areas. The general orientation of the party is expressed in

representative of the Disciples of Christ both attacked, by implication, the role of Jews in the press and in the liquor industry at a Senate investigation into liquor advertising. U.S. Congress, Senate Committee on Interstate and Foreign Commerce, *Liquor Advertising* (Washington, D.C.: Government Printing Office, 1950), p. 112.

[35] *The National Prohibitionist* (February, 1961), p. 1.

a letter to *The Indianapolis Star* by Earl Dodge, Chairman of the Prohibition Party: "We oppose Federal aid to education, support right-to-work laws, oppose socialistic policies such as are being practiced right now in our government and call for an end to foreign aid to Communist nations and other dictatorships. We are the only party on the Indiana ballot this year which stands for conservatism."[36]

The anti-Communism of the radical right appears both in their condemnation of foreign policy and in their orientation to domestic groups. This is an attitude which identifies sources of dominance in American life as distrustful and alien. Insofar as the groups that hold power in America cannot be identified with cultural fundamentalism, with the orientations of the old middle class, their actions are responded to by a sense of fear and loss. In antifluoridation and mental health opposition they express their suspicion of the role of science and the carriers of its culture. The attack of the Prohibition Party on federal aid makes the point of cultural struggle quite clear. They assert that the Department of Health, Education, and Welfare employs "one-third of the top echelon of Communist conspirators in the United States." Hence the objection to placing "our children's education under the control of the most extreme radicals in our government."[37]

Within the WCTU there has been a less extremist trend in the same direction, toward a more hostile and critical posture with respect to international alliances. Both the WCTU and the Prohibition Party had been antimilitaristic, in the periods before and after World War II. Both organizations had supported American participation in the League of Nations in 1919 and after. In the 1930's both manifested the neo-Populist isolationism represented in attacks on military profiteers and the investigations of the munitions industries, which they demanded. They supported disarmament conferences and the passage of the Ludlow-Ware bill to provide referenda on declarations of war. In the 1930's the WCTU in Kansas fought against the introduction of ROTC into Topeka high schools and after World War II both organizations opposed peacetime con-

[36] Quoted in *ibid.* (November, 1960), p. 2.
[37] Harry Everingham, "Federal Aid—Enemy of Education," *ibid.* (May, 1961), pp. 1, 4.

scription and also the adoption of universal military training.[38]

In the 1950's there is a more pronounced antipathy to symbols associated with antimilitarism and with international cooperation. The UN is especially a target for criticism. It is the style of the organization, as a vehicle of nonfundamentalist culture, which attracts the negative response in the WCTU. While the UN was at first supported, the resolutions of the 1950's became more negative and qualified. The secular and cosmopolitan image of the UN was singled out as the aspect which caused the Temperance adherent most concern. Mrs. D. L. Colvin devoted a portion of several annual addresses to criticism of the UN for failure to observe prayer in opening their meetings or to recognize God or the Bible as an aid in their deliberations. "The Prince of Peace, through whom peace can and will come to the world, is absolutely ignored. King Alcohol is on the throne at Lake Success."[39] This is a clear admission of the way in which the association of the UN with styles of life that oppose the old middle-class symbols are experienced as threatening.

In similar vein, the opposition to conscription has been muted and softened. A leading WCTU official during recent years was much opposed to universal military training and was much more negative toward the UN: "The United Nations, now there's something. . . . I believe in supporting it when it's an instrument for peace, but not when it's an instrument for appeasement and dishonor."

This remains, however, a most diffuse undertone of rightist sentiment. The Communist issue has been virtually ignored in WCTU materials, either as an issue of importance per se or as tied to Temperance issues. The WCTU presents the appearance of an organization which adheres to cultural fundamentalism but can hardly be said to have embraced the radical right, as the Prohibition Party has. While political issues are perceived in status terms,

[38] See the 1948 platform of the Prohibition Party, Porter and Johnson, *op. cit.*, p. 447, and the report of the WCTU Department of International Relations for Peace, *Annual Report of the NWCTU* (1952), p. 128. The antimilitarism of the Prohibitionists is consistent with their Populist ideology. Both posited a conspiracy of profiteers behind military alliances. See Wayne J. Cole's account of this in his history of the movement, *America First* (Madison: University of Wisconsin Press, 1953).

[39] Quoted in *The Chicago Daily News* (December 19, 1953), p. 24.

in terms of cultural loyalties and oppositions, extremist sentiment has not been given organizational expression.

THE DILEMMA OF THE TEMPERANCE MOVEMENT

A sense of isolation and rejection hangs over the Temperance movement like a persistent black cloud. It forms the atmosphere in which indignation and bitterness are nurtured. Whether to resolve that sense of rejection or to utilize it as a source of organized zeal is the basic dilemma of the movement.

Decline and Isolation

Despite the shifts in the prestige of drinking and the end of Temperance political dominance, total abstainers are still a large segment of the American population. In fact, "estimates of the proportion of drinkers suggest a levelling-off since World War II." [40] In 1945, 33 per cent of the adults surveyed by Gallup were abstainers. This slowly increased during the annual surveys to 45 per cent by 1958 and fell again by 1960. Nevertheless we can estimate, from the Gallup Poll and other studies, that at least one-third of the adult population do not drink. This has remained fairly constant during the past 15 years, as manifested by the similarity of this finding in studies taken by different observers at different times in the past two decades.[41] Whatever may have been the fate of Prohibition and the Temperance movement, total abstinence is a widely followed custom. The same studies also show that abstinence has declined among college-educated groups. This substantiates the decline in the prestige value of abstinence norms which we have found reflected in WCTU materials. Abstinence today is most frequent in the lower middle- and lower-class Protestant of the more evangelical and sectarian denominations. The Episcopalian and the Lutheran were seldom supporters. The Presbyterian, the Congregationalist, and the ·Methodist are less firm and the Baptist is wavering. It is among the Nazarene, the Church of God, the Jehovah's Witness and the less institutionalized and influential churches that Temperance seems to be growing most rapidly today.

[40] Raymond McCarthy (ed.), *Drinking and Intoxication* (Glencoe, Ill.: The Free Press, and New Haven, Conn.: Yale Center of Alcohol Studies, 1959), p. 179.
[41] See the discussion of this above, Chapter 5, pp. 134-135.

Local option results support a conclusion similar to that derived from survey results. There has been little loss of support for Dry measures during the past 20 years. The "hard core" of political following appears to have remained remarkably stable. The existent pattern of liquor control in the United States has been largely effected by local option elections at the county level. As stated above (Chapter 5), as a result of state and local Prohibition in 1939, 18.3 per cent of the American population lived in locally Dry areas. In 1959 this percentage had only declined to 14.7 per cent, despite the repeal of state Prohibition in Kansas and Oklahoma.[42] Dry strength had increased in 16 states while Wet strength had increased in 15 states.

Despite intense local activity in elections, there has been remarkably little change during the past decade.[43] During the period 1947-59 there were 12,114 local elections held in the United States on issues of liquor control. Most of these left the existent situation intact. In 10.8 per cent of the elections there was a change from one direction to another. Even here the forces were well balanced. In 45.3 per cent (592) of the 1,307 cases the voting unit went from Dry to Wet. In 54.7 per cent (715) of the cases the unit went from Wet to Dry.[44]

As an active movement, however, Temperance support is declining drastically. There is much concern in the WCTU, voiced in its journal and in interviews, for the future of the organization. It appears increasingly difficult to recruit young people into the movement. As the older members die out, the organization is not fed new membership from younger generations.[45] Table VI shows how WCTU membership has declined since 1930. The past decade has even shown a reversal in the small growth of the 1940-50 decade.

The decline of the past decade has been consistent in all parts of the country. No state showed an increase in membership. While there has been a consistent increase in percentage of WCTU membership in the South and Midwest and a consistent drop since 1930 in percentage of membership from New England and the East,

[42] Based on statistics compiled by the Distilled Spirits Institute, *Annual Report* (1939), Appendix E; (1959), p. 51.
[43] *Ibid.* (1959), pp. 46 ff.
[44] *Ibid.*, p. 54.
[45] This is described further in my article "The Problem of Generations in an Organizational Structure," *Social Forces*, 35 (May, 1957), pp. 323-330.

TABLE VI. WCTU MEMBERSHIP BY SELECTED YEARS [46]

Year	Number
1921	344,292
1931	355,355
1941	216,843
1951	257,548
1960	195,327

there has been an over-all decline in membership while the total population of the country has been increasing.

The same phenomenon of declining support is manifest in the electoral strength of the Prohibition Party. The Prohibition Party is the oldest third party in the United States. It has placed a candidate in every presidential election since 1872. While it has never been strong enough to capture an electoral vote, its strength has been significant in local and state elections in certain periods and in certain areas. Measured as a national party, the Prohibition Party has declined in strength since the pre-Prohibition era.

Even with a larger total electorate, the total Prohibition vote is lower than pre-Prohibition. Since Repeal, however, it has fluctuated considerably, although the past two elections have seen a lower vote than at any time since 1936.

The Future of the Temperance Movement

At present the Temperance movement is a declining but still functioning phenomenon. Three alternative approaches have emerged to the dilemma of the movement in contemporary America. While all of them, to some extent, are found in all facets of the movement, each tends to dominate one wing of the movement more than the others.

One approach is a narrowed concern with drinking and drinking legislation to the exclusion of other reforms or of general political participation. The National Temperance League follows this policy. Unlike its forerunner, it no longer places Prohibition, either at the national or the state level, at the head of its aims. The work is more modest, confined to local option, to maintenance of existing

[46] Based on the treasurer's reports, *Annual Reports of the NWCTU*. These figures can be presumed fairly accurate. A state is required to pay a uniform dues to the national treasury for each member enrolled. The vote of the state delegation to the national convention is based on this. Hence the importance of accurate reporting to the national treasurer.

antiliquor legislation, and to education in Temperance sentiment. As a political pressure group it serves to marshal the limited power of the movement largely as a defensive maneuver, to prevent the Wets from eradicating the legal and political measures which limit the expansion of liquor sales. As a pressure group, the movement has been moderately successful in maintaining present restrictions on liquor advertising on radio and television. Especially when it operates with other, nonideological interests, the Temperance movement has been a fairly successful "veto group," preventing the passage of legislation detrimental to its interests but unable to pass its own.

A second approach, especially manifested in the WCTU, lies in spreading the cluster of activities to which the movement is oriented so as to include a number of reforms acceptable in middle-class church circles. This functions to mitigate the isolation of the

TABLE VII. **TOTAL VOTE FOR PRESIDENT ON PROHIBITION TICKET BY YEAR** [47]

Year	Total Vote
1872	Not tabulated
1876	Not tabulated
1880	10,305
1884	150,369
1888	249,506
1892	264,133
1896	132,007
1900	208,114
1904	258,536
1908	253,840
1912	206,275
1916	220,506
1920	189,408
1924	57,520
1928	20,106
1932	81,869
1936	37,847
1940	57,812
1944	74,758
1948	103,224
1952	72,949
1956	41,937
1960	46,239

[47] U.S. Bureau of the Census, *Historical Statistics of the United States* (Washington, D.C.: Government Printing Office, 1960), p. 682. These figures may be grossly underenumerated. Officials of minority parties claim that their votes are often not tabulated. The matter has never been studied, but the author's personal experience at one precinct suggests there may be merit to this claim.

movement from social areas of prestige and from major institutions. Among such reforms are narcotics prevention, chronic alcoholism, juvenile delinquency, censorship of obscene literature, and religious devotions. The emphasis of these activities is on assimilative reform and on cultural fundamentalism. The organization will work with groups in areas of alcoholism even though they are opposed to Prohibition and total abstinence. The thrust of the effort in this wider policy is toward eradicating the stereotype of the narrow, fanatical, and doctrinaire "blue-nose" of the famous Rollins Kirby cartoon of the Dry. The WCTU has even cautioned its members to dress with some gaiety, to be tactful toward non-members, and to avoid the mannerisms and actions of the "fanatic." Prohibition, while not disowned, is not emphasized, and the educational and pressure group aspects of the organization are given primacy. The subtitle of the WCTU periodical, "A Journal of Social Welfare," suggests the tone which is followed. Political issues outside of these generally accepted areas are excluded from organizational interest.

The third approach lies in capitalizing on the sources of isolation and protest among old middle-class citizens as they feel the discontents of a fading social status. This approach is clearly that of political extremism and middle-class protest. The platform of the Prohibition Party illustrates how Prohibition and total abstinence, as issues, are brought within the syndrome of the radical right. This is the classic position of the third party as a vehicle of generalized protest.

The prospect that any of these approaches will succeed in achieving a significant change in American drinking norms appears slim. As long as the Temperance movement is dependent on the Protestant churches for political, organizational, and cultural support it is doubtful that a firm rejection of moderate drinking in favor of total abstinence will occur. Protestantism no longer represents a cultural group sufficiently uniform to support the mobilized Temperance opinion it mustered in the 1920's. The socialization of each succeeding generation reduces the importance of abstinence as a symbol differentiating the respectable middle class from the nonrespectable drinkers. In order to stay within the orbits of churchgoing respectability the Temperance movement must minimize its indignation, accept Repeal, and be largely a vehicle of middle-class reform without any distinctive properties, except as a veto group for a constituency which is growing smaller.

The chance that the demand for liquor reform as a status symbol will again return in America is not dependent on drinking habits. In fact, while Americans have become less alcoholic they have accorded alcohol greater prestige. The future of alcohol reform depends on the general future of fundamentalist protest in the United States. Liquor control can become imbedded in the syndrome of political fundamentalism if the Temperance movement becomes allied to right-wing radicalism or if other radical rightist organizations absorb Temperance issues and present demands for alcohol reform. Something of this nature has begun to occur with the absorption of the position of the Southern white supremacist by the radical right. Both as an opportunistic measure and as expressive of the fundamentalist-modernist conflict, states' rights has become a symbol to which the political fundamentalist attaches himself.

In short, while the future of the movement as a direct attack on drinking seems to be limited, its role as a "holding movement" may possess greater possibilities. By a "holding movement" we refer to the fact that future crises unconnected with drinking may change the movement in directions which will be more significant for political success. There are many Americans who do not drink but to whom Temperance is not a burning issue. Any crisis which may create a generalized rightist neo-Populist movement contains the possibility that it may utilize the liquor industry as one of several bêtes noires and liquor reform as a symbol of revived prestige.

The separation of the old middle class from a specific role of dominance in major institutions, especially the churches, severely limits their role in politics. Cut adrift from a specific institutional mooring, their very weakness leads to the divergent tactics of extremism and of accommodation.

7

A Dramatistic Theory of Status Politics

Political action has a meaning inherent in what it signifies about the structure of the society as well as in what such action actually achieves. We have argued that Prohibition and Temperance have operated as symbolic rather than as instrumental goals in American politics. The passage of legislation or the act of public approval of Temperance has been as significant to the activities of the Temperance movement as has the instrumental achievement of an abstinent society. The agitation and struggle of the Temperance adherents has been directed toward the establishment of their norms as marks of social and political superiority.

The distinction between political action as significant per se and political action as means to an end is the source of the theory underlying our analysis of the Temperance movement. We refer to it as a dramatistic theory because, like drama, it represents an action which is make-believe but which moves its audience. It is in keeping with Kenneth Burke's meaning of dramatism, "since it invites one to consider the matter of motives in a perspective that, being developed from the analysis of drama, treats language and thought primarily as modes of action." [1] It is make-believe in that the action need have no relation to its ostensible goal. The effect upon the audience comes from the significance which they find in the action as it represents events or figures outside of the drama.

[1] Kenneth Burke, *A Grammar of Motives* (New York: Prentice-Hall, 1945), p. xxii.

Throughout the analysis of Temperance we have referred to the symbolic nature of Temperance goals. Our theory is further dramatistic in its perspective on political action as symbolic action, as action in which "the object referred to has a range of meaning beyond itself." [2] As we have pointed out in Chapter 1, this is the literary sense of the symbol as distinguished from the linguistic. It is in this sense that we refer to the flag as a symbol of national glory, to the cross as a symbol of Christianity, or the albatross as a symbol of charity in *The Rime of the Ancient Mariner*.

The dramatistic approach has important implications for the study of political institutions. These will be analyzed in this chapter, in the light of our study of the Temperance movement. Governments affect the distribution of values through symbolic acts, as well as through the force of instrumental ones. The struggle to control the symbolic actions of government is often as bitter and as fateful as the struggle to control its tangible effects. Much of our response to political events is in terms of their dramatic, symbolic meaning.

This is especially the case where elements of the status order are at issue. The distribution of prestige is partially regulated by symbolic acts of public and political figures. Such persons "act out" the drama in which one status group is degraded and another is given deference. In seeking to effect their honor and prestige in the society, a group makes demands upon governing agents to act in ways which serve to symbolize deference or to degrade the opposition whose status they challenge or who challenge theirs. We have seen this in the ways that Temperance goals symbolized victory or defeat for the devout native American Protestant.

This view of social status as a political interest enables us to solve some of the ambiguities about noneconomic issues and movements with which we began our study. It also provides us with a useful addition to the economic and the psychological modes of analysis current in the study of political and social movements.

SYMBOLIC ISSUES IN POLITICS

The State and the Public

Following Max Weber, it has become customary for sociologists to

---

[2] M. H. Abrams, quoted in Maurice Beebe (ed.), *Literary Symbolism* (San Francisco: Wadsworth Publishing Co., 1960), p. 18.

define the state as the legitimate monopolizer of force.[3] A major defect of this view, however, is that it minimizes the extent to which governments function as representatives of the total society. Other organizations or institutions claim to represent the values and interests of one group, subculture, or collectivity within the total social organization. Government is the only agency which claims to act for the entire society. It seeks its legitimation through the claim that it is effected with a "public interest" rather than with a special, limited set of goals. Much of the effective acceptance of government as legitimate rests upon the supposition that it is representative of the total society, that it has the moral responsibility "to commit the group to action or to perform coordinated acts for its general welfare."[4]

The public and visible nature of governmental acts provides them with wider consequences for other institutions than is true of any other area of social life. The actions of government can affect the tangible resources of citizens but they can also affect the attitudes, opinions, and judgments which people make about each other.

It is readily apparent that governments affect the distribution of resources and, in this fashion, promote or deter the interest of economic classes. The passage of a minimum wage law does affect the incomes of millions of laborers and the profits of thousands of owners of capital. The Wagner Labor Relations Act and the Taft-Hartley Act have changed the conditions of collective bargaining during the past 26 years. Tariff laws do influence the prices of products. While these legislative actions may not direct and control behavior as much as was contemplated in their passage, they nevertheless find their *raison d'être* as instruments which have af-

[3] Max Weber, *Theory of Social and Economic Organization,* tr. A. M. Henderson and Talcott Parsons (New York: Oxford University Press, 1947), p. 156. "The claim of the modern state to monopolize the use of force is as essential to it as its character of compulsory jurisdiction and of continuous organization." This definition is open both to the objection discussed above and to the inadequacy of singling out "force" as a major method of compulsion. Other institutions compel behavior by effective means other than violence, such as the ecclesiastical controls of a priesthood or the employment powers of management. The phenomena of "private governments" is not included in Weber's definition but the only ground of exclusion which is sociologically significant is the public character of governing bodies.

[4] Frances X. Sutton, "Representation and the Nature of Political Systems," *Comparative Studies in Society and History,* 2 (October, 1959), 1-10, at 6. Sutton points out that in primitive societies the political officers are often only representatives to other tribes rather than agents to enforce law.

fected behavior to the delight of some and the dismay of others. They are instruments to achieve a goal or end through their use.

That governmental acts have symbolic significance is not so readily appreciated, although it has always been recognized. We see the act of recall of an ambassador as an expression of anger between one government and another. We recognize in the standardized pattern of inaugural addresses the gesture toward consensus after the strain of electoral conflict. These acts, of ambassadorial recall and of presidential oratory, are not taken at face value but as devices to induce response in their audiences, as symbolic of anger or of appeal for consensus.

Not only ritual and ceremony are included in symbolic action. Law contains a great deal which has little direct effect upon behavior. The moral reform legislation embodying Temperance ideals has largely been of this nature, as have other reforms, such as those directed against gambling, birth control, and prostitution. The impact of legislation on such problems as civil rights, economic monopoly, or patriotic loyalties is certainly dubious. While we do not maintain that Temperance legislation, and the other legislation cited, has had no effect on behavior, we do find its instrumental effects are slight compared to the response which it entails as a symbol, irrespective of its utility as a means to a tangible end.

Nature of the Symbol

In distinguishing symbolic from instrumental action we need to specify the way in which a symbol stands for something else. It is customary in linguistic analysis to distinguish between "sign" and "symbol." [5] The former points to and indicates objects or experiences to our senses. The latter represents objects and events apart from any sensory contacts. Thus the ringing of the doorbell is a sign that someone is at the front door. The word "doorbell" is a symbol, as is the concept of "democracy." Our usage is not linguistic in this sense,[6] but literary. We are concerned with the mul-

---

[5] See the discussion of signs and symbols in Susanne K. Langer, *Philosophy in a New Key* (Baltimore, Md.: Penguin Books, 1948), pp. 45-50.

[6] Neither is our usage to be equated with the discussion of symbolic behavior used in the writings of the symbolic interaction school of social psychology, best represented by the works of George H. Mead. The idea of symbolic behavior in that context emphasizes the linguistic and imaginative processes as implicated in behavior. It is by no means contrary to our usage of symbols but the context is not specifically literary. The symbolic interactionists call attention to the fact that objects are given meanings by the systems of concept formation. We emphasize one aspect of this process.

tiplicity of meanings which the same object or act can have for the observer and which, in a society, are often fixed, shared, and standardized. The artist and the writer have developed language and visual art with the use of symbols as major tools of communication. Religious institutions have developed a rich culture around the use of objects whose meanings are symbolic. The wine and wafer of the Mass are but one example of objects which embody a multiple set of meanings for the same person at the same time.

This distinction between instrumental and symbolic action is, in many ways, similar to the difference between denotative and connotative discourse. In denotation, our eyes are on the referent which, in clear language, is the same for all who use the term. Instrumental action is similar in being oriented as a means to a fixed end. Connotative references are more ambiguous, less fixed. The symbol is connotative in that "it has acquired a meaning which is added to its immediate intrinsic significance." [7]

It is useful to think of symbolic acts as forms of rhetoric, functioning to organize the perceptions, attitudes, and feelings of observers. Symbolic acts "invite consideration rather than overt action." [8] They are persuasive devices which alter the observer's view of the objects. Kenneth Burke, perhaps the greatest analyst of political symbolism, has given a clear illustration of how a political speech can function rhetorically by the use of language to build a picture contradicting the instrumental effects of political action. For example, if action is proposed or performed which will offend the businessman, language is produced in speeches which glorify the businessman. In this context, language functions to persuade the "victim" that government is not really against him. It allays the fears and "softens the blow." Burke refers to this technique as "secular prayer." It is the normal way in which prayer is used, "to sharpen up the pointless and blunt the too sharply pointed." [9]

---

[7] Talcott Parsons, *The Social System* (Glencoe, Ill.: The Free Press, 1954), p. 286.

[8] Phillip Wheelwright, *The Burning Fountain* (Bloomington: Indiana University Press, 1954), p. 23.

[9] Burke, *op. cit.*, p. 393. My debt to Burke's writings is very great. He has supplied the major conceptual and theoretical tools for bridging literary and political analysis. In addition to *A Grammar of Motives*, see his *Attitudes Toward History* (Los Altos, Calif.: Hermes Publications, 1959), and *Permanence and Change* (New York: New Republic, Inc., 1935). Two sociologists, heavily influenced by Burke, have been extremely useful in developing attention to symbolic behavior in the sense used here. They are Erving Goffman, whose works are cited throughout this study, and Hugh D. Duncan, *Language and Literature in Society* (Chicago: University of Chicago Press, 1953).

It is not only language which is utilized in symbolic fashion by political agents. Any act of government can be imbued with symbolic import when it becomes associated with noninstrumental identifications, when it serves to glorify or demean the character of one group or another. Ceremony and ritual can become affected with great significance as actions in which the political agent, as representative of the society, symbolizes the societal attitude, the public norm, toward some person, object, or social group. Law, language, and behavior can all function ceremonially. They persuade men to a form of thought or behavior rather than force them to it. "The officer who doubts the obedience of his men may meet the situation by raising his voice, adopting a truculent tone, and putting on a pugnacious swagger." [10] This, too, is a form of rhetoric, of persuasive art.

Types of Political Symbolism

We find it useful to distinguish between two forms of political symbolism: *gestures of cohesion* and *gestures of differentiation*. The first type, gestures of cohesion, serve to fix the common and consensual aspects of the society as sources of governmental support. They appeal to the unifying elements in the society and the grounds for the legitimacy of the political institution, irrespective of its specific officeholders and particular laws. They seek to mobilize the loyalties to government which may exist above and across the political conflict of parties, interest groups, and factions. National holidays, inaugural addresses, and the protocols of address and behavior are ways in which the President of the United States attempts this function in his actions and words. The coronation of the monarch in Great Britain represents a highly ritualized method of symbolizing legitimacy. [11]

[10] Harold Lasswell, "Language of Politics," in Ruth Anshen (ed.), *Language* (New York: Harper and Bros., 1957), pp. 270-284, at 281.

[11] Edward Shils and Michael Young have studied the consensual effects of the coronation ceremony in England. See their "The Meaning of the Coronation," *Sociological Review*, 1, n.s. (December, 1953), 63-81. The use of ritual and ceremony to establish cohesion and social control through historical pagents and holidays in modern society is studied empirically in W. Lloyd Warner, *The Living and the Dead* (New Haven, Conn.: Yale University Press, 1959), esp. Pts. I and II. These aspects of "political religion" have received comparatively little attention from students of modern societies although most recognize the importance of such rituals and would agree with Hugh Duncan that "Any institution can 'describe' the way it wants people to act but only as it develops rites, ceremonies and symbols for communication through rite in which people can act does it rise to power." Duncan, *op. cit.*, p. 18.

Gestures of differentiation point to the glorification or degradation of one group in opposition to others within the society. They suggest that some people have a legitimate claim to greater respect, importance, or worth in the society than have some others. In such gestures, governments take sides in social conflicts and place the power and prestige of the public, operating through the political institution, on one side or the other. The inauguration ceremonies of two presidents can be used as illustrations. In his 1953 inaugural, Dwight Eisenhower prefaced his address with a short, personally written prayer. Commenting on this freely, a WCTU officer remarked approvingly, "Imagine that prayer written in the morning in an offhand way! It's the finest thing we've had in years from a president's lips." This gesture placed government on the side of the traditionalist and the devout and separated it from identification with the secularist and freethinker. In the inaugural of John F. Kennedy, the appearance of the poet Robert Frost was greeted as a symbol of respect and admiration for art, conferring prestige upon the poets by granting them places of honor in public ceremonies.

Such gestures of differentiation are often crucial to the support or opposition of a government because they state the character of an administration in moralistic terms. They indicate the kinds of persons, the tastes, the moralities, and the general life styles toward which government is sympathetic or censorious.[12] They indicate whether or not a set of officials are "for people like us" or "against people like us." It is through this mechanism of symbolic character that a government affects the status order.

STATUS AS A PUBLIC ISSUE

Deference Conferral

In what sense can the prestige of a status group be a matter at issue? Conflicts about the appropriate deference to be shown can, and do, exist. Currently the relations between whites and Negroes in the United States are examples of a status system undergoing intensive conflict. An issue, however, is a proposal that people can

---

[12] Another example of this symbolic process in political issues can be found in the conflicts over city manager plans. Development of city manager government is usually supported by middle-class voters and opposed by the lower socioeconomic groups. The impersonal, moralistic, and bureaucratized "good government" is much closer to standards of conduct typical in middle classes. The machine politician is closer to the open, personalized, and flexible government that represents the lower-class systems of social control. The issue of the

be for or against. A public issue has status implications insofar as its public outcome is interpretable as conferring prestige upon or withdrawing it from a status group.

Desegregation is a status issue par excellence. Its symbolic characteristics lie in the deference which the norm of integration implies. The acceptance of token integration, which is what has occurred in the North, is itself prestige-conferring because it establishes the public character of the norm supporting integration. It indicates what side is publicly legitimate and dominant. Without understanding this symbolic quality of the desegregation issue, the fierceness of the struggle would appear absurd. Since so little actual change in concrete behavior ensues, the question would be moot if it were not for this character as an act of deference toward Negroes and of degradation toward whites.

Unlike the desegregation question, many public issues are confrontations between opposed systems of moralities, cultures, and styles of life. Examples of these are issues of civil liberties, international organizations, vivisection, Sunday "blue laws," and the definition and treatment of domestic Communism. Probably the clearest of such issues in American public life has been the one studied in this book, the issue of restrictive or permissive norms governing drinking. Status issues indicate, by their resolution, the group, culture, or style of life to which government and society are publicly committed. They answer the question: On behalf of which ethnic, religious, or other cultural group is this government and this society being carried out? We label these as *status issues* precisely because what is at issue is the position of the relevant groups in the status order of the society. Such issues polarize the society along lines of status group differentiation, posing conflicts between divergent styles of life. They are contrasted with *class issues*, which polarize the society along lines of economic interests.[13]

city manager poses the two subcultures against each other. One study of the advent of city manager government reported that the first thing the new council did was to take away jobs from Catholic employees and, under merit employment, give them to Protestants. The city manager people celebrated their political victory with a banquet at the Masonic hall. See the discussion in Martin Meyerson and Edward Banfield, *Politics, Planning and the Public Interest* (Glencoe, Ill.: The Free Press, 1955), pp. 290-291.

[13] Essentially the same distinction is made by students of the voting process. Berelson, Lazarsfeld, and McPhee distinguish between issues of style ("ideal" issues) and issues of position ("material" issues). Bernard Berelson, Paul Lazarsfeld, and William McPhee, *Voting* (Chicago: University of Chicago Press, 1959), p. 184.

Status issues function as vehicles through which a noneconomic group has deference conferred upon it or degradation imposed upon it. Victory in issues of status is the symbolic conferral of respect upon the norms of the victor and disrespect upon the norms of the vanquished. The political institution or public is thus capable of confirming or disconfirming the individual's conception of his place in the social order.[14] Such actions serve to reconstitute the group as a social object by heaping shame or honor upon it through the support or rejection displayed toward its tastes, values, and customs. When the indignation of the abstinent toward the drinker is publicly confirmed by prohibitory legislation it is, in Harold Garfinkel's analysis of degradation ceremonies, an act of public denunciation: "We publicly deliver the curse: 'I call upon all men to bear witness that he is not as he appears but is otherwise and *in essence* of a lower species.'"[15]

Symbolic properties of deference and degradation can be involved in a wide range of issues and events. They may be implicated as a major theme in some issues or as a peripheral element in other issues, where the groups and themes are more directly those of specific economic interests. David Riesman and Ruel Denney have given us an excellent analysis of American football as a carrier of symbols which served to heighten the prestige of some social groups at the expense of the degradation of others.[16] The victories of Knute Rockne and Notre Dame over the previously championship teams of the Ivy League symbolized the growing social and educational equality of the non-Protestant middle-class Midwest vis-à-vis the Protestant upper-class East. Fans could identify themselves with football teams as carriers of their prestige, whether or

[14] ". . . the individual must rely on others to complete the picture of him . . . each individual is responsible for the demeanour image of himself and deference image of others, so that for a complete man to be expressed, individuals must hold hands in a chain of ceremony, each giving deferentially with proper demeanor to the one on the right what will be received deferentially from the one on the left." Erving Goffman, "The Nature of Deference and Demeanor," *American Anthropologist*, 58 (June, 1956), 473-502, at 493. Goffman's writings constitute an important discussion of deference and degradation ceremonies in interpersonal interaction. In addition to the article cited above see *The Presentation of Self in Everyday Life* (New York: Doubleday Anchor Books, 1959), and *Encounters* (Indianapolis, Ind.: Bobbs-Merrill, 1961).

[15] Harold Garfinkel, "Conditions of Successful Degradation Ceremonies," *American Journal of Sociology*, 61 (March, 1956), 420-424, at 421.

[16] David Riesman and Ruel Denney, "Football in America," *The American Quarterly*, 3 (Winter, 1951), 309-325.

not they were college graduates themselves. Knute Rockne was football's equivalent of Al Smith in politics.

Status Interests

Precisely because prestige is far from stable in a changing society, specific issues can become structured as tests of status when they are construed as symbols of group moralities and life styles. A civil liberties issue, such as domestic Communism, takes much of its affect and meaning from the clashes between traditionalized and modernist groups in American culture. Elements of educational sophistication, religious secularism, or political liberalism may appear as alien, foreign, and in direct contradiction to the localistic ways of life of the traditional oriented culture. Issues of civil liberties become fields on which such cultural and educational groups fight to establish their claims to public recognition and prestige.

In his analysis of McCarthyism, Peter Vierick has referred to just this kind of process in characterizing the attack on officials in the State Department. Vierick placed one source of this attack in the feeling of degradation which the Midwestern, agricultural, middle class felt at political domination by the aristocracy of the Eastern seaboard, educated at Ivy League schools and so prominent in State Department affairs. They symbolized the State Department personnel as "striped-pants diplomats" and "cookie-pushers." "Against the latter (the Foreign Service—ed.) the old Populist and La Follette weapon against diplomats of 'you internationalist Anglophile snob' was replaced by 'you egghead security risk.'" [17]

In the struggle between groups for prestige and social position, the demands for deference and the protection from degradation are channeled into government and into such institutions of cultural formation as schools, churches, and media of communication. Because these institutions have power to affect public recognition, they are arenas of conflict between opposing status groups. Their ceremonial, ritual, and policy are matters of interest for status groups as well as for economic classes.

It is in this sense that status politics is a form of interest-oriented politics. The enhancement or defense of a position in the status order is as much an interest as the protection or expansion of income or economic power. The activities of government, as the most

[17] Peter Vierick, "The Revolt Against the Elite," in Daniel Bell (ed.), *The New American Right* (New York: Criterion Books, 1955), pp. 91-116, at 103.

public institutions, confer respect upon a given style of life or directly upon a specific group. For this reason questions of institutional support of tastes, morals, and other aspects of life styles have consequences for the prestige of persons. Where status anxieties exist, they are then likely to be represented in the form of symbolic issues through which they are resolved.

To see that government, as do other institutions, is a prestige-granting agency is to recognize that status politics is neither extraordinary nor an irrational force in American history. Seymour Lipset appears to be quite mistaken when he writes, "Where there are status anxieties, there is little or nothing which a government can do." [18] Governments constantly affect the status order. During the 1930's the Democratic Party won many votes by increasing the number of Jews and Catholics appointed to state and federal judgeships. Such jobs did little to increase the total number of jobs open to these ethnic and religious groups. They did constitute a greater representation and through this a greater recognition of the worth of these groups. In this sense they were rituals of prestige enhancements, just as Andrew Jackson's inauguration symbolized the advent of the "common man" to power and prestige by the fact that rough men in boots strode across the floors of the White House.

It is just this consequence of the Temperance movement for the public designation of respectability that we have seen throughout this study. We have been interested in the efforts of Temperance people to reform the habits of others. While such efforts have indeed been motivated by the desire to perfect others in accordance with the reformer's vision of perfection, they have also become enmeshed in consequences affecting the distribution of prestige. Temperance issues have served as symbols around which groups of divergent morals and values have opposed each other.[19] On the

[18] Seymour Lipset, "The Sources of the Radical Right," in *ibid.*, pp. 166-234, at 168.

[19] This is evident in Lee Benson, *The Concept of Jacksonian Democracy* (Princeton, N.J.: Princeton University Press, 1961), esp. Ch. 9. Benson's work appeared too late to have been used in earlier sections of the book. It provides valuable evidence for the role of moral issues, and especially Temperance, in developing party loyalties in New York state in the 1840's. Using the concept of negative reference groups, Benson shows that economic interests played less of a role than did religious, cultural, and moral differences as influences on voting. Voters tended to see the two major parties as linked to one or another ethnocultural group.

side of Temperance there has been the rural, orthodox Protestant, agricultural, native American. On the side of drinking there has been the immigrant, the Catholic, the industrial worker, and the secularized upper class. In more recent years the clash has pitted the modernist and the urbanized cosmopolitans against the traditionalists and the localites, the new middle classes against the old.

When Temperance forces were culturally dominant, the confrontation was that of the social superior. He sought to convert the weaker members of the society through persuasion backed by his dominance of the major institutions. Where dominance of the society is in doubt, then the need for positive governmental and institutional action is greater. The need for symbolic vindication and deference is channeled into political action. What is at stake is not so much the action of men, whether or not they drink, but their ideals, the moralities to which they owe their public allegiance.

POLITICAL MODELS AND STATUS POLITICS [20]

Our analysis of symbolic acts has implications for traditional theories of American politics. In attempting to understand political processes and movements sociologists, political scientists, and psychologists have operated with two major models of political motivation. One model has been drawn from economic action and reflects the struggle for economic interests. This model we have designated *class politics*. The other model has been drawn from clinical psychology and reflects a view of politics as an arena into which "irrational" impulses are projected. The latter model, which we have called *psychological expressivism*, has been utilized by others to describe movements of status politics. Our use of a model of symbolic action has been intended to distinguish movements of status politics from both economic interest on the one hand, and psychological expressivism on the other. This section of the chapter indicates the implications of our analysis for theoretical political sociology.

Class Politics and the Pluralistic Model

The view of the political process as a balance of economic forces organized as classes has led to a compromise model of political

[20] Some of the matters discussed in this section are treated in greater detail in my "Mass Society and Extremist Politics," *American Sociological Review*, 27 (February, 1962), 19-30.

actions. The pluralistic model assumes a multiple number of specific interest groups whose demands conflict with and contradict each other. Farmers, bankers, skilled workers, unskilled workers, and professionals are represented through pressure groups and occupational associations. Political decisions are resultants of the compromises mediated between the various groups in accordance with the distribution of political power. Each group tries to get as much as they can but accepts partial losses in return for partial gains.

Compromise and the model of the political arena as one of mutually cooperating yet antagonistic groups presupposes a "political culture" in which victory and defeat are only end points on a continuum. An expediential attitude of calculation and exchange must govern the trading and bargaining. The language and imagery of compromise is drawn to a considerable extent from the marketplace, where monetary transactions enable interaction to be expressed in measurable quantities and mutual advantages. We "meet people halfway," develop political programs that are "deals," and operate through political parties talked about as "brokers of interests."

The "rules of the game" governing pluralistic politics are sharply antithetical to the "poor loser," the "sorehead," the intolerant ideologue who considers himself morally right and all others morally evil. He cannot accept the legitimacy of an institution in which even partial defeat occurs. For him politics is not a search for benefits in his work and life but a battleground between forces of good and evil. He reacts with passion in ways which contradict the rules of pluralistic politics. He rejects the presupposition that everybody in the political arena has a legitimate right to get something and nobody has a legitimate right to get everything. He typifies the moralizer in politics, described by Riesman and discussed in connection with the contemporary Temperance movement in Chapter 6.

Psychological Expressivism as a Model of Status Politics

The analytical scheme of pluralistic politics is most applicable to movements of class politics and instrumental action. Movements such as Prohibition, civil rights, religious differences, and educational change are puzzles to the sociologist and political scientist precisely because they cannot be analyzed in instrumental terms.

Their goals and major images appear 'irrational" and unrelated to the content of their aims. Being puzzles, a resort is often made to schemes which stress the impulsive, uncontrolled elements of spontaneous and unconscious behavior. Thus Lipset writes of status discontents as one source of rightist extremism: "It is not surprising therefore that political movements which have successfully appealed to status resentments have been irrational in character and have sought scapegoats which conveniently serve to symbolize the status threat." [21]

The essential idea in psychological expressivism is that the adherence to the movement is explainable as an expression of the adherent's personality. "Thus the mass man is vulnerable to the appeal of mass movements which offer him a way of overcoming the pain of self-alienation by shifting attention away from himself and by focussing it on the movement." [22] Unlike instrumental action, which is about conflicts of interest, the substance of political struggles in expressive politics is not about anything because it is not a vehicle of conflict but a vehicle of catharsis—a purging of emotions through expression. The analysis of politics as expressive takes on the attributes of magic, as in Malinowski's classic definition: "Man, engaged in a series of practical activities, comes to a gap . . . passive inaction, the only thing dictated by reason, is the last thing in which he can acquiesce. His nervous system and his whole organism drive him to some substitute activity." [23]

If we utilize only the two models of instrumental actions and psychological expressivism we tend to divide political and social movements into two categories—the rational and the irrational. Status politics, as we have seen in both Lipset and Hofstadter, gets readily classified as "irrational": "Therefore, it is the tendency of status politics to be expressed more in vindictiveness, in sour memories, in the search for scapegoats, than in realistic proposals for concrete action." [24] Between instrumental and expressive politics there is no bin into which the symbolic goals of status move-

[21] Lipset, op. cit., p. 168.
[22] William Kornhauser, The Politics of Mass Society (Glencoe, Ill.: The Free Press, 1959), p. 112.
[23] Bronislaw Malinowski, Magic, Science and Religion (New York: Doubleday Anchor Books, 1954; orig. pub., 1925), p. 79.
[24] Richard Hofstadter, "The Pseudo-Conservative Revolt," in Bell (ed.), op. cit., pp. 33-55, at 44.

ments can be analytically placed. Our usage of symbolic politics is an effort to provide such a bin.

Symbolic Politics and Status Interests

The consequences of interpreting status movements in the language of psychological expressivism is that the analyst ignores the reality of the status conflict. Expressive politics cannot be referred back to any social conflict which is resolved by the action taken. It is not a vehicle through which conflicts are mediated or settled. We have tried to show, in the instance of the Temperance movement, that the attempt to utilize political action was not only expressive but was a way of winning a concrete and very real struggle over the distribution of prestige in American society.

Discontents that arise from the status order are often as sharp and as powerful as those that emerge in the struggles over income and employment. In a society of diverse cultures and of rapid change, it is quite clear that systems of culture are as open to downward and upward mobility as are occupations or persons. Yesterday's moral virtue is today's ridiculed fanaticism. As the cultural fortunes of one group go up and those of another group go down, expectations of prestige are repulsed and the ingredients of social conflict are produced.

The dramatistic approach we have used in this study includes language but is by no means only a linguistic analysis. It is applicable to acts of legislation, such as Prohibition or fluoridation, to court decisions, and to official ceremony. Arguments about symbolic action are real in the sense that men's regard for respect, honor, and prestige is real. We do live in a forest of symbols, and within that forest there is disagreement, conflict, and disorder.

We are not maintaining a symbolic approach to politics as an alternative to instrumental or expressive models. We conceive of it as an addition to methods of analysis but an addition which can best help us understand the implications of status conflicts for political actions and, vice versa, the ways in which political acts affect the distribution of prestige. Most movements, and most political acts, contain a mixture of instrumental, expressive, and symbolic elements. The issues of style, which have troubled many social scientists in recent years, have not lent themselves well to political analysis. Those issues which have appeared as "matters of principle" now appear to us to be related to status conflicts and understandable in symbolic terms.

An example of what we have in mind can be seen in the political issues presented by controversies over school curricula in American municipalities. During the 1950's there has been much agitation to force American schools and universities to require more American history or courses on Communism as ways to establish patriotic loyalties among students and oppose Communist doctrine. Observers of American life are likely to deride these actions as pathetic attempts to control a situation with ineffective weapons or denounce such actions as coercion over the content of education. Beneath these programs, however, is the assumption that the school personnel are not succeeding in transmitting some value which the pressure groups feel important. The symbols of "Communism" are related to the cultural conflicts between fundamentalist and modernizing forces in American life, as well as the foreign policy conflicts between Russia and the United States. Cultural conflicts become easily centered upon school curricula because the content of education depends upon cultural assumptions. As our schools are increasingly manned by professionalized, college-trained personnel they come to represent modern, cosmopolitan values against which fundamentalists struggle.[25] Whose values shall the school system enunciate? Whose values shall be legitimized and made dominant by being the content of education? The manifest intent of such curricular changes may be inducement of patriotic feeling, but the latent, symbolic issue is not so directly educational. Psychologists may show that the pledge of allegiance every morning has no discernible effect upon patriotic feeling, but this is not the issue as status elements are involved. What such curricular changes "bear witness" to is the domination of one cultural group and the sub-

[25] For an analysis of one such school controversy in which "Communism," "human relations," "progressive education," and UNESCO were symbols of a feared cosmopolitanism see National Education Association of the United States, *The Pasadena Story* (Washington, D.C.: National Education Association, 1951). This same use of these symbols is linked to group conflict in many of the speeches and pamphlets of the extreme right wing in the 1950's and early 1960's. They underline the cultural values which are the center of the struggle. One example is the following from a reprinted speech: "Our most dangerous enemies are the thousands and thousands of disguised vermin who crawl all around us and, in obedience to orders from their superiors in the conspiracy, poison the minds of those about them with glib talk about 'social justice,' 'progressive education,' 'civil rights,' 'the social gospel,' 'one world' and 'peaceful coexistence.' You will find them everywhere: in your clubs, in your schools, in your churches, in your courts." R. P. Oliver, "Communist Influence in the Federal Government," speech to the fifth annual convention of We, the People! Chicago, September, 1959.

ordination of another. As most educators know, schools are run for adults, not for children. There is more than expression of feeling in such demands. There is an effort to dominate the rituals by which status is discerned.

A political model that ignores symbolic action in politics would exclude an important category of governmental action. It is a major way in which conflicts in the social order are institutionalized as political issues. Groups form around such issues, symbols are given specific meaning, and opposing forces have some arena in which to test their power and bring about compromise and accommodation, if possible. This is precisely what the issues of Prohibition and Temperance have enabled the status groups involved as Wets and Drys to accomplish. Turning status conflicts into political conflicts is precisely what Lasswell seems to have meant when he described politics as "the process by which the irrational bases of society are brought out into the open." [26]

Our approach also differs somewhat from that of Murray Edelman, who has been the most salient political scientist to recognize the role of symbolic action in legislative acts. He has pointed out that groups frequently seem satisfied by the passage of legislation, even though the execution of the acts often contradicts the intent of the legislation. This has been true in cases such as antitrust laws, the work of the Federal Communications Commission and other regulatory commissions, and in much civil rights legislation. "The most intensive dissemination of symbols commonly attends the enactment of legislation which is most meaningless in its effects upon resource allocation." [27] Edelman's analysis assumes, however, that this discrepancy is a result of the "psychological reassurance" given to such groups that their interests are being protected. We suggest that while this is a credible theory, especially in economic issues, there are some real interests at stake as well.

These can be specified as two different types of ways in which status interests enter into political issues. First, any governmental action can be an act of deference because it confers power on one group and limits some other group. It bolsters or diminishes the claims of a group to differential treatment. Second, the specific

[26] Harold Lasswell, *Psychopathology and Politics* (Chicago: University of Chicago Press, 1930), p. 184.
[27] Murray Edelman, "Symbols and Political Quiescence," *American Political Science Review*, 54 (September, 1960), 695-704, at 697.

status order, as distinct from the constellation of classes, is affected by actions which bear upon styles of life. The issues of Temperance and Prohibition have had particular relevance to the prestige of old and new middle-class ways of life.

We live in a human environment in which symbolic gestures have great relevance to our sense of pride, mortification, and honor. Social conflicts and tensions are manifested in a disarray of the symbolic order as well as in other areas of action. Dismissing these reactions as "irrational" clouds analysis and ignores the events which have significance for people. Kenneth Burke has pointed out the pejorative implications which emerge when noninstrumental usages are described as "magical." He distinguishes between poetic language, which is action for its own sake, scientific language, which is a preparation for action, and rhetorical language, which is inducement to action or attitude. If you think of acts as either magical or scientific there is no place to classify symbolic acts of the kind we have been considering, where an interest conflict is resolved but in noninstrumental symbolic terms. Consequently, a great deal of political activity is dismissed as ritual, magic, or irrational waste when "it should be handled in its own terms as an aspect of what it really is: Rhetoric." [28]

THE VOLATILITY OF STATUS POLITICS

Issues invested with status interests are not easily handled by political institutions oriented to the model of a pluralistic class politics. In American politics such issues are likely to be most difficult to regularize within the structure of the American political framework. Their volatile nature is further accentuated by recent changes in American culture and society which make such issues emerge even more explosively than they have in the past.

Status Conflict and the Political Process

It is the issues of morals and style, of religious belief and ethnic loyalties which searchers for political harmony most often implore be kept out of politics. Such pleas are recognition of the intensity with which status loyalties and aspirations prevent the operation of the culture of bargaining, compromise, and detached trading so necessary for a pluralistic politics. The introduction of status issues

[28] Kenneth Burke, *A Rhetoric of Motives* (New York: Prentice-Hall, 1950), p. 42.

cuts deeply at the sources of political consensus by converting political questions into moral ones.

The language of status issues, essential to their symbolic import, is the language of moral condemnation. In the confrontation of one culture with another, each seeks to degrade the other and to build its own claims to deference. The sources of conflict are not quantitative ones of the distribution of resources. Instead they are differences between right and wrong, the ugly and the beautiful, the sinful and the virtuous. Such issues are less readily compromised than are quantitative issues. When politicians argue about the definition of sin instead of being uniformly opposed to it, then the underlying political consensus is itself threatened.

The discontents generated by social change become fixed upon groups which are in status opposition. Each becomes the symbol of the other's obstacle in objectifying its view of its proper position. Each seeks to wrest from the other the admission of its place in the order. An issue like fluoridation, for example, carries the status struggle between the culturally modern and cosmopolitan middle classes and the culturally fundamentalist and localistic old middle classes.

The association of an issue with the styles of life of its supporters enhances the tendency of political issues to turn into matters of "face," freezing the adherents to a given program and further diminishing the possibilities of compromise or graceful defeat. When participants have become committed to a "line" which makes retreat and compromise immoral, discontinuance of the stance will be more painful than if they had entered with a bargaining orientation. In the former case, they invested their egos. In part, compromise is possible at all because the parties to the action will help each other maintain the illusion that a victory has been achieved. In human encounters, as Goffman has shown, parties to the interaction help maintain each other's "face." People mutually accept each other's lines—the consistent pattern of acts expressing the actor's evaluation of himself and the participants. The hostess covers over the embarrassment of the guest who has just broken a new and expensive piece of glassware by minimizing the importance of the breakage. She maintains the guest's "face" as a considerate person and permits him to "erase" the act by mumbling apologies. "Should the person radically alter his line, or should it become discredited, then confusion results, for the participants will have prepared and committed themselves for actions that are now unsuitable." [29]

Status conflicts, however, involve just such "face-smashing" operations. The pretense that one's values and morals are prestigious and powerful is undermined whenever public actions contradict such assertions. Loss of face becomes degrading. Since status conflicts involve opposition between styles of life, it is necessary to break the "face" of the opponent by degrading his cultural content. Ego is invested in status claims and degradation is keenly felt. The inability of the forces of North and South to reach compromise on the eve of the Civil War is a good illustration of how investment in a line made compromise less possible. ". . . after years of strife the complex issues between the sections assumed the form of a conflict between *right* and *rights*. . . . They suggested things which cannot be compromised." [30]

Political Structure and Status Politics

The institutionalization of status conflicts occurs less frequently than the institutionalization of class conflicts. Class organization develops out of stable, institutional positions in the occupational and economic structures. Labor unions, businessmen's associations, professional organizations are constructed on the basis of institutional roles and statuses. The organization of conflict associations is a necessary step in the structuring of conflict relationships. It enables political accommodations to be worked out among contending groups. Institutional ties operate both to promote the formation of "pressure groups" and to integrate the occupant into organizations on this basis.

Some historians have recently suggested that American politics has displayed a higher degree of consensus than has been true in Europe.[31] The sharp antagonisms between economic and social classes described by Marx have been avoided in the United States, with its higher available level of resources and the absence of a feudal past. Because economic conflicts have been less salient,

---

[29] Erving Goffman, "On Face-Work," *Psychiatry*, 18 (August, 1955), 213-231, at 216.

[30] Avery O. Craven, "The Civil War and the Democratic Process," in Kenneth Stampp (ed.), *The Causes of the Civil War* (Englewood Cliffs, N.J.: Prentice-Hall, 1959), pp. 150-152, at 152.

[31] See the presentation of this point of view with additional references in Benson, *op. cit.*, pp. 272-277.

American politics has been open to the interjection of status issues to a very great degree.[32]

We lack the techniques to measure accurately the degree to which European politics displays more or less class conflict than American politics. Certainly issues of cultural conflict have often been significant in European politics. ". . . every significant stratum (in Europe) is divided between support for a modern, secular, industrial society and preference for the values, if not the fact, of a clerical, non-industrial order." [33] The presence of a multiple party system, however, enables such elements to be introduced into politics within the structure of political institutions.

In American politics, especially in recent decades, issues involving cultural conflict appear to find less place in the structure of the two-party system than was the case in past historical periods. The designation of either major party as predominantly Catholic or immigrant or the voice of Puritan morality is less accurate today than it might have been in the nineteenth century and even in the first third of the twentieth. The studies of national voting behavior during the last 20 years indicate the saliency of economic differences between Republicans and Democrats and the lack of any sharp relation between party preference and orientations toward such issues as civil liberties, race relations, internationalism, and religious education.[34]

The exclusion of status elements from institutionalized politics imparts an erratic, highly emotional, and disturbing character to such issues when they do find their way into politics. They emerge in highly diffuse forms. The separation of the issue from any specific party location destroys the control of the institution, the political party system, over it. Support in the form of sentiments are just as likely to come from one class as another, from Republicans as well as Democrats. Since status issues are likely to be highly symbolic, the absence of fixed political connotations enables people to provide their own connotations. In this fashion a bewildering array of diverse groups can become attached to any set of symbols when

[32] *Ibid.*, p. 275.

[33] Seymour Lipset, "Party Systems and the Representation of Social Groups," *European Journal of Sociology*, 1 (1960), 50-85, at 60.

[34] Berelson, Lazarsfeld, and McPhee, *op. cit.*, pp. 189 ff.; Samuel Lubell, *The Future of American Politics* (New York: Doubleday and Co., Inc., 1956); Angus Campbell, Philip E. Converse, and Warren Miller, *The American Voter*, (New York: John Wiley, 1960), Ch. 9, esp. pp. 194-195.

they lack clear location in the political spectrum. Almost every major social segment in the United States has been included by some writer as one of the major supports of Senator Joseph Mc-Carthy. Pro-McCarthyism has been attributed to highly diverse and often conflicting groups, sometimes by the same author. Neo-Populists, Catholics, anti-Catholics, isolationists, downwardly mobile people, upwardly mobile people, Protestant fundamentalists, small businessmen, and industrial workers have all been held "responsible" for McCarthyism.[35] This "looseness' is seldom the case with economic issues.

Status constituencies, however, are looser collections of adherents than are economic interest groups. Formed out of sentiments rather than concrete, objectified interests, commitment is less structured. The organization is less able to speak for its constituency, less able to "deal" with opposing groups in the negotiations on which the model of class politics has been built. The constituency of doctors is more clearly represented by the American Medical Association than the constituency of birth control adherents is represented by the Association for Planned Parenthood.

We have pointed out in the previous chapter that the institutional and communal differences of the past are becoming muted in American life. They are replaced by conflict between characterological and cultural groups within the same institution and community. In our terminology, status communities are breaking up and cultural conflicts emerging in the form of status collectivities. This means that the differences in life styles between Protestants and Catholics or between urban and rural people are lessened. Differences between cosmopolitan and local, between fundamentalist and modernist remain but they are not connected to specific institutions, such as the church or the local community.

Ethnic and religious groups are better structured than social classes, generations, or stylistic groups. Catholics, Jews, Negroes, Protestants, Italians, rural people, or urban people possess stable relationships to churches, communities, or political units which serve to structure their relation to the political institutions. The effectiveness of the Anti-Saloon League as a "pressure group" rested on the consensus within the Protestant churches on the Temperance issue. As social and cultural cleavages cease to be superimposed on

---

[35] See the array of theories and groups in Bell, *op. cit.*

religious, residential, and communal groups the institutional basis for status group representation is lessened.

The isolation of status collectivities from the political party structure is double-edged. We have seen how it operates to push some elements of the Temperance movement toward an extremist response in political programs. On the other hand, as status communities are less salient as political forces, the volatility of status issues cuts across party lines and minimizes the bitterness of party differences. Had the Democrats been clearly pro-McCarthy and the Republicans clearly anti-McCarthy the issues surrounding his actions would have generated as intense conflict as did the nominations of Al Smith and Abraham Lincoln.

Temperance has receded as an issue of paramount significance in American life. It is highly doubtful that the status conflicts which it represented have disappeared from the American scene. The quest for an honored place in society is likely to persist. Social changes are likely to continue to upset old hierarchies and develop new aspirations. Cultural transformations are to be expected and resistance to them is almost certain. Status politics is neither a new nor a transient aspect of American society.

Index